Soft Shepherd or Almighty Pastor?

Soft Shepherd or Almighty Pastor?

Power and Pastoral Care

EDITED BY
ANNEMIE DILLEN

☙PICKWICK *Publications* · Eugene, Oregon

SOFT SHEPHERD OR ALMIGHTY PASTOR?
Power and Pastoral Care

Copyright © 2014 Wipf and Stock Publishers. All rights reserved. Except for brief quotations in critical publications or reviews, no part of this book may be reproduced in any manner without prior written permission from the publisher. Write: Permissions, Wipf and Stock Publishers, 199 W. 8th Ave., Suite 3, Eugene, OR 97401.

Pickwick Publications
An Imprint of Wipf and Stock Publishers
199 W. 8th Ave., Suite 3
Eugene, OR 97401

www.wipfandstock.com

ISBN 13: 978-1-62032-531-5

Cataloging-in-Publication data:

> Soft Shepherd or Almighty Pastor? Power and Pastoral Care / edited by Annemie Dillen.
>
> p. ; cm. —Includes bibliographical references and index.
>
> ISBN 13: 978-1-62032-531-5
>
> 1. Pastoral care. 2. Church and social problems. I. Dillen, Annemie. II. Title.

BV4012.2 .S655 2014

Manufactured in the U.S.A.

Contents

Preface | vii

INTRODUCTION
Power, Church, and Pastoral Care: Beyond the Taboo | ix
Annemie Dillen

PART 1
Fundamental Philosophical and Theological Reflections on Power and Pastoral Care

1. A Web of Power: Toward a Greater Awareness of the Complexity of Power | 3
   Machteld Reynaert

2. Power and Compassion in Pastoral Work: From the Perspective of Michel Foucault | 17
   Roger Burggraeve and Anne Vandenhoeck

3. Beyond the Almighty Pastor: On Three Forms of Power in Pastoral Care | 28
   Stefan Gärtner

PART 2
Power and Interculturality

4   Self-Affirming Prejudice and the Abuse of Pastoral Power | 57
    Carrie Doehring

5   "When I Am Weak, Then I Am Strong": An African Christian
    Reflection on the Ambiguities, Paradoxes, and Challenges of
    Pastoral Power | 79
    Emmanuel Lartey

PART 3
Power and Sexual Abuse

6   Intimacy in Pastoral Care: Ethical Notes on the Use of
    Power in Pastoral Guiding | 101
    Didier Pollefeyt

7   A Wolf in Sheep's Clothing: Dealing Honestly
    with Pastoral Power | 122
    Cristina Traina

PART 4
Challenges for Theology and Pastoral Praxis

8   Empowerment in Pastoral Care for Persons with a
    Psychiatric Disorder: Towards Human Flourishing | 147
    Jana Binon

9   The Meaning of Informed Consent in Pastoral Counseling | 171
    Axel Liégeois

Contributors | 193

Index | 195

Preface

This volume contains a selection of papers presented at the expert seminar on power and pastoral care in Leuven, *"Soft Shepherd or Almighty Pastor?" Power (im)balances in Pastoral Care*, 5–8 January 2012, complemented by a few new chapters written for this volume.

After my introductory chapter on various meanings of power in relation to church, theology, and pastoral work, there are nine other chapters. The volume is divided into four main parts, each reflecting a different aspect of power. The first part deals with fundamental philosophical and theological reflections on power and pastoral care. This part opens with the contribution of Machteld Reynaert, titled "A Web of Power." She shows the complexity of power and thus stimulates awareness that power is everywhere and needs to be recognized. The second chapter is a reflection of Roger Burggraeve and Anne Vandenhoeck about power and compassion in pastoral work, inspired by Michel Foucault. In the third chapter, Stefan Gärtner offers his fundamental reflections on power and pastoral care under the title "Beyond the Almighty Pastor: On Three Forms of Power in Pastoral Care."

The second part of this volume deals with aspects of interculturality. The relations between power and cultural identity, intercultural relations and prejudices are deepened in two chapters, one of Carrie Doehring ("Self-Affirming Prejudice and the Abuse of Pastoral Power") and one of Emmanuel Lartey ("'When I Am Weak, Then I Am Strong': An African Christian Reflection on the Ambiguities, Paradoxes, and Challenges of Pastoral Power").

Preface

The third part deals explicitly with power and sexual abuse, although the contributions in this part also offer insights that go much further than sexual abuse. Didier Pollefeyt reflects on the use of power in pastoral guiding, centered around the theme of intimacy. Cristina Traina reflects on the role of eros, under the title "A Wolf in Sheep's Clothing: Dealing Honestly with Pastoral Power." Both authors offer also insights for dealing in an adequate way with power in order to avoid power abuse. In the concluding, fourth part, specific issues in relation to pastoral work form the starting point of reflections on power. Jana Binon speaks about empowerment in relation to persons with a psychiatric disorder. The concept of human flourishing is central in this contribution. Axel Liégeois concludes with a specific reflection on preventing power abuse in pastoral settings. He explores the role of informed consent and its complexities in pastoral counseling. Each author has his or her specific terms and ideas about power and pastoral work. As a whole, these contributions offer a complementary view alongside one another for consideration.

This book is the result of a longer research project, sponsored by the research council of the KU Leuven on power and pastoral care. The expert conference in 2012 received additional financial support from the Fund for Scientific Research, Flanders (FWO). Thanks to both institutions for making this publication possible, but especially thank you to the publisher Wipf and Stock for their enthusiast support of this volume.

I wish to thank all the contributors of the chapters for their cooperation in the process of editing this volume. Special thanks goes to the reviewers of the different chapters, Stephen Bullivant, Bridie Stringer, Marie Keenan, Sheelah Treflé Hidden, Gloria Braunsteiner, Slavka Karkoskova and especially to Jennifer Besselsen for the English editing. Machteld Reynaert (KU Leuven) deserves a very special thank you for the assistance in the entire editing process and the organization of the expert seminar in 2012.

Annemie Dillen

Leuven, August 2014

INTRODUCTION

Power, Church, and Pastoral Care: Beyond the Taboo

Annemie Dillen

INTRODUCTION

Soft shepherd or almighty pastor? Or should it be "almighty shepherd" or "soft pastor"? The title of this book, which was also the title of the expert seminar we organized in January 2012 in Leuven (Belgium), is still puzzling me. Most shepherds are not really soft—they are courageous,[1] both in the biblical stories as in daily life, and have to take risks in order to save the sheep. But if they are soft, they might be dangerous, at least when "shepherd" is considered here as a metaphor for "pastor." Being friendly, sweet or even "soft" as not being very strong and lacking power, seeking harmony and avoiding conflict, might disguise forms of power abuse for victims and bystanders. This attitude might function as an easy way to manipulate the other or might be an euphemism for a form of neglect of courageous speaking up for the dignity of others. Soft shepherds are to be shirked, because they might be disguised "almighty pastors." The same is

---

1. See the image of the "Courageous shepherd," in Campbell, "The Courageous Shepherd."

true for soft pastors or almighty shepherds. Sometimes the metaphor of the shepherd is used in the way it has functioned for many years within the catholic church, namely as the image a powerful clergyman, to be respected and to be honored. This image of powerful shepherd might also be dangerous, and does not sound very attractive to many people, although for some it awakens a form of nostalgic desire. The popularity of pope Francis, who led down quite a few of his privileges associated with power and a high hierarchical position, shows how many people prefer a form of "authenticity": a church that criticizes power, should incorporate this in her deeds, at least also in the agency of the pope. But, even if some of the formal symbols of power (luxary, protection, . . .) are less visible, this does not mean that the church and pastoral caregivers do not have power or have lost all their power during the last decades. In this volume, the multiplicity of power will be demonstrated. Power abuse, but also feelings of powerlessness pastoral caregivers encounter in themselves and in others, cannot be neglected.

These puzzling associations, and the image of the pope and the lack of power-attributes, show us that a reflection on power in relation to church and pastoral relation is really timely and relevant. Power abuse, especially also sexual abuse, should be prevented and dealt with adequately. Before presenting the content of this book, I will explore the theme of power in relation to the church and pastoral care in its broadness. I will give some interpretations and preliminary ideas about the topic. Attentive readers will find different accents in all the texts in this book, but also many similarities. With this first chapter, I hope to raise the interest in the theme and to deepen the awareness of the relevance of more reflection on power in relation to pastoral issues. I write this chapter from my own Belgian Catholic perspective, hoping that many readers will recognize similar aspects in their own context.

DISCUSSING THE THEME OF POWER

Taboo

Power has for many people negative connotations. In church contexts in particular, the word is often taboo. There are many and diverse reasons for this.

In the first place, many pastors and pastoral workers in the church frequently camp with the feeling of impotence. This can be related for example

INTRODUCTION

to a sense of impotency in relation to systems, or to people's suffering, to the context in which they work such as a hospital, prison, or parish, to contemporary post-modern society and its individualized approach to life, and, not infrequently, to other actors in the church. Speaking about power does not always coincide with this experience. At the same time, the experience of impotency does explain, in some cases, why people begin to exert power over others.

Furthermore, a number of people in the church seek positions that offer considerable (hierarchical) power. The latter cannot be openly recognized however, as it is at odds with a number of Christian views on, for example, humility or the attitude of service. The power of every Christian should moreover be considered in the light of God's power. This paradoxical relationship between the fantasizing about and seeking of more power on the one hand, and the theology that calls power into question and the actually experienced powerlessness on the other hand, often makes the discussion of power very difficult. In the words of the German theologian Gärtner: "It is the taboo surrounding power that makes power so powerful."[2]

What Is Power?

Breaking the taboo on power requires that we first reflect on the meaning of power. Power is present everywhere in society in many and diverse ways and in both a positive and a negative sense. Power can be described as "every opportunity in social relationships for asserting one's own will, even in the face of opposition."[3] A person can consequently exercise this power in concrete situations.

Sometimes we are not even aware of resistance and it is especially in such situations that power is often "hidden," but is all the same subtly at work and asserted for good or for evil. Consider for example a priest who preaches—this too can be seen as a form of power that can be used positively or negatively and that does not necessarily arouse opposition. In other situations, in spite of significant resistance, for example from those with less authority, decisions may still be imposed.

In a positive sense, the concept of "power" has associations with the English "agency," which indicates the opportunities persons have to determine their own agenda and to make decisions themselves concerning their

2. Gärtner, "'Doe maar gewoon'?," 260.
3. Weber, *Wirtschaft und Gesellschaft*, 38.

INTRODUCTION

actions, in order not to be merely a victim, or determined by others, or by a particular situation.

Power can be described in many ways. One approach is the threefold distinction: "power over" (hierarchical power), "power within" (internal power, indicating personal power), and "power with" (where several parties are acting together).[4] In general, when thinking of "power," it is "power over" that comes to mind.

Power does not necessarily coincide with a person's hierarchical position. The situation comes to mind of a colleague who has worked in the same place for twenty years and who at every new suggestion makes the comment, "We have done it this way for years, why should we change?"[5] Another example relates to teaching practice. I have power over my students, whom I expect to be more or less silent when I speak, and, I am in a position to enforce this. They exert power over me when they are continually disruptive, or simply do not come to class. Every master is also dependent on the slave, or, to put it another way, almost every sort of assertion of power goes hand in hand with the power that is conferred on a person by someone else (or by others).

Power is also closely linked with the privileges a person has. I possess power in being able to determine, to a great extent, how I do my work, choose how I dress, buy something when I wish to do so, and so forth. I have many privileges that many others do not have because of their financial situation and working circumstances, for example: because of the social pressure they are under compulsion to conceal their sexual preference, because their name alone betrays that they are a foreigner and are therefore frequently dependent on the goodwill of others, and so forth.

Power is extremely complex, that is already obvious. Power can be very easily "abused," or in other words, it can easily be asserted at the expense of others or of oneself. Below, I will analyze the phenomenon of power and the church from three perspectives, each of which is challenged by the experience of victims. I will first give consideration to the tradition and to theology, subsequently to the church itself and the context in which power functions, and, in conclusion, to the individual.

---

4. Stortz, *PastorPower*, 43–68

5. Van Damme, "Macht en mechanismen in conflicten in organisaties," 21.

POWER, TRADITION AND THEOLOGY

There are many elements in Catholic theology that legitimate certain forms of power. In the theological formation of priests and laypersons in the church, it is important to critically reflect on the images of being a Christian, leadership, sexuality, relationships, family, in relation to power. I will consider here a number of images specifically from the perspective of power.

The theology relating to the priesthood puts the priest in a certain sense in a class of his own. There is also the fact that the "priest" is a believer, together with and in the same way as other Christians. We are reminded here of the words of Augustine, recalled in the Second Vatican Council text, *Lumen Gentium* 32: "For you I am a bishop, but with you I am a Christian."[6] A priest acts "in the context of the community" and he is situated "in the midst of" the community. At the same time, the priest is ordained to act "in the name of Christ, who is the Head of the Church." In this sense, the priest is also positioned "facing" the faith community, implying in a certain sense that the priest is "set apart," although of course many different interpretations may be given to this—in both a more positive and a more negative sense. Celibacy contributes to some extent to this "setting apart" of priests.

Some people use the argument that the place reserved for the priest in the liturgical setting (the celebrant's chair) is not a form of clericalism, but an expression of the Catholic theology of the priesthood. The latter is certainly true, but this theology of priesthood can however give rise to forms of clericalism. What I mean here is an attitude that makes a great distinction between the clergy and the laity, through which a minority comes to possess numerous privileges, while others, on the basis of their being or not being a priest, receive, or do not receive access to, for example, the exercising of certain functions, or the right to make certain decisions. A dualistic approach (as is the clear-cut distinction between priest and laity, but also between man and woman, black and white and so on) is not purely neutral, but is often charged with many value associations, where one side is consequently considered to be more important and more valuable than the other.

In consequence, priests often have many privileges, with the implication that priests can appropriate much power. They can assert this power in diverse ways. Chances are high that "power over" will be opted for,

---

6. Augustine, "Sermo 340:1."

certainly in concrete situations. This hierarchical form of power provides great opportunity for power abuse—even although the two are not necessarily linked, and many positive things can also be done with the "power" invested in priests.

The following quotation illustrates the idea of clericalism and the possible dangers it may entail: "They (priests) may moreover always depend on being defended by their own group and by their superiors. The clergy demonstrates moreover the characteristics of a sub-culture: there is considerable group solidarity (*esprit de corps*), what takes place within the group must remain within the group (secrecy), and the sub-culture is characterized by a general attitude of us (priests) against them (laity). The sub-culture, united with the status of holiness and unsupervised power presents a structural occasion for power abuse."[7]

The strong emphasis on the special status of priests can also give rise to the fear of facing up to abuse, in particular among those who have been abused. I refer here to an example from one of the testimonies of victims of sexual abuse in the Catholic Church in Belgium and demonstrate in this way that sexual abuse always takes place in combination with power abuse. A woman writes, "He (the priest who abused her) was the man who could do everything and I had no respect for him, my mother reproached me constantly for this . . . the 'Reverend Father had to be respected for all that he had done for us.'"[8]

Power abuse linked to a form of hierarchical power is of course something to which many functions may lead, also the positions of teachers and educators, sport trainers and in particular parents.

I will here further consider church positions and theological legitimation of power and do not want to limit myself solely to theology concerning the priesthood. The metaphor of the good shepherd is another example of a theological perspective that may legitimate power in pastoral settings. The word "pastor" and "pastoral" refer in themselves to the image of the good shepherd. Pastors are too often depicted as shepherds on the basis of the story of the good shepherd. The picture of the shepherd can illustrate how the shepherd risks his own life in order to take care of the lost sheep, but it can also be interpreted as a person who knows what is best for the

7. Demasure, "Na schandalen seksueel misbruik. Kerk moet in eigen boezem kijken," 51.

8. Adriaenssens, "Verslag activiteiten Commissie voor de behandeling van klachten wegens seksueel misbruik in een pastorale relatie (onafgewerkt wegens inbeslagname op 24 juni 2010)," 65.

sheep, which follow him obediently. It is the person of the shepherd who is central in the metaphor and not so much the community of believers (the sheep), or their reciprocal care. A form of clericalism is concealed here in which an excessive emphasis is put on the person with the "priestly office," in contrast to the "herd," or to the laity, who are expected to obediently follow. The risks inherent in this shepherd metaphor also exist where the pastoral worker is a layperson.

The picture of the pastor as a good shepherd refers to the shepherd as a metaphor for Jesus Christ, the Good Shepherd (see John 10:1–21), who even gave up his own life for the sheep. This Christological reference can on the one hand encourage pastors to put their own power in perspective and to relate it to the broader framework of who Christ is. Some individuals will however interpret the reference to Christ as a legitimation of their own power (often understood as "power over")—and in this case the picture of the good shepherd is "abused" in order to exercise power "over" others and possibly also to legitimate power abuse.

It is however not so that power abuse only occurs when there is a great difference in power between different actors, where the weakest person has the least possibility of protesting, involvement, or self-determination. Power abuse also occurs in relationships where there is a perspective that minimizes the distinction between the pastor and the person being ministered to, namely where the picture of "friendship" is used to describe a pastoral relationship.

The picture of "friendship" suggests a form of symmetry and seems to rule out the possibility of differences in power playing a role in pastoral relationships. Types of sexual abuse in pastoral relationships, in particular between adult partners, are often legitimated on the basis of "friendship" being characteristic of the pastoral relationship. This example illustrates the dual character of "friendship" in a pastoral context. A woman speaks of the sexual abuse she endured from the chaplain responsible for the youth movement, "He was of course very friendly toward me. Nothing was too difficult for him . . . After a folk-dancing party we were allowed to sleep over at his house. Very kind of the man! But he evidently meant this very literally."[9] Friendliness and intimacy may conceal forms of abuse. This example demonstrates how hierarchical functions and intimacy often go together and in some instances lead to power abuse.

---

9. Ibid., 16.

INTRODUCTION

Sometimes we lose sight of the fact that the function of pastor involves a form of "power" and that complete symmetry is impossible in a pastoral relationship. It is therefore very important to recognize differences in power, to dare to mention them and, in light of the differences in power, for those in a pastoral relationship to subsequently seek an appropriate way of relating to each other.

The power of the individual can thus be legitimated on the basis of certain theological concepts. This does not mean that this will happen, nor does it mean that the theology is problematical as a whole, but it means that certain theological perspectives should be subject to critical questions since they are more likely to lead to abuse than other perspectives.

Additionally, there is also the power of the church as an institution, which is legitimated by theology and tradition. One of the central tasks of the church is to develop a (ethical and theological) perspective on all dimensions of life and a neutral position is neither possible nor desirable. It is however important to realize that every ethical statement is in some way an assertion of power, which as a consequence (whether justifiably or not) bestows more "power" on some than on others . . . In terms of liturgy or dogmatics, some positions may also include or exclude people. A theologically educated women who was extensively involved in the church, experienced this power that excluded her by a "simple" question. After she had expressed her opinion, a clergyman responded, "have you been baptized?" Such a comment is a form of asserting power over another person (power over). Many people today are afraid of expressing their opinion because they are wary that others are going to consider me as "not being Catholic enough." Reflection on power also means that we consider to what extent the church and theology allows for diversity.

It is in the first place important to be aware of the fact that power mechanisms are at work and subsequently, in theological reflection and writing, to take these mechanisms into account so that a theological legitimation of power abuse may be avoided as much as possible.

POWER, CHURCH AND SOCIETY

Another way of looking at power and the church today does not start from "tradition" and "theology" as we have developed in the previous part, but starts from an analysis of the situation and the processes that are taking place in church and society today.

Disciplinary Power

Michel Foucault speaks of disciplinary power as a phenomenon that is present throughout society.[10] Many norms exist in our society that determine what is normal and what is not normal, which may or may not be endorsed within the church.

Not infrequently, pastors also experience forms of powerlessness in this sort of context in relation to the system. This is something that happens with great frequency in juridical contexts and in the army. At the same time, the pastor may also assert a particular form of power in such contexts, for example by expressing criticism of the system, or of those higher up in the hierarchy. We speak here of prophetic pastoral situations, with the possibility of proceedings being taken against the pastor as a consequence. Criticism of the system is not always appreciated. The pastor's use of such a form of power in the context of disciplinary systems—for example in the form of the breaking of set opinions determined by for example the logic of financial power—are however a very important and pre-eminent form of Christian response. It is the pursuit of more structural justice that is involved here. In other words, pastors, and more broadly the whole church, are called to condemn contextual, systematic forms of repression that obstruct the positive exercise of power (as in *empowerment*) by others.

There are also forms of "disciplinary power" within the church itself, for example in the area of territorial pastoral service. People who volunteer in diaconal services are not considered to be part of the "church community" as quickly as those who attend Mass every week. If a new pastor wants to become a part of the new local community, it is in most cases the Eucharist in particular that counts, much more than social welfare activity. Certain norms regarding what it is to be "church" make their influence felt in local church communities.

Consider also for example the norm that continues to be implied that one should be well dressed to go to church. A child who does not wear special clothing for his or her first communion or confirmation is likely to be looked down upon.

---

10. See Foucault, *Surveiller et punir*. See also Part 1, "Fundamental Philosophical and Theological Reflections on Power and Pastoral Care."

Identity

On giving further consideration to what characterizes church and society today, we come face to face with post-modernity.

Our post-modern society is characterized by a multiplicity of perspectives, opportunities and points of view both inside and outside the church. For many people, this creates a need for new certainties. The identity discourse often takes the form of a quest to distinguish oneself from others, which not infrequently involves reacting against perspectives and people who are outsiders. Power is also involved here and differences in power and privileges are created. The theological and ethical discourse also plays a role here and contributes to the creation of "identity" for certain groups within the church. Where not so long ago the power of the church could also be considered as "territorialism," the attempt to "have an influence" on all aspects of life, to be present as church in every town and in every facet of society, in our postmodern society, where the gap between church and society is much greater, power comes to the fore particularly in the creation of image and identity.

The Continuity of the Power

In a hierarchical structure where "power over" is a very much present form of power, the phenomenon that power is self-perpetuating also plays a role. Many people within the Church seek (whether explicitly or not) an increasingly higher office in the hierarchy, but to achieve this demands however adherence to the predominating dynamic of the institution and to its hierarchical thinking. People holding a certain office are on the one hand "kneaded" by the dominating views within the institute, and on the other hand, they also help to keep the institute as it is. In the light of the revelations concerning sexual abuse, we likewise see how many attempt to defend the church.

POWER AND THE SUBJECT

A third way of reflecting on power relates in particular to the person and the professionalism of the individuals who are engaged in the church. To speak of power as though it only relates to the theology and the church institution (including the ordained clergy) presents a false picture. There is also a personal component linked to power abuse, one that often goes back to a person's having been himself a victim of others who abused their power, or is linked to a strong sense of powerlessness. There may be moments when people who are themselves vulnerable, or have been violated, take it out on others. They are themselves responsible for their actions, but it may be helpful to consider these in the context of their life history. What is important in this context is that in the supervision of those who are engaged in the church (priests and laity), specific attention is given to the theme of power and that adequate supervision, coaching or spiritual direction is provided.

Similarly, it is important to give attention to a spirituality that recognizes its own power, both in a positive sense and with awareness for its possible abuse. Didier Pollefeyt calls the "desire for power" a "daily vice," something with which every person wrestles and that every person needs to dare to recognize as a possible risk, one that should be avoided as much as possible.[11]

In this context it is important to encourage a spirituality in which it is not the ideal of self-sacrifice that is central, since the discourse on self-sacrifice can conceal power mechanisms ("look at all I do for you," "you should be thankful for me"), or which in the end implicitly put the person himself in a more central position. In the literature, reference is made to the "messiah complex" or to "the helper's syndrome."[12] A healthy spirituality takes power into account by consciously recognizing it and by striving for forms of shared power (power with) without obscuring or magnifying differences in power.

FURTHER REFLECTIONS

This short overview of the vastness of the field of power in relation to church and society is not complete. This whole book is required in order to gain a glimpse of what power may involve, to reflect on power in relation to the church and pastoral relationships. And, far more than this one book is needed. But it may help researchers, students and practitioners to reflect on their own ideas and practices in relation to the theme of power.

---

11. Pollefeyt, "Ethics, Forgiveness and the Unforgivable after Auschwitz." See also the contribution of Pollefeyt in this volume.

12. See Dillen, "The Complexity of Power in Pastoral Relations."

BIBLIOGRAPHY

Adriaenssens, Peter, et al. "Verslag activiteiten Commissie voor de behandeling van klachten wegens seksueel misbruik in een pastorale relatie (onafgewerkt wegens inbeslagname op 24 juni 2010)." http://www.deredactie.be/polopoly_fs/1.860520!file/Eindrapport.pdf.

Augustine. "Sermo 340:1." In *Patrologia Latina* 38, 1483.

Dillen, Annemie. "The Complexity of Power in Pastoral Relations: Challenges for Theology and Church." *ET-Studies* 4 (2013) 221–35.

Demasure, Karlijn. "Na schandalen seksueel misbruik: Kerk moet in eigen boezem kijken," *Tijdschrift voor geestelijk leven* 6 (2010) 45–53.

Campbell, Alastair, V. "The Courageous Shepherd." In *Images of Pastoral Care: Classic Readings*, edited by Robert C. Dykstra, 54–61. St. Louis: Chalice, 2005.

Foucault, Michel. *Surveiller et punir. Naissance de la prison*. Paris: Galimard, 1975.

Gärtner, Stefan. "'Doe maar gewoon'? De pastor en de macht." *Tijdschrift voor Theologie* 44 (2004) 259–73.

Pollefeyt, Didier. "Ethics, Forgiveness and the Unforgivable after Auschwitz." In *Incredible Forgiveness: Christian Ethics between Fanaticism and Reconciliation*, edited by Didier Pollefeyt, 121–59. Leuven: Peeters, 2004.

Stortz, Martha Ellen. *PastorPower*. Nashville: Abingdon Press, 1993.

Van Damme, Caroline. "Macht en mechanismen in conflicten in organisaties." In *Ga nu allen in vrede! Omgaan met macht en conflicten in pastorale contexten*, edited by Annemie Dillen and Didier Pollefeyt, 11–32. Leuven: Davidsfonds, 2010.

Weber, Max. *Wirtschaft und Gesellschaft. Grundriss der verstehenden Soziologie*, edited by Johannes Winckelmann. Keulen: Kiepenheuer & Witsch, 1964.

PART 1

Fundamental Philosophical and Theological Reflections on Power and Pastoral Care

1

A Web of Power
Toward a Greater Awareness of the Complexity of Power

Machteld Reynaert

POWER IS A COMPLEX phenomenon. The different ways and contexts in which power is used, indicate this clearly. In general practical theological literature and in practical theological literature relating to power, power relations, or power abuse, power is often endowed with different meanings and a (clear) definition of power is often lacking.

It is not easy to give a clear general definition of power that is applicable in every context, and perhaps this is not necessary. Nevertheless, such a definition is important in order to gain insight into the phenomenon of power and to reveal power in all its complexity. A clear description of power can create a greater awareness of the power present in every relationship and may increase the possibility of power being dealt with in an appropriate way.

The purpose of this chapter is to reveal the complexity of power on the basis of the insights of the German sociologist Max Weber (1864–1920) and of the French philosopher Michel Foucault (1926–1984) on power. These insights will be completed with the insights of some practical theologians on power.

EVERYONE HAS POWER

Everyone has power or at least everyone has a certain access to or—as Weber argues[1]—everyone has the opportunity for power. Foucault,[2] and some other practical theologians,[3] describes this with the term "circular power." According to Foucault, power may not be seen as something that only can be made use of by certain people. He states that power is a dynamic phenomenon that is always in motion and that is available to all, but does not structurally belong to a subject.

Everyone has a certain access to power, but how much power a person possesses, and to what extent he or she can exercise this power depends on several factors. First, it depends on the situation.[4] A professor has for example a certain power over his or her students in an auditorium. But outside of this auditorium, one of the professor's students can also have power over the professor, for example if the student happens to be the professor's gym teacher at the sports club. The meeting place determines in this example how much access a person has to power. Another possible example, in which the situation clearly plays a role, is the example of a teacher who has at one moment much power over the class because the students find the topic very interesting, but who has less power at another moment because the students are not interested in the topic and therefore refuse to cooperate.

Secondly, social identity plays a role in how much access a person has to power.[5] Characteristics such as gender, age, ethnic origin, social status, class, and sexual inclination determine the access to power. The social identity determines which "position" a person has in society and is thus

---

1. Weber, *Wirtschaft und Gesellschaft*, 38.
2. Foucault, "Cours du 14 janvier," 26.
3. See e.g. Redekop, "Power"; Neuger, "Power and Difference in Pastoral Theology"; Stortz, *PastorPower*.
4. See Stortz, *PastorPower*, 9.
5. See for example Neuger, "Power and Difference in Pastoral Theology," 66–67; Ganzevoort and Veerman, *Geschonden lichaam*, 42; Doehring, *Taking Care*, 74–78.

closely linked with positional power.⁶ For example, a thirty year old Western man has more chance of finding a job in Belgium than a fifty year old Western man, or than a African peer of the same age. A person's position (of power) in society is connected to a large extent with the social identity of the person, which determines the access to certain means of power and the possibility of exercising power.⁷ Since every person has a social identity, and this social identity determines a person's position of power, it may be said that, although in theory, social identity not should lead to hierarchical power, it does in fact involve thinking in terms of hierarchical power. Because of their social identity, some people are considered to be "superior" and therefore as "more powerful" than other persons.

By stating that every person has, in principle, the possibility of exercising power, this also means that no one person is completely powerless. Even if one is in a situation in which he or she has a sense of powerlessness, there is still the possibility of using power when one has a certain access to it. The constant access to power ensures that in every situation—even where the situation seems hopeless—the possibility of resistance exists. For example, if an employer announces a collective redundancy, employees can resist by striking. By means of a strike, a certain pressure on and certain power over the employer can be exerted, in the hope that the redundancy will be avoided. Since every person has access to power, a glimmer of hope always exists. There is always the hope that the situation can be improved and that the balance of power can change. The present situation does not need to remain as it is. Furthermore, the fact that no one is completely powerless offers the possibility of, and opportunity for empowerment. The idea that one has always a certain power may empower a person and may give the person the strength to use this always available power.

The circular thinking relating to power makes mutuality possible in a relationship. A mutual relationship is often considered as a "perfect" relationship, one without any abuse of power. In this respect, mutuality is often seen as the solution for preventing power abuse in a relationship.⁸

---

6. See, e.g., Ganzevoort and Veerman, *Geschonden lichaam*, 41–42; Poling, *The Abuse of Power*, 30–31.

7. Ganzevoort and Veerman, *Geschonden lichaam*, 41–42.

8. In the "boundary wars," a discussion in the nineties about boundaries in an asymmetrical relationship between the "radicals" (e.g., Heyward, SteinhoffSmith) and the "pastoral professionals" (e.g., Fortune, Doehring, Cooper-White), the radicals state for example that mutuality is the solution to prevent power abuse in an asymmetrical relationship. For more information about this discussion see Ragsdale, *Boundary Wars*;

But even in a mutual relationship, power abuse can occur and usually does so in a subtle way. Mutuality should then rather be seen as an ideal that should be pursued in every relationship. The existence of mutuality in a relationship creates space for "give and take" and demands that the other person is considered as a subject with a certain power. Mutuality in a relationship does not imply that the relationship has to be symmetrical or that the power in the relationship has to be symmetrical. In an asymmetrical relationship, and in a relationship with an imbalance of power, mutuality is also possible. Mutuality may not be seen as equality in the relationship, but must rather be thought of in terms of equivalence.[9] It is important to recognize that each person in the relationship is fundamentally equal. But being fundamentally equal does not mean that each person should be treated in the same way. Equivalence in a relationship implies that the personhood of each person is recognized and that each person is approached on the basis of his or her own capabilities. This means that the interpretation of mutuality is dependent on each individual relationship.[10] By considering each person in the relationship as equal and as a person with a certain power, the power present in the relationship can be dealt with in a more conscious and adequate way.

In conclusion, everyone has access to power, but not everyone possesses the same power. How much power a person has depends on the situation and the social identity of the person. Because of this, power in society is always asymmetrical. But this may not exclude mutuality in the relationship.

POWER IS EVERYWHERE

Power is not just present in some places, or in some relationships, but is to be found everywhere. Power is everywhere and all things involve power. Weber positions power in a social relationship.[11] This means that where another person is present, there is power. In contrast, Foucault argues that power is relational and that every relationship involves power.[12] Power is

---

SteinhoffSmith, "The Boundary Wars Mystery."

9. Bruinsma-De Beer, "Pastoraal leiderschap," 26; Dillen, *Het gezin*, 355; Browning et al., *From Culture Wars to Common Ground*, 271.

10. Miller-McLemore, *Let the Children Come*, 130–31.

11. Weber, *Wirtschaft und Gesellschaft*, 38.

12. Foucault, *Histoire de la sexualité*, 123; Foucault, "The Subject and Power," 219;

about how individuals interact.[13] We can say that Weber situates power with the persons involved in the relationship, while Foucault designates the relationship in itself as power. By combining Weber and Foucault's perspectives on power, we can state that power is everywhere. Power is present between persons—so power is also present in the pastoral relationship—but power is also present in the relationship with the self (the inner-relationship) and in relationships between institutions or groups. A relationship of power demands a broad interpretation. A relationship of power is more than a relationship in which one person has power over the other person or over a whole group. It also has to do with how groups or institutions interact.

Martha Ellen Stortz adopts this relational aspect of Foucault's analysis of power and discerns three forms of power in a (pastoral) relationship.[14] However, she remarks that in reality these forms will never occur in their pure form, but that they are usually mixed up. A first form of power is "power over" or the power to influence the behavior of the other. People usually spontaneous think of this kind of "visible" power when mentioning the word power. "Power over" is often interpreted as hierarchical because this form of power clearly indicates that one person has (more) power over the other. However, this does not mean that the other person has no power—as pointed out above, no one is completely powerless—or that it is bad. Power, even when it is interpreted more hierarchically, is not necessarily negative. The other two forms of power belong rather to the category of "invisible" power and are often not recognized as power.

"Power within" refers to inner power, the power that is in every person and that is related to the capacities and the charisma of the person. It is the power that something or someone has set in motion. Because this inner power is present in every person, the possibility of empowerment exists. The other person can be "empowered" by being awakened to the fact that he or she is never completely powerless and by being stimulated to use the power to which the person has access, in a positive way. Empowerment has to be seen as a process of awakening to power. A process that is only possible if we see ourselves as persons who have a certain power and if we consider power as something positive.

The third form is power as "power with" or co-active power. It exists when people have more power together than one of them would have

---

See also Steinkamp, *Die sanfte Macht der Hirten*, 126; Tran, *Foucault and Theology*, 33.

13. Stortz, *PastorPower*, 17–20.

14. See ibid.

individually. "Power with" is a shared form of power that can best be compared with friendship and solidarity because it is characterized by choice, similarity, mutuality, equality, benevolence, and so forth. By describing this form of power in terms of friendship and solidarity the power that is present is veiled. For this reason, one is often not aware of the power in the relationship, which means that the power that is present can easily be abused.

DIFFERENT EXPRESSIONS OF POWER

Everyone has power and power is everywhere. However, we are not always aware of this. In some relationships it is very clear that power is at hand. In such cases, power expresses itself mostly in its hierarchical form and through a negative use of "power over." When we are aware of the power that is present, power is usually defined as being negative. In other relationships, we have the feeling that there is no power present at all. Many relationships seem at first sight to be free of power, or we think that we act without any recourse to power. However, this is—as stated above—impossible. Where we consider or expect no power to be present, power is subtly at work.

Power abuse is often linked with power in its hierarchical form. But whatever form power takes, whether it is visible or not, it can always be abused. To judge whether there is an abuse of power, first, the personhood of a person has to be taken into account. Is the personhood of the other person respected and promoted? When the other person is regarded as an object without any autonomy or freedom and without any agency, this interaction may be judged as an abuse of power. Secondly, the (power) action in itself, the motivation of the person who asserts power, the context in which power is used, and the effect of the use of power have to be taken into consideration to properly judge whether or not there is an abuse of power. Power abuse can be, as can be the positive use of power, either perceptible or invisible, and it expresses itself mostly in the form of domination, exploitation or subjugation.

Expressions of Pastoral Power

Power is always present, but often hidden. Power can take for example the form of loving care and service, of self-giving and self-sacrifice, of social support or well-intended guidance.[15] Even though it is stated that something is done "out of love," or that something is done "with pleasure" or "just for fun," there is always a certain power present. People see in this case primarily the good intentions and not the power that lies behind them. The subtle character of power makes it sometimes difficult to detect power and power abuse.

Foucault has paid great attention to this subtle character of power and entitles it "pastoral power" (*pouvoir pastoral*).[16] Pastoral power is a power that fully penetrates and shapes the life of an individual in a subtle way. Foucault viewed it as a new form of power in modern society that no longer can be understood as a hierarchical form of power, characterized by a direct exercise of power by authorities, or described in terms of sovereignty. Foucault used the image of the "shepherd/pastor" (*berger/pasteur*) as model for this form of power.[17] A shepherd is a person who gathers, guides, and leads the herd, and who assures the herd's well-being, even if this drives him or her to extremes. The shepherd is responsible for and has to focus on the entire "herd," but this is only possible when no "sheep" escape. Everything that the shepherd does has to be done both for the benefit of the herd and for each individual sheep. The shepherd has to assure both the general well-being of the herd and the individual salvation of each sheep. Through the image of the shepherd, Foucault makes clear that pastoral power is both an individualizing and a totalizing power. Pastoral power also has a disciplinary aspect.[18] The shepherd can influence the life of the sheep through his or her power and can lead and direct the sheep as he or she desires. This requires a certain knowledge of the sheep. Knowledge can in this respect be seen as a means of power to exercise (disciplinary) power.

Pastoral power also expresses itself through the care for the herd—a shepherd has the duty of caring for the salvation and well-being of the herd. Therefore, pastoral power can also be called a power of care (*pouvoir de soin*).[19] His or her care for the herd gives the shepherd a certain power over the sheep, a power that manifests itself in the diligence, dedication and end-

---

15. Steinkamp, *Die sanfte Macht der Hirten*, 9–10.

16. See Foucault, *Sécurité, Territoire, Population*, 111; Foucault, "Cours du 14 janvier," 32; Devisch, "'Wie niet ziek is, is gezien,'" 77–78.

17. Foucault, "Omnes et Singulatim," 227–30.

18. Foucault, *Surveiller et punir*. See also Gärtner, *Zeit, Macht und Sprache*, 175–80; Smith, *Who's Afraid of Postmodernism?*, 101.

19. Foucault, *Sécurité, Territoire, Population*, 131. "Le pouvoir pastoral est un pouvoir de soin."

less attention to all. This intertwinement of power and care is, according to Herman Steinkamp very dangerous in a pastoral relationship.[20] It is dangerous because it is not obvious that power is an issue since the attention is focused on the "good care." Under this guise of care, the pastoral caregiver can control the life of its recipient of pastoral care. This is why it is important to distinguish and separate care and control in pastoral care. "To care for" someone in a pastoral relationship may not be equated with "controlling" the person.

Stefan Gärtner mentions that in pastoral care, power is mostly at play in a subtle way. He argues that power is often subtle and is present in concealed ways in the profession of pastoral caregiver, but we are often not aware of it because power is not immediately associated with the caring and "gentle" character of this profession. Nevertheless, the pastoral caregiver possesses (pastoral) power.[21] In the first place, pastoral caregivers possess a certain pastoral power through the institutional embedding of pastoral care. A pastoral caregiver usually works under the authority of the church and has through this statute a "legitimated" power. But at the same time, he or she is also "powerless," because of the dependency on the church. In addition, the pastor also possesses a certain power through the professionalization of pastoral care. Pastoral caregivers will present themselves more and more as an expert, in order to position themselves in relation to other health care providers and to demonstrate the necessity of their profession.

We are often not aware of this (pastoral) power in a care relationship because the work of the pastoral caregiver is often seen as a "service." We do not see the pastoral caregiver as a "powerful" person, but as a "servant." The kenotic use of the power of a pastoral caregiver, inspired by the example of Jesus in his dealing with power, reinforces this idea. A kenotic power structure for the pastoral caregiver implies a "downward" movement toward the experience of the recipients of pastoral care, as well as an "upward" movement rooted in the hope of resurrection. This kenotic use of power is, according to Gärtner, a possible way of dealing adequately with power in pastoral care.[22] However, this kenotic use of power holds certain danger. This use of power reinforces for example the ideas of the "gift of

20. Steinkamp, *Die sanfte Macht der Hirten*, 21–24.

21. See Gärtner, *Zeit, Macht und Sprache*; Gärtner, "'Doe maar gewoon'?." See also the contribution of Gärtner in this volume.

22. Gärtner, *Zeit, Macht und Sprache*, 219, 234–35.

self," of humbling oneself, of service, ideals that in themselves conceal a notion of power.

Expressions of Hierarchical Power

When the word power is mentioned, people think often spontaneously of power as control and coercion. Power is often put on a par with these two terms. The phenomenon power is broader than this interpretation. Power and coercion may be considered as expressions of hierarchical power.

Power takes the form of control when a person is clearly the more powerful one in the relationship and when the person tries to fully control the life of the other person by means of this position. When this control is observable, it can be considered to be an excessive form of hierarchical power, or "power over," where the circularity is reduced to the minimum. However, control is not always visible. Controlling the life of another can also take place in a subtle way. The concept of "governmentality" (*gouvernementalité*)—introduced by Foucault—can be seen as an example.[23] The government tries to keep the life of the inhabitants firmly in hand and to control their lives by means of a certain method of governing the society. This (subtle) control can rather be seen as an expression of disciplinary power.

Coercion is another expression of hierarchical power. Coercion aimed at the complete obedience of a person. This goal can be achieved, for example, by controlling and obstructing a person's freedom, or by means of physical punishment.[24] In this respect, coercion is often considered as being violent, as it may harm a person and may decrease the person's freedom. When this coercion involves an infringement of personal freedom, and when coercion is used exclusively for the benefit of the person exerting it, there is abuse of power. However, coercion must not always be interpreted negatively. Coercion can also be positive. For example, when parents coerce their child to take the medication that the child refuses because of its nasty taste, then the parents use coercion in a positive way. Even though the freedom of the child is obstructed, it is not labeled as power abuse, as the motivation and effect is positive and the conditions permit it. After all, the parents only want their sick child to recover quickly and, as they know that the medication works, they give the medicine for the good of the child.

---

23. See Foucault, *Sécurité, Territoire, Population*.
24. Redekop, *Power*, 932.

PART 1—Fundamental Philosophical and Theological Reflections

Authority

The term authority is often considered to be a synonym of power. Yet, there is a difference. Authority should rather be considered as a specific form of power.[25] When someone with authority gives an order, people obey more quickly and adapt their behavior to the given order. Authority is a legitimate form of power that is accepted and recognized by most people and for this reason it can determine their actions over a longer period. Weber discerns three forms of authority, namely traditional, rational-legal, and charismatic authority.[26] Ruard Ganzevoort links these three forms of power to three types of pastoral caregivers, namely the pastoral caregiver as witness, the pastoral caregiver as expert, and the pastoral caregiver as companion.[27]

Through the use of the term "authority" to indicate legitimate power and because of the general recognition and acceptance of authority, it is often forgotten that authority implies power. In consequence, the danger arises that the existing power is disguised and even abused. For example, when a pastoral caregiver is solely considered as a person with authority, and authority is not associated with power, the danger exists that the power imbalance between the pastoral caregiver and the recipient of pastoral care will not be recognized. The pastoral caregiver can then easily abuse his or her power under the guise of his or her status of authority.

POWER IS POSITIVE

In the previous sections, power is analyzed as an phenomenon that is present everywhere, but often on a subtle way, and present in areas to which all people have access. The question is then: "How should power be evaluated?" Is power positive or negative? An initial reaction is often the tendency to conclude that power is negative and dangerous and that it creates conflicts. This is confirmed by the fact that there is a kind of taboo concerning power.[28] The consideration of power in terms of expressions of hierarchical power particularly stimulates this negative interpretation of power.

---

25. Weber, *Wirtschaft und Gesellschaft*, 38, 159, 691; Redekop, "Power," 932; Stortz, *PastorPower*, 32.

26. Ibid., 159.

27. See Ganzevoort and Visser, *Zorg voor het verhaal*.

28. Gärtner, "'Doe maar gewoon'?," 260–263; Gärtner, *Zeit, Macht und Sprache*, 163–73.

The definition of power as a means to achieve a goal[29] or to suppress and overcome resistance,[30] also results in a negative interpretation of power.

However, it is important not to place power solely in a negative atmosphere. Power is not necessarily negative or discordant. The aim of using power is, according to Foucault, not to exclude people, but to produce reality.[31] Power is necessary for society because it shapes society and the relationships within society, and it produces knowledge. According to Gärtner, a positive interpretation of power could break the taboo concerning power.[32]

Emmanuel Lartey adopts this positive interpretation of power and states that power is a (productive) asset.[33] Lartey nuances this positive interpretation of power and states that we may not lose sight of the fact that power can also be dangerous and negative. The possession or the exercise of power as such is, according to him, not negative, but the way in which power is dealt with can be negative. He compares power with a knife: sometimes it can be very useful, but sometimes it can also be very dangerous. Therefore it is important that power is dealt with in a responsible way. The notion of power as "premoral evil" fits in with this. Axel Liégeois considers power as a premoral evil, because it possesses the possibility to threaten human life and because it runs counter to the fundamental equality between people. But depending on how the power that is present is dealt with, power can become a moral good or evil.[34]

It is important that power is considered in a positive way. Power as a positive phenomenon contains an appeal to deal with power in a right way, one which enhances the chance that through using power, something good can be achieved. However, it is also important not to extol power and the use of it. We may not lose sight of the negative side of power. It is not

---

29. Redekop, "Power," 932.
30. Neuger, "Power and Difference in Pastoral Theology," 67.
31. See Foucault, "Entretien avec Michel Foucault," 148–49. "Ce qui fait que le pouvoir tient, qu'on l'accepte, mais c'est tout simplement qu'il ne pèse pas seulement comme une puissance qui dit non, mais qu'en fait il traverse, il produit les choses, il induit du plaisir, il forme du savoir, il produit du discours; il faut le considérer comme un réseau productif qui passé à travers tout le corps social beaucoup plus que comme une instance négative que a pour fonction de réprimer."; Smith, *Who's Afraid of Postmodernism?*, 91.
32. Gärtner, "'Doe maar gewoon'?," 260.
33. See the contribution of Lartey in this volume.
34. See Liégeois, "Asymmetry and Power in Pastoral Counselling." See also his contribution in this volume.

PART 1—Fundamental Philosophical and Theological Reflections

because power is positive that it cannot be asserted in a negative way. An important question in this regard is: "How is one to use power?" Is power used in a positive or negative way? The boundary wars demonstrate that the boundary between a positive and negative use of power is very thin and ambiguous.[35] Drawing boundaries is very personal and everyone draws his or her boundaries at a different place. If power is considered as positive, and if there is a recognition of the fact that power also can have negative effects, it may be concluded that the responsibility for a proper use of power is borne by the one who has power.[36] In other words, everyone has the responsibility for using the power that he or she possesses in a sensible way. The person with the biggest responsibility in a relationship possesses the most power, and the person with the most power bears the greatest responsibility for a proper use of power in the relationship. In a pastoral relationship this is the pastoral caregiver. So it is important that the pastoral caregiver is aware of his or her power and responsibility. Self-care and supervision can be aids in becoming aware of the responsibility and of the power possessed by the pastoral caregiver, whenever he or she uses this power, and for employing this power in a positive way.

CONCLUSION

Power can be described as a positive phenomenon that is present everywhere and to which every person, depending on the situation and social identity, has a certain access. Sometimes power is very visible, but other times it is very subtly at work. Power is a phenomenon that expresses itself in different forms, for example in coercion, control, or authority, but also in loving care and service.

This description of power clearly indicates that every person needs to be aware of the power that one has: "I have power. In everything that I do, in all my relationships, in all my activities there is some power present. Moreover, in the way I (and all others) do (practical) theology, there is power." But this always present power is often a hidden power. The concept of pastoral power makes for example clear that our behavior and everything that we say has an influence on others. We direct (sometimes unconsciously) people on the basis of our own opinion. This is an important

---

35. Ragsdale, *Boundary Wars*; SteinhoffSmith, "The Boundary Wars Mystery."

36. Ganzevoort and Visser, *Zorg voor het verhaal*; Liégeois, "Is Physical Touch a Prophetic Act?," 51.

insight, especially for pastoral care. It also makes clear that we have the tendency to veil the power that is present, for example by saying "I just do it out of love." This description alerts us to the importance of questioning even trivial matters with regard to power.

This description also counteracts the taboo of power and the thinking that power can only be negative. As long as power remains a taboo in pastoral care, the pastoral caregiver can exercise their power over the recipient of pastoral care without the latter, and sometimes even the pastoral caregiver, being aware of it. Power as something positive implies that we can and have to use the power we possess in a good way, and that we can achieve something by using our power. The advantage of this description is that it encompasses the possibility that people can be empowered. But it is important to take care that we do not lose sight of the negative side of power. Power can also be abused.

BIBLIOGRAPHY

Browning, Don S., et al. *From Culture Wars to Common Ground: Religion and the American Family Debate*. 2nd ed. Louisville: Westminster John Knox, 2000.

Bruinsma-De Beer, Joke. "Pastoraal leiderschap: Komen we er nog met herders en schapen?" *In de Marge* 16 (2007) 23–27.

Devisch, Ignaas. "'Wie niet ziek is, is gezien'. De pastorale macht en de zorg voor het alledaagse leven." *De uil van minerva* 23 (2010) 75–87.

Dillen, Annemie. *Het gezin: à Dieu? Een contextuele benadering van gezinnen in ethisch, pedagogisch en pastoraaltheologisch perspectief*. Brussel: Koninklijke Vlaamse academie van België voor wetenschappen en kunsten, 2009.

Doehring, Carrie. *Taking Care: Monitoring Power Dynamics and Relational Boundaries in Pastoral Care and Counseling*. Nashville: Abingdon, 1995.

Foucault, Michel. "Cours du 14 janvier 1976." In *Il faut défendre la société. Cours au Collège de France. 1976*, edited by Mauro Bertani et al., 21–36. Paris: Gallimard/Seuil, 1997.

———. "Entretien avec Michel Foucault." In *Dits et écrits 1954-1988. Tome III 1976-1979*, edited by Daniel Defert and François Ewald, 140–60. Paris: Gallimard, 1994.

———. *Histoire de la sexualité 1. La volonté de savoir*. Paris: Gallimard, 1976.

———. "Omnes et Singulatim: Towards a Criticism of Political Reason." In *The Tanner Lectures on Human Values*, edited by Sterling M. McMurrin, 223–54. Salt Lake City: University of Utah Press, 1981.

———. *Sécurité, Territoire, Population. Cours au Collège de France. 1977-1978*. Paris: Gallimard/seuil, 2004.

———. "The Subject and Power." In *Michel Foucault: Beyond Structuralism and Hermeneutics*, edited by Hubert L. Dreyfus and Paul Robinow, 208–26. Brighton: Harvester Press, 1982.

———. *Surveiller et punir. Naissance de la prison*. Paris: Gallimard, 1975.

PART 1—Fundamental Philosophical and Theological Reflections

Ganzevoort, Ruard, and Alexander L. Veerman. *Geschonden lichaam: Pastorale gids voor gemeenten die geconfronteerd worden met seksueel geweld*. Zoetermeer: Boekencentrum, 2000.

———. *Zorg voor het verhaal: Achtergrond, methode en inhoud van pastorale begeleiding*. Zoetermeer: Meinema, 2007.

Gärtner, Stefan. "'Doe maar gewoon'? De pastor en de macht." *Tijdschrift voor Theologie* 44 (2004) 259–73.

———. *Zeit, Macht und Sprache. Pastoraltheologische Studie zu Grunddimensionen der Seelsorge*. Freiburg: Herder, 2009.

Liégeois, Axel. "Asymmetry and Power in Pastoral Counselling: The Need for Ethical Attitudes." In *'After You!'. Dialogical Ethics and the Pastoral Counselling Process*, edited by Marina Riemslagh, Axel Liégeois, Jozef Corveleyn, Roger Burggraeve, 201–15. Leuven: Peeters, 2013.

———. "Is Physical Touch a Prophetic Act? A Case Study." In *Prophetic Witness in World Christianities: Rethinking Pastoral Care and Counseling*, edited by Annemie Dillen and Anne Vandenhoeck, 47–57. Zürich: LIT, 2011.

Miller-McLemore, Bonnie J. *Let the Children Come: Reimagining Childhood from a Christian Perspective*. San Francisco: Jossey-Bass, 2003.

Neuger, Christie C. "Power and Difference in Pastoral Theology." In *Pastoral Care and Counseling: Redefining the Paradigms*, edited by Nancy J. Ramsay, 65–86. Nashville: Abingdon, 2004.

Poling, James N. *The Abuse of Power: A Theological Problem*. Nashville: Abingdon Press, 1991.

Ragsdale, Katherine H. *Boundary Wars: Intimacy and Distance in Healing Relationships*. Cleveland: Pilgrim, 1996.

Redekop, Calvin. "Power." In *Dictionary of Pastoral Care and Counseling: Expanded Edition*, edited by Rodney J. Hunter, 931–34. Nashville: Abingdon Press, 1990.

Smith, James K.A. *Who's Afraid of Postmodernism? Taking Derrida, Lyotard and Foucault to Church*. Grand Rapids: Baker Rapids, 2006.

SteinhoffSmith, Roy H. "The Boundary Wars Mystery." *Religious Studies Review* 24 (1998) 131–42.

Steinkamp, Herman. *Die sanfte Macht der Hirten. Die Bedeutung Michel Foucaults für die praktische Theologie*. Mainz: Matthias Grünewald, 1999.

Stortz, Martha Ellen. *PastorPower*. Nashville: Abingdon, 1993.

Tran, Jonathan. *Foucault and Theology*. London: T. & T. Clark, 2011.

Weber, Max. *Wirtschaft und Gesellschaft. Grundriss der verstehenden Soziologie*. Edited by Johannes Winckelmann. Keulen: Kiepenheuer & Witsch, 1964.

2

Power and Compassion in Pastoral Work
From the Perspective of Michel Foucault

Roger Burggraeve and Anne Vandenhoeck

INTRODUCTION

ASK ANY RANDOM GROUP of pastoral workers which words or images best express what they do and it is more than likely that the following words will appear on the list: compassion, listening, attention, being a shepherd, nearness and care. The context of these core words is the relationship with the other. The pastor is someone who sees the other, becomes moved or touched in that seeing, and in that being moved, the pastor acts himself or herself and begins to care for the other. In the Christian tradition, the word and metaphor pastor has become an expression of being a shepherd, being near people, listening to people, helping them to recuperate, to support them in their search for meaning, to be near them with signs, and to allow them experience that God, the fullness of salvation and healing, wants to be near. In this manner, pastors and other members of the church community are the expression of the pastoral care of the church where being shepherd and compassion or mercy for the other take a central position. Little, however, has been said or reflected on of late regarding the aspect of power in that pastoral care of the church.

The French historian and philosopher, Michel Foucault (1926–1984), studied the pastoral care of the church in function of his reflections on management and democracy. Foucault starts with the conviction that the image of management and of politicians in present society is strongly influenced by Christianity. Moreover, the pastoral concept creates the present expectations with regard to politicians who, in a certain secularized sense, also have to be shepherds. In his reflections, he links pastoral care especially with power, not with compassion, and makes use of the expression *le pouvoir pastoral*. His view on pastoral power highlights a tension in the church's pastoral care and can be an interesting addition to the current debate on power in pastoral relationships.

In this contribution, starting from the analysis of Foucault's *le pouvoir pastoral*, we emphasize that the tension between compassion and power is inherently present in pastoral work and in being a pastor. More so, the aspect of power comes to us through the core metaphor of the shepherd. Pastors are challenged to deal with that tension as best they can.

FOUCAULT'S VIEW ON PASTORAL POWER[1]

God as King and Shepherd

Foucault's point of departure is the conviction that contemporary political power is a secularized form of pastoral power. This is why he first investigates the concept of pastoral power. For Foucault, power belongs fundamentally to pastoral work. He thus delves into the biblical and theological roots of the metaphor of the shepherd. In the Hebrew tradition, God is at the same time king *and* shepherd. He is creator and ruler and is so in a shepherd-like manner. The concurrence of ruler and shepherd automatically brings about an asymmetry and includes power. Foucault comments that the Greek tradition separates kingship and being shepherd, but the Jewish tradition enthusiastically embraces a merger of shepherd and ruler. God is the only true and good shepherd, who asks Moses, Aaron, and

---

1. This article mainly uses the following text of Foucault: Foucault, *Dits et écrits*. We also refer to the following discussions on Foucault: Büttgen, "Théologie politique et pouvoir pastoral," and Chevallier, *Michel Foucault et le christianisme*. We are grateful to Mark Lambrechts for the literature suggestions.

David, among others, to be shepherd to the people in imitation of himself.[2] Psalm 78 refers explicitly to David as such a shepherd.[3] The Midrash states that God concerns himself with the one lost sheep, and that he asks Moses to care for the other ninety nine. The merging of power and protection makes pastoral work a paradoxical concept. The biblical roots speak of majesty and nearness, of being ruler and good shepherd, of being king over all and caretaker. All Christian thought of Jesus as the good shepherd, and the pastor as shepherd in imitation of him, is rooted in the Jewish thought of God as shepherd. Through our contemporary neglecting of the original meaning of that pastoral care, we have separated power and pastoral work in a nearly schizophrenic way.

God's Style of Shepherding

A first characteristic that Foucault ascribes to *le pouvoir pastoral*, the direction and guidance of God, is that it thereby concerns not a territory, but a flock.[4] God is in the first place king and shepherd over a people and not over a territory. This determines the relationship between God and the people where the land is rather a promise for the future.

A second characteristic is that the shepherd is the one who brings together what is scattered and is concerned for the flock as a whole, as a community. In the Gospel story, the shepherd leaves the ninety-nine sheep behind in order to seek the one lost sheep, while the Midrash narrates that God looks for the one sheep and asks Moses to care for the other ninety-nine.[5] The fact that it is the shepherd who keeps his flock together assures a bond between shepherd and flock. The biblical tradition indicates that the people know the voice of its shepherd. In addition to Foucault's perspective, it is also evident that the bond between the people and the shepherd is expressed ultimately in the covenant. However, Foucault thus states, it is indeed the shepherd who gathers and goes in search; it is not a sheep that

---

2. Foucault, *Dits et écrits*, 137. "Yahvé est le seul et unique véritable berger. Il guide son peuple en personne, aidé de ses seuls prophètes."

3. Psalm 78:70–72: "He chose his servant David, and took him from the sheepfolds; from tending the nursing ewes he brought him to be the shepherd of his people Jacob, of Israel, his inheritance. With upright heart he tended them, and guided them with skillful hand."

4. Foucault, *Dits et écrits*, 137. "Le pasteur exerce le pouvoir sur un troupeau plutôt que sur une terre."

5. Luke 15:3–7.

PART 1—Fundamental Philosophical and Theological Reflections

is safe that goes in search of the lost sheep. The paradox of nearness and power is always kept in play. It is God who determines who he is as shepherd and not the people. This tension between majesty and care is, according to Foucault, absorbed into a secularized version by politics. A politician is someone who stands above the people and yet must care for the people.

Foucault distinguishes a third characteristic at the point where the task of the shepherd is orientated toward salvation. A shepherd does not act without a goal. He is involved in the salvation of his flock, in their ups and downs. He wants the flock to stay together and does not want any sheep to be lost. God wants what is good for his flock, and Foucault calls that the benevolence or the *bienveillance* of the shepherd.[6] This *bienveillance* is first of all permanent or constant. In contrast to the Greek tradition, where the king does not concern himself with the fate of the people, except in exceptional circumstances, God is always concerned with his people. In the metaphor of being shepherd, He cares constantly for their nourishment, rest, and well-being. This aspect of being shepherd has certainly slipped into the image that pastors often have of themselves in their vocation. A pastor is always a pastor, and not only from nine to five. Secondly, God's benevolence as shepherd is not only directed at the flock, but also at every individual sheep. He knows each sheep by its name and does not simply generalize. Later on, the evangelist John says the same thing about Jesus.[7] Thirdly, the benevolence of the shepherd also has a final goal. The shepherd's plan remains that of keeping his sheep together and leading them to green pastures. God's intention is to fulfill the covenant so that the people can truly be the people of God, not only as a means, but also as a final goal.

The final characteristic that Foucault distinguishes is in every way related to the same *bienveillance*. God's majesty as king, his glory, is always related to God's benevolence as shepherd. God's glory and transcendence have no meaning without his benevolence. Foucault then analyses the term *bienveillance* and brings out the meanings of "to watch over" and "being

---

6. Foucault, *Dits et écrits*, 138. "Tout est une question de bienveillance constante, individualisé et finale."

7. John 10:1–5: "Very truly, I tell you, anyone who does not enter the sheepfold by the gate but climbs in by another way is a thief and a bandit. The one who enters by the gate is the shepherd of the sheep. The gatekeeper opens the gate for him, and the sheep hear his voice. He calls his own sheep by name and leads them out. When he has brought out all his own, he goes ahead of them, and the sheep follow him because they know his voice. They will not follow a stranger, but they will run from him because they do not know the voice of strangers."

vigilant."[8] It is remarkable that God as king is not distant, but involved. He is committed to and watches over his flock. The only place in the Old Testament to be found where positive statements are made about God as watchman and of his watching over his people is in Psalm 121.[9] From the perspective of this positive meaning, Cain asks God indignantly whether he is his brother's keeper or watchman![10] The image of watching over and of the watchman likewise includes a certain asymmetry. It is thus noteworthy that Foucault pays insufficient attention to the reciprocity between God and the people. The concept of the covenant between the people and God allows one to reflect more from the perspective of a certain reciprocity: I shall be your God and you shall be my people.[11] In the covenant both partners have rights and duties.

The Good Shepherd

It is clear for Foucault that politics today have become so secularized that politicians no longer realize that their profile has been influenced by the biblical linking of power and benevolence. A politician should not only make laws, but also demonstrate that he cares. If a politician is not present at a time when people are suffering (for instance during the closing of a factory), then he loses respect and popularity. In order to further analyze this biblical influence, Foucault considers how Christianity has dealt with the combination of being both shepherd and king. It is clear that within the Christian tradition the title of shepherd has also been ascribed to Christ and to all who follow him and take up responsibility in the church community. Is the function of the pastor still linked to power and benevolence? A certain antipathy or resentment seems to hold sway among pastors regarding

---

8. Foucault, *Dits et écrits*, 139. "La bienveillance pastorale, en revanche, est beaucoup plus proche du <dévouement>. Tout ce que fait le berger, il le fait pour le bien de son troupeau. C'est sa préoccupation constante. Quand ils someillent, lui veille."

9. Ps 121:3–8: "He will not let your foot be moved; he who keeps you will not slumber, He who keeps Israel will neither slumber nor sleep. The Lord is your keeper; the Lord is your shade at your right hand. The sun will not strike you by day, nor the moon by night. The Lord will keep you from all evil; he will keep your life. The Lord will keep your going out and your coming in from this time on and forevermore."

10. Gen 4:9.

11. Lev 26:11–12: "I will place my dwelling in your midst, and I shall not abhor you. And I will walk among you, and will be your God, and you shall be my people."

PART 1—Fundamental Philosophical and Theological Reflections

the pole of power. The Foucault's perspective on *le pouvoir pastoral* can help to clarify this resentment.

Foucault first notes the central place of Jesus in Christianity. The title Good Shepherd is given to him.[12] Jesus' being shepherd goes hand in hand with his being Son of God. Jesus is the Son of God and watches over his flock, the church. Even here, power is integrated into Jesus' pastoral care and in the pastoral responsibility of all who take up leadership in the church community in his name. Secondly, Foucault seeks to better understand the transformation of the Hebrew interpretation that has taken place in Christianity. Although Foucault does not always succeed in clarifying this transformation accurately, it is significant and can be a mirror.

A first transformation that occurs in Christianity relates to the concept of responsibility.[13] In the Jewish tradition, God as shepherd is responsible for his flock and for the fate of each individual sheep. This typical Jewish thought is further developed, for instance, by Emmanuel Levinas, a Jewish philosopher, who understands the relationship between God and humans, in its entirety, as responsibility. Christianity adopts the concept of responsibility and gives it a central place in its conceptualization of pastoral work. Bishops and all pastors are responsible for the well-being of the faithful. But due to the re-contextualization in Greek and Roman cultures, this responsibility acquires a moralizing emphasis. The desert fathers and monasticism witness to the introduction of a striving for perfection and an emphasis on asceticism that stands in tension with God's offer of salvation. Foucault labels the transformation of responsibility into a responsibility for behavior as well as a transformation to the disadvantage of salvation. The church and her servants are thus not only responsible for the salvation of each of the faithful, but also for the actions of each of the faithful. Pastors should see to it that the faithful not only receive, but also do, that which is good. By exposing the tension in the church between grace and behavior, Foucault puts his finger on an actual source of resentment. Pastors feel resentment toward the moralizing aspect of responsibility in the church's pastoral care. They want to act out of mercy, but do not want to exert any moralizing

---

12. John 10:11: "I am the good shepherd. The good shepherd lays down his life for the sheep."

13. Foucault, *Dits et écrits*, 144. "Dans la conception chrétienne, le pasteur doit rendre compte—non seulement de chacune des brebis, mais de toutes leurs actions, de tout le bien ou le mal qu'elles sont susceptibles de faire, de tout ce qui leur arrive. De surcroît, entre chaque brebis et son pasteur, le christianisme conçoit un échange et une circulation complexes de péchés et de mérites."

influence, or become knights of morality for the simple reason that power is linked to a moralizing responsibility.

The second transformation of this Jewish body of thought in Christianity has to do with obedience. In Hebrew thought, the flock is obedient to the shepherd. Foucault points out that the people subject themselves to the Torah and to the will of God. The transformation in Christianity occurs because the relationship between the shepherd and the flock is conceived from the perspective of individual and integral dependence. Each of the faithful should not only obey God's will, but also God himself. As a believer, one therefore also binds oneself to all those representing God's will and thus, who are exercising a certain power. Consequently, forms of spirituality arose in early Christianity that emphasized subjugation and obedience, as a result of which these are seen as virtues. Foucault additionally touches upon a source of real resentment felt by many Christians toward obedience to the church or to her servants and toward the power that accompanies this obedience. This resentment is reinforced in the era of neo-liberalism, where no person wished to any longer be subject to anyone or anything.

A third transformation in Christianity is linked to individualization. The Hebrew tradition highlights that the shepherd knows each one of his sheep, and each sheep knows the shepherd. This individualization is expanded in Christianity: the shepherd must know the individual needs of each sheep, their innermost soul and the relationships among the sheep themselves. According to Foucault, forms of spirituality arose in early Christianity that emphasized asceticism and the growth toward perfection. Foucault again ascribes this to Christianity's rootedness in the Greco-Roman culture. Christianity has adopted from the Stoics, for instance, the examination of conscience and counseling. These Romans and Greeks were familiar with the custom of examining one's conscience daily in function of one's duties. This examination of conscience became a kind of measure on the road to perfection and provided a certain control over one's own passions. The concept of counseling was also well known. In the face of difficult decisions, one sought the advice of a counselor, usually a philosopher. According to Foucault, Christianity has adopted these practices and reinforced them by not limiting the examination of conscience and counseling to difficult circumstances, but by integrating them into daily life.[14] In

---

14. Foucault, *Dits et écrits*, 146. "La direction de conscience constituait un lien permanent: la brebis ne se laissait pas conduire à seule fin de franchir victorieusement quelque passe dangereuse; elle se laissait conduire à chaque instant."

PART 1—Fundamental Philosophical and Theological Reflections

the cultural context of early Christianity, therefore, striving for perfection was integrated in such a manner that asceticism was strongly emphasized, and all its necessary measures, to the disadvantage of soteriology. In spite of the fact that Foucault admits that a search for a synthesis between salvation and the striving for perfection has existed within the church, he still emphasizes the moralizing influence of the church and her legalistic thinking. In this way, Christianity has had a huge influence on the development of consciousness. In all likelihood this interpretation is also related to Foucault's perception of the church and with his personal biography.[15] Augustine emphasized, for instance, both asceticism and salvation. A person must renounce this world, but grace comes from God. The imbalance between salvation and behavior again touches on a resentment pastors still feel today. Pastors prefer to put all moralizing interpretations aside and to focus rather on salvation and caring for people. They would rather distance themselves, as Protestantism has done, from controlling the behavior of people, or from a one-sided asceticism as the way to holiness. They feel resistance to the great power that accompanies the control over the examination of conscience of the faithful.

CRITICAL COMMENTS AND SUGGESTIONS

Foucault's view unmasks and particularly brings to the fore the fact that compassion, in its biblical and theological roots, includes a strong element of power. In the course of the development of the Catholic faith, this aspect of power is strengthened, among others, by the ordained ministers and the way in which the sacraments were ministered. In Foucault's view, this therefore concerns a paradox between two elements, compassion and power, which at first sight hardly goes hand in hand, but which cannot be divided in the pastoral care of the church. Applied concretely to pastors, this means that being pastor is both a service and a mandate.

Going against the Current

How, in that legacy of power and compassion, do we act as pastors? A first step is to go and stand in the given-ness of compassion *and* power. Pastoral

---

15. Foucault was homosexual and in all likelihood, from that perspective, had difficulty with the church.

work can never be solely compassion; increasingly, it is also mediation. Jewish and Christian thought point out that the human person can never save herself, or pull himself out of the quagmire; one always needs an other (Other). The one who saves or mediates introduces a certain asymmetry whereby an element of power enters into the relationship. We cannot redeem ourselves; we need God or other people in his service who set us on the right path. Our existence is never autonomous, but received. In our contemporary culture that glorifies autonomy, this tension between compassion and power is very much a challenge for pastors. Mindfulness, in the way it is observed here in the West, starts from the premise that the human being is the only true manager of his or her own existence. The human being alone can, as it were, care for and liberate himself or herself. There is no mediator necessary. However, self-realization that is totally free of power is an illusion. Heteronomy is thereby at odds with liberalism. The Christian, and especially the Catholic tradition, however, has interpreted the mediating role in a very moralistic manner and has consequently reinforced the element of power. This has generated resentment among the present generation of pastors and Christians. Justifiably, more emphasis is now put on compassion than on power, but neither element can be detached from the other. Every pastor mediates and thus has to deal with the element of power that this implies.

De-ecclesiologizing among Pastors

The resentment among pastors also brings about a de-ecclesiologizing. Not only does resentment toward power exist, but it also exists toward being a representative of an institution that in a certain sense stands as a symbol of that power. An institution that has acted, through its power structure, in a moralizing way. Thus the trend of approaching an individual as another individual is reinforced. In so doing the pastor becomes a kind of mediator of meaning who may also possibly have a Christian content. In this context, opening up the priesthood to married men and to women as a response to the disappearance of the sacraments of the Eucharist and the anointing of the sick is not a solution, because even then, few will want to enter into such a power structure. The Judaeo-Christian tradition, in its central thesis of heteronomy, demands above all a counter-figure. If there is no counter-figure there can be no belief in a personal God. God is then often reduced to a part of one's own interiority. God then is, for instance, a collective name for the good in people, but not a counter-figure. Without heteronomy there can be no mediation. According to this ideology, not only is the pastor a mediator of God's salvation, but also a representative of the church community. Both relationships include a form of power. Foucault pays insufficient attention to the power that goes hand in hand with being the representative of an institution and a community. The specific challenge for pastoral-theological thought is to reflect on and give shape to this possession of power and submitting to power.

Room for Boldness

As mentioned above, Foucault defaults, in his analysis of *le pouvoir pastoral*, as far as reciprocity is concerned.[16] The people of God fulfill their obligations by keeping the Torah, and the covenant accords rights and duties to both partners. He emphasizes rightly that the Catholic tradition has given too much room to moralism and to the power that accompanies it, but, by shedding less light on reciprocity, he actually contributes to the enhancement of the perception of power. Whereas, some form of reciprocity and maturity is indeed present in the Jewish and Christian tradition. In order to clarify this critical reflection on Foucault, we now appeal—oh the irony!—once again to Foucault, namely to his work on the *parrèsia*.[17]

Although in *parrèsia* the emphasis is on "speaking frankly" *(le franc-parler)*, bold speech, according to Foucault, is active not only on the interindividual level, but also and especially on the social and political level. From the outset, it stands in relation to the administration and to the community. What is central is not the openness of direct and—nearly—brutal speech in itself, but daring to voice the truth in the community. There may be, on the part of the organization and authority structures of the community, a form of pressure and intimidation not to speak, or to weaken contrarian positions and to voice only what people want to hear. But the *parrèsiastès*—the bold one—endeavors not to let the close bond between conviction and truth be overwhelmed by the dominance of structures and "powers" in the community. Speaking boldly is thus more than a figure of speech, and in fact more than rhetoric or "good words." It wants to "speak the truth" in the context of the community, at the service of the community. This indeed requires courage, especially because this speaking the truth is

16. Chevallier, *Michel Foucault et le christianisme*.
17. Foucault, *Parrèsia*.

not without risk, namely when it says—precisely with regard to the "established order" in the community—something "dangerous." *Parrèsia* is a way of speaking the truth out loud: it is thus a speaking that comes "from below" and is directed "to the above." In addition, the bold speaker feels "obliged" to speak, even although he or she is free to remain silent or to be "circumspect." Hence, according to Foucault, the *parrèsia* is also an "art," albeit a difficult—but at the same time indispensable—art that every community requires in order to secure its future.

This also applies to the church community and to the pastors in the church community that is dear to them. Standing in the tension between compassion and power in the pastoral care of the church and proceeding from heteronomy, we argue for more institutional room for empowerment and boldness. This room within the institution would make standing within the tension more bearable and achievable. Boldness is a Jewish idea that can also be found among the Church fathers. Today we miss an objectively organized structure for boldness that is moreover canonically recognized and protected. Only thus can boldness, of which Foucault speaks, become effectively employed. "Pastoral *parrèsia*" is not frankly saying what is wrong with the other, but daring, in a relationship of asymmetry, to question the other: the pastor against the institution, the faithful against the pastor, in the context of—at the service of!—the community. Pastoral *parrèsia* seems to be a necessary way of limiting power, of leaving room for compassion, and for a pastor to be a representative of the church as "community of salvation."

BIBLIOGRAPHY

Büttgen, Philippe. "Théologie politique et pouvoir pastoral." *Annales. Histoire, Sciences Sociales* 5 (2007) 1129–54.
Chevallier, Philippe. *Michel Foucault et le christianisme*. Lyon: ENS Éditions, 2011.
Foucault, Michel. *Dits et écrits, 1954–1988*. Vol. 4, *1980–1988*. Edited by Daniel Defert and François Ewald. Paris: Gallimard, 1994.
———. *Parrèsia: Vrijmoedig spreken en waarheid*. Translated by Ineke Van der Burg. Amsterdam: Parrèsia/De Balie, 2004.

3

Beyond the Almighty Pastor
On Three Forms of Power in Pastoral Care

Stefan Gärtner

DURING ONE OF MY *first days of internship at the hospital, I walked into the room of a seriously ill patient who was recovering from a failed surgery she had undergone the day before. The tumor in her stomach had proven inoperable. I asked the gynecologist if the patient would be able to talk so soon after her surgery. She answered affirmatively. Beforehand, I had also spoken to the nurse, and she assured me that I should feel free to wake the patient if she was sleeping.*
I walked in and woke the patient gently by saying her name.

  P1: Mrs. D., I am the chaplain of the hospital and have come to see how you are doing.

  D1: That's very nice of you. I would have gone to church on Sunday, but I had to cancel.

  P2: No, that's not why I'm here. I only want to ask how you are. I come every week to give people support when they need it. I just drop in on people. And now I have come to see you. There is absolutely no obligation.

The above recounts the beginning of a conversation that one of our students at Tilburg University initiated as part of the pastoral training required for her master's of theology. It contains at least three aspects of power in pastoral care interaction.

One could call the first aspect the traditional one. Pastors had and still have power because they are pastors. Their ministry makes them respected persons with authority—whether they like it or not and whether they are aware of it or not. This *traditional power* makes the patient in our example justify herself for her absence at the Sunday service. She interprets the visit of the pastor as a visit with a controlling purpose. She implies a position of power that, given her apologetic answer in P2, the chaplain herself does not want to assume. I call this aspect of power in pastoral care traditional, because in late modern society, it is losing its significance more and more. The role of pastor as a person with a quasi natural authority is increasingly less accepted, even by loyal parishioners. We are beyond the almighty pastor. Nevertheless, this still plays a role in everyday pastoral practice.

The chaplain in the above dialogue also has power of a different kind. A power that is not of the kind she denies for herself in P2. Already before the conversation begins, the student puts herself in a superior position. She seeks collaboration with other professionals in the hospital and trusts in their appraisal of the state of health and the needs of the patient. She gathers information about the client and bases her interaction with the patient on it. Then she wakens the patient, an act that ordinarily only occurs in family and partnership relationships. In the logic of the hospital, however, this intimacy can be broken, if the timetable of the care-giving action requires it. This logic seems to be quite natural for the student. One must know that she was studying to become a nurse before she began studying theology.

We see another aspect of power in pastoral care. It concerns the fact that a pastor generates knowledge about his clients in coalition with other professionals and that he participates in a coordinated action. This gives him power. At the same time, pastoral care and counseling can be affected in subtle ways by other sources of plausibility than that of the Gospel. In our example, the boundaries of intimacy melt. In addition, the patient becomes an object or *sujet* who requires treatment. One could call this aspect *pastoral power*.

The patient in our verbatim is not exclusively an object of the chaplain's power. Although she is inferior and in need of help due to her illness, she has power on her part too. This is a third aspect of power in pastoral

PART 1—Fundamental Philosophical and Theological Reflections

care. One might speak of *client power*. A pastor depends on others who accept his role and his help. Power comes to nothing if individuals and communities no longer accept the agents of this power. We saw in our remark about traditional power that such power was produced by the anticipation of the patient even contrary to the explicit intention of the chaplain. It is not only his ministry, or the collaboration with other professionals that makes the pastor powerful. He also receives this position from the complementary expectations of his parishioners. The pastor is both powerful and dependent.[1] Power in pastoral care proves to be mutual.

TRADITIONAL POWER

I have already indicated that the foundation for the traditional power of the pastor has disappeared to a great extent in late modern societies. Parishioners are in a position to evade this power by repudiation. This occurs, for example, in relation to the sexual teachings of the Roman Catholic Church, or in the acts of choice which parishioners make between different pastoral offers. In late modernity, much has changed from the past, "neither internal personal sanctions, set up for example by means of a 'pastoral' approach based on fear, nor the threat of social ostracism compel people . . . to become involved with the church."[2]

After the decline of the church of the masses in many countries of the Western world, pastors cannot guarantee that they will have a direct influence on "souls." Pastoral care is no longer associated with effective social control, although this is sometimes still attempted, especially in connection with the provision of the sacraments. However, as a rule many pastors themselves are overwhelmed by the plurality of late modern life patterns. Their old answers no longer seem to be appropriate. On this basis alone, the claims of their traditional power come to nothing.

Pastoral care has become part of what is called the late modern "vicarious religion." A majority recognizes religion as important; however, this may not be connected with personal consequences. Religion is assigned to the professional pastor instead. He should take care of it on behalf of others, so that they can enlist pastoral care and counseling selectively in periods of crisis.[3] This undermines the traditional power of the pastor.

1. Gärtner, "Powerful and Dependent," 157–67.
2. Bucher, "Body of Power," 121.
3. Davie, *Religion in Modern Europe*, 177–80.

The Past of the Traditional Power

In the past, people continued to be confronted with the exercise of power by church authorities. These authorities had distinctive instruments to sanction and control in order to assert and to protect their influence. Opposition to this form of power could be met with exclusion from the congregation, or even from the social community. In this model, power worked top down reflecting a pyramidal structure. The pastor had a firm place in this pyramid. He could avail himself of a complex set of tools to check, regulate and sanction people's behavior. This enabled him to make his influence felt.

This traditional power of the pastor involved the idea that parishioners were no longer solely responsible for their own lives or their souls. They could transfer this responsibility to somebody who fulfilled this task by virtue of his ministry: the pastor. The character of his work is best described in the metaphor of the shepherd and his flock.[4] Just as the shepherd looks after his herd, the pastor looked after every single sheep of his congregation.

This model helped to bring about "the development of 'pastoral technology' in the management of men"[5] in the church. It has seven basic characteristics.[6]

1. The ultimate goal of the pastor and his flock was not in this world. On the contrary, distance was taken from the (negatively valued) influences of earthly reality. The focus was the salvation of the individual soul in heaven.

2. The pastor had a personal responsibility for guiding his congregation, for it was his duty to justify his acts toward God. This comprehensive responsibility left its mark on the self-awareness of pastors in the form of readiness, absolute servitude, and self-sacrifice.[7]

3. Between the pastor and his parish a complex and paradoxical network of dependencies developed. On the one hand, the good behavior of

---

4. Foucault, "Omnes et Singulatim," 223–54.

5. Ibid., 231.

6. Ibid., 223–54; Foucault, *Security, Territory, Population*, 165–83; Foucault, "Subject and Power," 208–26.

7. Zulehner, *Priester im Modernisierungsstress*, 221–25.

PART 1—Fundamental Philosophical and Theological Reflections

the sheep commended the shepherd. On the other hand, he could only prove his real skills in light of a recalcitrant flock.

4. Pastoral guidance was not only directed toward the congregation as a whole, but also toward every individual. The traditional power of the pastors is "an individualizing power."[8] It is based, in the end, on the personal relationship between the pastor and each parishioner.

5. Traditional power encompassed all aspects of life, just as a shepherd would take care of the flock's every need. This structure of subject-object led to a "usually unquestioning, sometimes even infantile care-mentality"[9] among the sheep.

6. For the exercise of his power, the pastor used an economy of rewards and punishments. Its ultimate aim was pure obedience.

7. Traditional power is not just about outward behavior, but also about an individual's inner life, his soul, his consciousness, and his suppressed thoughts. Comprehensive techniques for guiding and controlling souls and for moral education were developed. As a result of this, the individual internalized an introspective perspective. This completed the combination of guidance and self-restraint.

This traditional form of ecclesial power represented a unique type of power. "It is oblative (as opposed to the principle of sovereignty); it is individualizing (as opposed to legal power); it is coextensive and continuous with life; it is linked with a production of truth—the truth of the individual himself."[10] Superficially the issue appears to be the care and support for each parishioner. This manifests itself as power, however, and it created a disciplining effect. In other words: the traditional power of the pastor is "a power of care."[11]

The Bipolar Structure of Traditional Power

This form of power has of course not simply disappeared in late modernity. However, Foucault makes it clear that the power relations of the present time are more differentiated. His aim was to think of "power without the

8. Foucault, *Security, Territory, Population*, 128.
9. Steinkamp, *Macht der Hirten*, 16.
10. Foucault, "Subject and Power," 214.
11. Foucault, *Security, Territory, Population*, 127.

king."[12] We could complement this: to think of power without the pastor. The model of hierarchical power imbalances can no longer be regarded as exclusive. Nowadays, we face a much more diffuse form of power. It is effective not by direct exclusion, but, on the contrary, by enclosing everything and everyone. It operates by influencing our conceptions of what we believe is ordinary, prohibited, allowed, normal, true, healthy, and acceptable. It appears these are not as obvious as they would seem. They are actually very powerful structures that form our day-to-day reality, down to every relationship.

Instead of the traditional, symbolically, and institutionally anchored power of ecclesial authorities, we are confronted with a much more subtle power today. "Power is not an institution, and not a structure; neither is it a certain strength we are endowed with; it is the name that one attributes to a complex strategical situation in a particular society."[13] This power works by influencing our images of what we think is normal. These images seem to be quite natural in our social contacts, and mark our self-awareness as well.[14] This type of power is all-pervasive. It is a circulating phenomenon and a component of all relationships, thus also of the pastoral relationship. Power comes from all directions. Power "from above" is merely an expression of this disciplining power at all levels of our daily life.

Contrastingly, the traditional power in pastoral care was primarily based on the polarity between authorities and the oppressed, between the powerful pastor and the powerless parishioner.[15] An unequivocal distribution of power takes place: one has all power, the other none. A one-sided dependency is indicated from the bottom upward, from parishioner to pastor. Our case study has already made clear, however, that the latter is also actively involved in maintaining this traditional monopoly of power in the church.

Nevertheless, in late modernity, fewer and fewer people are willing to do so. The steering and controlling function of the ecclesial authorities, as it is suggested in the model of traditional power in pastoral care, has dramatically lost significance. The direct, authoritarian implications of the shepherd's role have become outdated. They represent a hierarchical type

12. Foucault, *History of Sexuality*, 91.

13. Ibid., 93.

14. Neuger, "Power and Difference," 65–85.

15. Pollefeyt, "Intimiteit in de pastoraal," 230–34; Bauer, "Macht und Gnade," 54–55; Doehring, *Taking Care*, 19.

of power that is less significant today.¹⁶ Its bipolar structure does not do justice to the comprehensive and subtle way power works under the conditions of late modernity.

In addition, the bipolar structure of the traditional power concept insinuates an one-sidedness that overlooks the reciprocity of power in pastoral care and counseling. This reciprocity exists, even if there is always (and must always be) an asymmetrical relationship between pastor and parishioner, or between chaplain and client. One may not think of power unilaterally from top down. One must assume that *both* sides prolong the traditional power of the pastor. Every one-sided model must be complemented, because the parishioner is actively involved in the preservation of the superior position of the pastor.¹⁷ Without his or her interventions, a dominant position for the latter would not exist.

Finally, it is worth noting that the overall balance of power between pastors and their parishioners is never constant. This is simply an insinuation that stems from the traditional concept of power. It entails the idea that the increased influence of one side would automatically be balanced out at the expense of the other side. However, pastors and parishioners could also intensify each other's power through their actions. In the ideal case, this results in a mutual empowerment.¹⁸ This possibility is ignored in the traditional concept of power in pastoral care. The problems of this model, therefore, arise not only from the extensive repudiation by parishioners and clients or from the advent of a new form of pastoral power in late modernity. This model is also contradictory in itself.

Adopting the Traditional Power

In late modernity, the idea of linear, one-sided, and stable power relations from top down in pastoral care needs to be complemented with a deeper lying modus of exercising power. A modus that allows a varied, permanent, and liquid influence at all levels of social life. This power does not achieve its status through orders and prohibitions, nor through rewards and punishments, as was typical for the traditional model. It works by a movable arsenal of regulation, education, and correction, the ultimate purpose being

16. Steinkamp, *Macht der Hirten*, 15–17.

17. Hochschild, "Was mich rettet," 65–67; Sander, "Gott im Zeichen der Macht," 111–15.

18. Karle, *Pfarrberuf als Profession*, 165–68.

to "homogenize" the individuals. It "is both strong and shapeless."[19] The individual is not an offender or a victim in the first place; power was already circulating prior to and independent of the person. "In other words: power is not applied to the individuals, it goes right through them."[20]

The traditional power of the church and her ministers has played an essential historical role in making this effective. Although her current significance as an authority has all but vanished for the reasons mentioned above, the church has created important preconditions for the effectiveness of the disciplining power in late modern societies. The latter can thrive through by making use of the Christian practice of confession and spiritual care, both of which have existed since the third century.[21]

Due to the traditional power of the church, individuals grew ever more aware of the inner causes of their acts. This has become an essential part of a ritual of remembrance: "Thoughts, desires, voluptuous imaginings, delectations, combined movements of the body and the soul; henceforth all this had to enter, in detail, into the process of confession and guidance."[22] This gradually causes the individual to develop a fitting *habitus*, which has provided a perfect basis for the disciplining effect of power since the modern age. The church's practice of penance and spiritual guidance paved the way for the all-encompassing internalization of the late modern registers of power.

According to Foucault, the modern state integrated a power strategy that, for a long time, was practiced exclusively in Christian institutions. The state integrated it into its own political form, combining the totalizing tendency of its authority, which desired to have everybody and everything under control, with the individualizing tendency of the traditional ecclesial power. It could fall back upon certain attitudes and habits that individuals had developed within the church to allow the disciplining effect of its own power to flourish in the form of concrete governmental technologies.

It is understandable why the modern state fell back on the traditional form of individualizing and disciplining power to exercise its authority. In some respects its political power filled a certain vacuum that had developed with the Enlightenment. From this period onwards, the church began to lose her influence, due to the dissident behavior of the believers. Her

19. Sennett, *Corrosion of Character*, 57.
20. Foucault, *Dispositive der Macht*, 82.
21. Foucault, *Security, Territory, Population*, 147–56.
22. Foucault, *History of Sexuality*, 19.

sovereignty was seriously undermined.²³ By then, however, she had already made essential historical contributions in terms of "mentality" to the "civilization process" (N. Elias) simply by exercising her traditional power.

The government merely had to secularize the original goal of this power—obtaining the salvation of souls.²⁴ The issue is no longer the future in heaven, but the prosperity of the individuals here and now. The way in which the government provides for this is comparable to the comprehensive ways the church did this in the past: health care, safety, solidarity, education et cetera. Meanwhile, the role of the shepherd becomes increasingly anonymous, bureaucratic, and differentiated. Several institutions, such as hospitals, schools, the police, prisons, the psychiatry, and employers, now play this role. Knowledge about the individual can be entered into a ubiquitous network that is connected to a complex register of power. At the same time, the network is used to encumber people with this normative register.

PASTORAL POWER

From the perspective of the pastor (the originally exclusive agent of the shepherd's role), this analysis raises the question of how he is confronted with this subject now that he and his congregation have to a great extent lost their traditional power. In late modernity, the pastor is primarily involved in the registers of power as a result of his institutional embedment. I will try to elaborate this thesis. Ecclesial and public organizations join together in coalition to form a common power complex. This is a typical example of the disciplining pastoral power effect we discussed in the previous section. It is neither his personal authority, nor is it his traditional role that gives the pastor power today. His influence stems from his participation in pastoral power, which affects the social world at all levels, and which manifests itself in different institutions responsible for the cure and care of people.

The Ambivalent Power of the Ministers

The pastors' institutional integration has consequences for their (power) position. Firstly, they answer to their role as ministers authorized and sent by their congregations; they are representatives of the religious institution

---

23. Foucault, *Security, Territory, Population*, 191–253.
24. Foucault, "Omnes et Singulatim," 240–45.

for which they work. Even if they choose to distance themselves from the church, they are still her agents. As ministers, pastors are authorities in themselves, if only because they are seen by others as representatives of the ecclesial authority.

This is still the case, despite the previously mentioned dwindling importance of the church as a factor of power in secularized late modern culture and the diminished reputation of the ministerial pastoral role, as well as the increased significance that is attached to the individual personality of a pastor.[25] The decline of traditional power expresses itself in these developments. Nevertheless, a pastor still symbolizes an authority for some, due to his position as minister and representative of his congregation.

This proposition of the pastor as an institutional figure of authority has both positive and negative implications that are quite different from any individual interpretation he himself might have about it. In this respect, the pastoral relationship is not primarily connected with the person of the individual pastor. It is dominated by the previous experiences of those seeking pastoral care with the church and her ministers.[26] In other words, the pastoral setting is already fixed before the pastor makes his appearance. He is stigmatized by the parishioners as "the" pastor, who is to them a positive or a negative figure of authority.

This stigmatization occurs only because the pastor is also a minister. It follows that the ecclesial authorization to act as a religious leader may have a problematic effect. It seems to affect the pastoral relationship without any personal interference. Even the pastor who chooses *not* to act on the basis of the authority of his ministry (as in our case study), he is still forced to do so through the expectations or the fears of his parishioners. Hence, pastors' ordination and the ministerial role given to them by the congregation are highly ambivalent for them.

The ambivalent feeling is strengthened by the fact that the power the church transfers to her ministers is a legitimizing power. It is external (it is received from the outside), public (it is transferred by means of a rite, a charter, an employment contract etc.), and institutional (it is given with the authority of a social organization).[27] This legitimization enables the use of power in pastoral care, but limits it at the same time. The pastor only possesses delegated power, which the institution can always take away or at

---

25. Klessmann, *Pfarrbilder im Wandel*, 27–65.
26. Pattison, *Critique of Pastoral Care*, 73–79.
27. Stortz, *PastorPower*, 36–40.

least limit. This becomes extra precarious when the congregation uses no transparent or adequate procedures for managing conflicts.[28]

This problem is aggravated in those cases where there is insufficient "concordance between responsibility and proficiency";[29] where, in other words, institutional authority is not combined with the personal abilities—of the pastor—necessary for carrying out the delegated tasks. The same holds true vice versa in cases in which the church, which equips her ministers with authority, falls short in her internal structure of the requirements and real developments in pastoral care and counseling.[30] Consequentially, pastors have certain competences, but are not allowed to exercise them due to the limitations of their ministry—for example because they are lay-ministers. Both experiences intensify feelings of ambivalence in the pastor when he uses the power he has been given by his congregation. This tension can lead to a diffusion of roles and to inner conflicts.

The institutional pastoral power, legitimized by his church, comes with major tension for the pastor. It puts him into a paradoxical situation. As a minister he is powerful and expected to exercise that power. Indeed, the backing connection of his authority with an institutional power can even be relieving for him. At the same time, his power is limited by the congregation, since he is sent by it and only for that very reason powerful. In essence, he is both powerful and powerless, as far as he is dependent.

Pastoral Professionalism

Institutional pastoral power as an authority transferred to him by his congregation must have a highly ambivalent effect on the minister. This does not only have an inner-ecclesial aspect, however. The ambivalence we have just identified will become stronger when he becomes as a chaplain part of the public care system.[31] The institution that ordinates and authorizes him is in some countries an essential part of this system.

This has consequences for the pastor as a representative of the church. He is once more confronted with the question of pastoral power. What is at stake here is the way in which he can take up and defend his position

---

28. Körver, "Conflicten in de context van het pastoraat," 37–47; Jähnichen, "Kirche mit Macht," 139–42.

29. Stenger, "Führen und Leiten," 20.

30. Karrer, "Seelsorger und Seelsorgerinnen," 240–48.

31. Haslinger, *Diakonie*, 100–61.

within the care system. This position is no longer uncontested. Psychologists, doctors, and social workers, and increasingly also volunteers,[32] are also offering their services. They are eager to take on those tasks that used to be obviously and exclusively the property of the chaplain. A struggle for the limited resources of social care has arisen between various types of caregivers.

This has an immediate effect on the work of the pastor. First of all, he is challenged to secure his position within the public system of social care. He often does so and is very conscious of his power. Trends toward pastoral professionalization in his training and his practice are part of this. From a power oriented perspective, these tendencies—apart from the competence profit linked with them—can be regarded as an attempt to defend the position of pastoral and spiritual counseling within the system of social care.[33] It is only logical that chaplains orientate themselves toward the standards that are used in the field of psychotherapy and in psycho-social disciplines, as this occurs for example within Clinical Pastoral Training programs.[34]

This type of professionalization leads to a development in which pastoral care in the self-awareness of the pastor "shows with regard to his own experience and to his profession more and more similarities with the . . . practice of other social care professions."[35] How does one still differ from what these others do, from the psychologist, the doctor, and the social worker?[36] We can interpret this uncertainty about his role as a result and a consequence of the professionalization of the pastor, which itself is a result and a consequence of the integration of pastoral counseling into the functionally differentiated public care system.[37] For such conflicts do not arise at all in a self-contained ecclesial context of pre-modern or modern provenance.

In the actual competition with other caregivers, it is all the more important to clearly identify the difference between a chaplain and other professionals. One way of doing so is by emphasizing the pastor's uniqueness.

---

32. Karrer, "Seelsorger und Seelsorgerinnen," 240–41; Rendle, "Reclaiming Professional Jurisdiction," 412–14.

33. Brouwer, *Pastor tussen macht en onmacht*; Schilderman, *Religion as a Profession*.

34. Rendle, "Reclaiming Professional Jurisdiction," 415–16.

35. Brouwer, *Pastor tussen macht en onmacht*, 173; Greenwald et al., "Identity of Pastoral Counselors," 51–69.

36. Gärtner, "Staying a Pastor," 48–60.

37. Karle, *Pfarrberuf als Profession*.

This is the best way to become indispensable as a professional. Pastors can achieve this by focusing their work on the "hopeless cases" that the competition is unable to help. Another possibility is to emphasize the ministerial character of liturgical acts and the exclusive part a pastor plays in these.[38] In this way, professionalization also leads to an increasing specialization and to a competition that undermines a real collaboration with others.

Pastoral professionalization trends, therefore, have different consequences. They force chaplains to face the experience "that the relevance and the status of their profession must be guaranteed by competence and not by institutional protection."[39] The social significance of the pastoral role crumbles in the late modern society. Within the public care system pastors now have to guarantee such social significance themselves, namely by being competent, by specializing their work, and by making it a professional practice. This is why pastoral professionalization within the scope of the public care system appears to be an adequate attempt to impose one's own interests while the institution distributes pastoral power.

Assignment of Roles

Apart from the *uncertainty* about roles, the strategy of professionalization, which is used to avoid the ambivalence stemming from this uncertainty, has some further effects. What is interesting here is that we face the exact opposite effect. The integration of the chaplain into the public care system and the resulting professionalization forces him to behave in a certain way. Therefore, there appears to be an *assignment* of roles too.

Relationships inside the system of institutional pastoral power are characterized by a role-specific asymmetry, which also influences the chaplain's professional contacts. He confirms this asymmetry by his institutional profile. The same applies to him as does to the therapist, the doctor, or the social worker. As a result of this, pastoral counseling cannot be based on real reciprocity, even if that notion is part of the self-awareness of the pastor, or is advocated in the practical-theological theory, for instance by referring to the equality that should take priority over the asymmetry between client and chaplain.[40] The institutional role of the latter constantly reaffirms a complementary structure in pastoral counseling. It manifests

---

38. Hoge and Wenger, *Evolving Visions*, 61–78.
39. Bucher and Ladenhauf, "Räume des Aufatmens," 174.
40. Vosman, "Macht en geweld," 33–49.

itself in the following polarities: helping–helpless; knowing–not-knowing; superior–inferior; active–passive. These polarities clearly form a powerful restraint in the pastoral setting.

The confidence, for example, with which the client treats a chaplain, and which manifests itself in the client's willingness to talk to a perfect stranger about intimate affairs, is an expression of their complementary relationship. Paradoxically, this confidence is based on a certain professional behavior that determines the pastor. It is based on the redemption of the client's expectations by his actual practice.[41] The client has confidence as soon as a chaplain responds with the expected behavior and acts as a typical pastor. The pastor who, in contrast to this, abandons his professional role causes a disturbance in the communication and confusion. At the same time, this is an aspect of power within the pastoral setting,[42] since pastoral care and counseling tend to an active–passive distribution between the involved parties.

There will inevitably be a role-specific asymmetry when a chaplain operates within the logic of a care institution. He will officially be expected to behave in a certain way. At the same time, this is an expression of pastoral power, for any contact will be that of a professional caregiver with a client seeking help. As a result of this, pastoral counseling duplicates the medical-therapeutic paradigm that is typical for social care institutions. The client faces a qualified professional who wants to contribute to his healing. The relationship between a chaplain and the one seeking help is characterized by an imbalance of power in which the client has a deficit that the pastor diagnoses and treats. A structure of subject versus object is established between them, for one is exclusively the helper, the other exclusively in need of help.

This is the beginning of a cycle of expectation and fulfillment that will gather a momentum of its own to such an extent that the congruence between expectation and fulfillment becomes the main criterion. In other words, the mere fact of there being pastoral and spiritual counseling becomes crucial. This can lead to a paradoxical situation in which the pastor, despite his original intention, is only interested in sustaining his activities because they allow him to continue his pastoral power. The authority connected with his practice entices him into striving predominantly for this

---

41. Karle, *Pfarrberuf als Profession*, 59–133.
42. Pollefeyt, "Intimiteit in de pastoraal," 227–30.

PART 1—Fundamental Philosophical and Theological Reflections

authority itself. He needs to retain the client in order to avoid losing his importance as a professional.

The Deficit Model of Care

Together with the medical-therapeutic paradigm, the chaplain will also adopt the ideas of what is "ill," "needy," "unhealthy," and "abnormal" in this sector. These conceptions are now applied to pastoral counseling as well. As clients, those asking for pastoral care see themselves both one-sidedly as deficient and confronted with the norm that their deficit can and must be conquered by the work of an expert.[43] The reintegration into normal, healthy life becomes the obvious goal of this deficit model of care. In addition, a holistic ideology, with optimistic expectations about curability,[44] and the late modern myth of a successful life[45] are expressed. These characterize the medical-therapeutic paradigm—and now pastoral care and counseling too.

The adoption of this paradigm is reinforced by the fact that the chaplain wants to cooperate both methodically and organizationally with the other caregivers on a comparable level. We saw this endeavor already in our case study. Cooperation with others is regarded as a hallmark of pastoral professionalism. Consequentially, a pastor tends to be less an advocate of the interests of his clients and more an advocate "of those who are currently in charge. The pastor obviously redoubles their pastoral power by the adoption of the 'power technique' psychology, aiming at normalization and discipline."[46] Clients are tied down to their object roles.

Action is taken on the clients' behalf. The medical-therapeutic paradigm clearly defines who gives care and who receives it. There is no middle course. If a chaplain completely adopts this thinking, he weakens any abilities the client may have for helping himself or herself. The latter will now think of himself or herself as in need of care, namely analogous to the behavior of the pastor. Of course, clients are, in fact, in need of care. Therefore, when criticizing the deficit model of care, one must distinguish between the overall structure of pastoral care and the concrete situation at

---

43. Luther, *Religion und Alltag*, 224–38.
44. Reuter, "Der heilsame Blick," 265–77.
45. Drechsel, "Der lange Schatten," 314–28.
46. Wittrahm, *Seelsorge, Pastoralpsychologie und Postmoderne*, 24.

hand. Yet, within the medical-therapeutic paradigm, any ability that the client might have to help himself tends to be pushed aside.

This fact cannot be refuted by claiming that the chaplain's main purpose is to help people to help themselves, and not the use of any form of pastoral power.[47] This popular notion simply expresses a "for the present pastoral care typical attitude of pastors, namely to relativize their own role."[48] Their primary purpose would involve becoming superfluous during the course of the pastoral contact.

The basis of this postulate and of a fitting behavior for pastors is yet another standard from the medical-therapeutic paradigm. From this perspective, one can only help the client efficiently if he can be made to understand his defects and deficits and to develop his own strategies to overcome them. The paradox of this approach arises from the fact that the aimed empowerment leads, in the end, only into the powerful registers of the putative normal and healthy.[49] In addition, the responsibility for reaching this goal is entrusted to the individual. Finally, this is merely about his ability to bow voluntarily to the registers of pastoral power.

Even a model of pastoral counseling that interprets the interventions of the chaplain as a more or less non-directive stimuli from the outside, the "system client" is thus confronted with the underlying tendency toward pastoral power—a tendency which is typical for the public care system. After all, this is where this type of pastoral care takes place. In particular, we must think of the internalization of the interventions of a pastor by his client within the dynamics of transference and countertransference.[50] The strategy outlined above only serves to disguise the implicit working of power. The paradox of care still exists within a systemic concept of pastoral care and counseling. The removal of the asymmetric structure of inequality between client and chaplain is one of its main goals. They both try to reach it, however, within an institutional framework that stands in the way of their endeavor.[51]

---

47. Janowski, "Theologia Gubernationis," 75–76.
48. Steck, *Praktische Theologie*, 604.
49. Petter, "Leiblichkeit als Machtinstrument," 189–202.
50. Hansen Robison, "Abuse of Power," 395–404.
51. Haslinger, *Diakonie*, 343–44.

PART 1—Fundamental Philosophical and Theological Reflections

A Pastoral Culture of Experts

One further effect of the integration of pastoral counseling in the public care system is the creation of a pastoral culture of experts. It is an expression of the true power relations. "The overvaluing of the caregiver's expertise and devaluing of the care receiver's expertise create a power imbalance which can become abusive of both caregiver and care receiver (noting that the care receiver is more at risk of being abused)."[52] In addition, this has a tendency toward devaluating forms of a day-to-day pastoral care and counseling given by volunteers, who are dismissed as unprofessional.

Exponents of this culture of the pastoral expert present themselves as irreplaceable. Their activities are packed in an aura of exclusivity and complexity. Parishioners and other volunteers do not even dare to begin with pastoral care. They immediately refer it to the responsible experts. This in turn only serves to strengthen their dominant role. The expert power of the pastor can develop to the full.[53] This again strengthens his power position as a professional and undermines day-to-day pastoral care.[54] At the same time, it makes those needing pastoral care "real cases" that have to be treated by an expert.

It has become clear that institutionally embedded pastoral care and counseling are part of the disciplining registers of power in late modern society. All developments mentioned result in a pastoral setting with very powerful implications. As a professional, the chaplain gathers knowledge about the inner life of his needy client and gains pastoral power over him. He does so within the public system of social care, in a well orchestrated harmony between Christian and secular care. This is how the pastor acquires his part in the overall registers of pastoral power. His authority merges with the power of the institution and, at the same time, affirms and strengthens it. Conversely, his power appears to be one of its typical modes of expression. Altogether we face a symbiotic power effect.

CLIENT POWER

I have already pointed out in the first reflection on our case study that the client is actively involved in preserving the power of the student or the

52. Doehring, *Taking Care*, 80.
53. Remmelzwaal, *Actief en afhankelijk*, 227–28.
54. Brouwer, *Pastor tussen macht en onmacht*, 58–60.

chaplain. The relationship between them is by no means one-sided, but reciprocal.[55] A pastor is always dependent on his parishioners. It is important to elaborate on this aspect in light of the clarification offered in the last chapter of the apparently encompassing effect of pastoral power on everything and everyone, and the special share that a pastor has in this. The client is not only an object of power in pastoral care, he also participates in it.

The Dependency of the Shepherd on the Flock

Firstly, this manifests itself through the strong impact that the passive and help-requesting attitude of a client has on a pastor. It is powerful because the pastor, as a professional and not as a private individual or a volunteer, can hardly escape it. A pastor should, and he always wants to, grant care and support. At the same time, he is confronted with the client's power. The role model associated with his profession, which was topic of the last chapter, results in a complementary dependency in pastoral care: because the client expects and may expect a certain form of help, the pastor, as a pastor, must provide it.

In addition, power exists only as long as a community implements a policy of cohesion and accepts its leaders and the agents of authority: "Power is never the property of an individual; it belongs to a group and remains in existence only so long as the group keeps together."[56] A pastor has power only because he can exercise it over a congregation that supports and accepts his leading position, as it is expressed in his ministerial role. The parishioners refer to this role when they enlist pastoral care and counseling resulting in the above mentioned complementary dependency. A pastor is much more than a private individual. As a minister, he is a public figure and a representative of the ecclesial community. He is a model believer. One can always count on him.

Vice versa, this means that the pastor's claim to power comes to nothing without a corresponding social basis, or it can only be enforced with violence. Since individuals do not have real power "as long as they cannot count on the open or implied assent of others."[57] Without roots in a com-

---

55. Remmelzwaal, *Actief en afhankelijk*, 225–39; Stortz, *PastorPower*, 40–43; Karle, *Pfarrberuf als Profession*, 298–99.

56. Arendt, *Violence*, 44.

57. Hübenthal, "Macht," 46.

munity that upholds it, power no longer exists. If one still tries to apply power despite lack of support from the community, the result is the abuse of power. According to Hannah Arendt, such abuse is actually no longer about power, but about violence: "Power and violence are opposites; where the one rules absolutely, the other is absent."[58]

This notion is especially interesting in view of the already mentioned secularization and the decline of the church's influence on late modern society. Today there is an actual loss of power within pastoral care caused by the erosion of its original social basis and of its self-evident, quasi natural plausibility. This melting of traditional power in pastoral care can result in the temptation to compensate for this loss. It can lead to the use of violence in various possible forms. Obviously there is a fluent boundary between power and the abuse of power within the church—and without it.[59]

It should be clear that this strategy of compensating for the decline of one's former position is very dangerous or at least little promising. That position is constantly threatened due to the effect of the client power. The church, as a social organization in late modern society, is dependent upon her members. The same holds true for the pastor. His position of leadership is similarly challenged by the possible rejection by his clients. This can no longer be concealed by the congregation through its support and legitimization of the authority of its leaders. The church's canonical or theological protection of a minister's position toward his parish, for example, does not neutralize the subtle, but nevertheless very powerful dependency of the shepherd on his herd. Since it has "an important instrument of power in the hands: check out and stay away."[60]

There is, in other words, a fundamental dependency of the shepherd on the flock. This becomes obvious when one recognizes that fewer clients enlist pastoral care and counseling as if they were a matter of course. A pastor finds himself torn between his actual authority on the one hand, and the dependency of his power on the wishes, expectations, imaginations, and needs of clients and parishioners on the other hand. What is useful for the clients, is what gives significance to pastoral care and counseling. Their needs become the norm. The work of a pastor is modified only to the extent that it matches the expectations of his parishioners.

58. Arendt, *Violence*, 56.
59. Kämpfer, "Macht," 273–82.
60. Brouwer, *Pastor tussen macht en onmacht*, 113.

This client power is even strengthened by subtle "processes of the proto-professionalization"[61] on the part of the clients. This concerns behavioral patterns that strategically anticipate the professional acts of the chaplain in the hope of attracting. Through such behavioral patterns, the client reaches his goal, namely to promote his own interests. He forces the pastor to grant help, care, and attention. The latter must answer this demand complementarily with pastoral care.

The Market Model of Pastoral Care

At this point, pastoral care is confronted with the same problems as all care professions. In return for the financial provision of the government, the church, the client, or the institution, a pastor cares, listens, gives advice, practices nearness and compassion, and performs rituals. Because he has been paid for it, it is almost impossible for him to refuse the parishioners their wishes. The neoliberal market model of the consumer society unfolds its dominant plausibility.[62] It induces a customer mentality on the part of the client. On such a basis, one has the right to claim good pastoral care, since one has "the freedom to treat the whole of life as one protracted shopping spree."[63] Furthermore, the pastor is in need of these customers to maintain his position in the public care system and also in his congregation.

In addition, the organization for which he works sometimes follows the logic of this market model without paying attention to its consequences.[64] Superficially this is about saving costs; subliminally, however, it again concerns the question of power. Since "the attractiveness of (neoliberal) management concepts in connection with the economically forced reorganization of ecclesial and diaconal care . . . has also to do with the old *pastoral power*. It returns in these concepts both familiar and stylish. It is now brought *à jour*."[65] For the individual pastor, this strengthens his feelings of dependency and of functional overload. He can escape

---

61. Baart, *Theorie van de presentie*, 810.
62. Bröckling et al., *Gouvernementalität der Gegenwart*.
63. Bauman, *Liquid Modernity*, 89.
64. Schlamelcher, "Unternehmen Kirche," 213–56; Schlamelcher, "Ökonomisierung der Kirchen," 145–77; Surzykiewicz, "Rezeption ökonomischer Führungstheorien," 560–73.
65. Halbe, "Chancen des Subjekts," 249.

neither the customer wishes of his parishioners, nor the cost-saving wishes of his congregation.

The power of the clients reaches into the last reserves of the pastoral activities. We have seen that it is important for the pastor to cultivate these reserves. For in doing so he is able to defend his independence and to indentify his significance in relation to other professional caregivers. The liturgical and ritual acts within pastoral counseling, for example, belong to these reserves. In the publicly funded care system, however, *kasualia*, as the anointing or blessing of the sick, or the viaticum, both of which ideally arise organically from the pastoral contact, easily gain the status of a service to be paid for—be it only in the perception of those who ask for it.

Therefore, the economic trends, which dominate the public care system and also churches and congregations, have an impact on the pastor.[66] They may result in parishioners acting as customers who have the right to his service. This is an expression of their client power. Pastoral care participates in the comprehensive and the whole-of-life-marking utilization trend, in which nearly everything can be defined as money. Pastoral practice is channeled into the economy of attention.[67] Client power is the power of customers who can enlist the time and the compassion of a pastor or a chaplain. "The balance of power between the religious individual and the former powerful religious authorities has turned around. The internal communication of the church has changed from domination-relationships between leaders and performers into exchange-relationships between service providers and people asking for this service."[68]

The Economy of Attention

What are the rules of this economy of attention? The attention, compassion, empathy, devotion and so forth, which a person gives, are longed for in late modern society. They have become scarce goods. Attention is "our scarcest resource."[69] It is fought for in a society in which the material basis to a great extent is considered to be secure, even if often it is not. Attention and time for each other are becoming increasingly more important.[70] According to

66. Schmälzle, "Monetarisierung von Religion," 262–81.
67. Franck, *Ökonomie der Aufmerksamkeit*.
68. Bucher, "Ehrenamt in der Transformationskrise," 69.
69. Bolz, "Die Splitter des Zeitpfeils," 131.
70. Nolte, *Kampf um Aufmerksamkeit*, 47–84.

the ruling logic of the market-model, both become goods of exchange that one must use cleverly and strategically.

With regard to the professional pastor, this means that his activity, as an object of exchange, is likewise involved in the powerful registers of strategy and utilization. Parishioners and clients use him and his attention while calculating the possible benefit for themselves. This cannot continue without consequences. Commercializing attention causes a semantic shift in the pastoral relationship, since the economic calculation contradicts the ideas and images that a pastor associates with his practice. He offers care according to the Gospel and for the sake of people, and not to be used by them.

Another aspect is that the pastoral activity now can be expressed as pecuniary benefit, and thus as money. Professional pastoral care is, after all, a paid occupation and not a private matter. Most pastors do their work with a very high personal commitment. As a result of this they suffer from the effects of the "mixed economy of attention and of money."[71] They suffer from the fact that the compassion, which they want to show their parishioners unconditionally and with much effort, is at the same time a paid good. A pastor wants to become involved with the life story of his client without reserve, yet he realizes that the contact between them becomes a matter of good service. Both economies, that of the attention and that of the finances, are actually connected in the professional pastoral practice. This connection stands in the way of the inner logic of pastoral care and the personal intentions most pastors and chaplains have.[72]

The same can be said for most clients. They expect to receive attention as a gift, to experience a real human encounter, to be accepted as a person, and to be important for their own sake and without executed consideration. The fact that one must not pay immediately for the pastoral communication—unlike, for example, for psychotherapy—only encourages this point of view. Nevertheless, one remains a customer who asks for and deserves a good service. As such, a client has power over the provider of this service.

Of course, even from a strict economic point of view, pastoral care and counseling with nearness, devotion, rituals, presence, empathy, time, and attention cannot be totally set off against pecuniary benefit.[73] But from this perspective, the problems of monetizing pastoral care become clear. The

---

71. Franck, *Ökonomie der Aufmerksamkeit*, 64.
72. Childs, "Pastoral Care," 47–56.
73. Franck, *Ökonomie der Aufmerksamkeit*, 88–111.

PART 1—Fundamental Philosophical and Theological Reflections

consequences of capitalistic thinking also reveal themselves in the pastoral relationship.[74] Clients receive power over the pastor. The pressure resulting from this can hardly be harmonized with his real intentions by, for example, using the common idea of customer orientation.[75]

On the other hand, it is recommended that pastoral care should avoid this pressure. It should offer an open space that is free from economic exploitation and utilization.[76] This can be achieved, so it is said, by the retreat from the public care system with its dominant economic logic since "pastoral counseling can fully exercise its healing ministry without participating in either private or federally managed care programs. It can practice the kind of counseling that it finds appropriate to each case without restraints by outside parties. This means that, to be true to itself, pastoral counseling needs to return to the direction of ecclesiastical authority, scripture, and tradition rather than regulation by managed care's administrative gatekeepers."[77] Whether such a return to the safe bosom of the church solves the indicated problems remains doubtful since she is as an organization likewise under the influence of the cost saving and economizing pressure.

It seems that none of the alternatives mentioned are completely convincing. On the one hand, a pastor may not give way to the trends toward a commercialization of his practice. He would do so if he affirmatively and without any resistance accepted the client power that is linked with this commercialization. On the other hand, he may not underestimate the effects of this on pastoral care, since "there is no way out the new, market-shaped religious reality."[78] If a chaplain denies this, the indicated problem would only become a blind spot for him.

We can conclude that one must avoid the extremes. As far as possible a pastor should insist "on forms of a non-economized presence."[79] He must try to make it felt in the concrete pastoral relationship and setting, be it in an ecclesial or a public care context. However, he should always bear in mind the way in which this contact is deformed by the economy of attention and how this manifests itself as client power.

74. Schmälzle, "Theologie und Qualitätsmanagement," 75–85.
75. Pott, *Kundenorientierung in Pastoral*, 202–345.
76. Reuter, "Seelsorge als eingeräumte Zeit," 282–83.
77. Childs, "Pastoral Care," 55.
78. Bucher, *Priester des Volkes Gottes*, 44.
79. Reuter, "Seelsorge als eingeräumte Zeit," 288.

In conclusion, a pastor as a powerful figure is at the same time at the client's mercy. He is dependent on the client, for the client's power has a strong impact on his profession. A unilateral dependence from the bottom upward, as it is suggested in the traditional model of power in pastoral care, does not exist. Parishioners are not just passive "victims" of the pastoral interaction. They are also customers and have as such power over the shepherd.[80] At the same time, this is in itself an expression of a certain register of (pastoral) power, in which even pastoral care and spiritual counseling can be transformed into economic categories.

BIBLIOGRAPHY

Arendt, Hannah. *On Violence*. New York: Harcourt, Brace & World, 1970.
Baart, Andries. *Een theorie van de presentie*. Utrecht: Lemma, 2001.
Bauer, Christian. "Macht und Gnade. Versuch einer Klärung der Begriffe angesichts von Ohnmacht und Gnadenlosigkeit heute." In *Macht und Gnade. Untersuchungen zu einem konstitutiven Spannungsfeld der Pastoral*, edited by Rainer Bucher and Rainer Krockauer, 45–60. Münster: Lit, 2005.
Bauman, Zygmunt. *Liquid Modernity*. Cambridge: Polity, 2000.
Bolz, Norbert. "Die Splitter des Zeitpfeils. Orientierung in der Nachgeschichte." In *Befristete Zeit. Jahrbuch Politische Theologie 3*, edited by Jürgen Manemann, 124–34. Berlin: Lit Verlag, 1999.
Bröckling, Ulrich, et al. *Gouvernementalität der Gegenwart. Studien zur Ökonomisierung des Sozialen*. Frankfurt am Main: Suhrkamp, 2000.
Brouwer, Rein. *Pastor tussen macht en onmacht: Een studie naar de professionalisering van het hervormde predikantschap*. Zoetermeer: Boekencentrum, 1995.
Bucher, Rainer. "Body of Power and Body Power: The Situation of the Church and God's Defeat." In *The Structural Betrayal of Trust*, edited by Regina Ammicht-Quinn et al., 120–29. London: SCM, 2004.
———. "Das Ehrenamt in der Transformationskrise der katholischen Kirche. Risiken und Perspektiven." In *Für Gottes Lohn?! Ehrenamt und Kirche*, edited by Walter Krieger and Balthasar Sieberer, 65–83. Linz: Wagner, 2011.
———. *Priester des Volkes Gottes. Gefährdungen, Grundlagen, Perspektiven*. Würzburg: Echter, 2010.
———, and Karl H. Ladenhauf. "Räume des Aufatmens. Welche Seelsorge brauchen Menschen heute?" In *Die Provokation der Krise. Zwölf Fragen und Antworten zur Lage der Kirche*, edited by Rainer Bucher, 154–76. Würzburg: Echter, 2004.
Childs, Brian H. "Pastoral Care and the Market Economy: Time-limited Psychotherapy, Managed Care, and the Pastoral Counsellor." *Journal of Pastoral Care* 53 (1999) 47–56.
Davie, Grace. *Religion in Modern Europe: A Memory Mutates*. Oxford: Oxford University Press, 2000.

---

80. Pott, *Kundenorientierung in Pastoral*, 307–319.

PART 1—Fundamental Philosophical and Theological Reflections

Doehring, Carrie. *Taking Care: Monitoring Power Dynamics and Relational Boundaries in Pastoral Care and Counseling.* Nashville: Abingdon Press, 1995.
Drechsel, Wolfgang. "Der lange Schatten des Mythos vom gelingenden Leben. Theologische Anmerkungen zur Angst vor der eigenen Endlichkeit und zur Frage der Seelsorge." *Pastoraltheologie* 95 (2006) 314–28.
Foucault, Michel. *Dispositive der Macht. Über Sexualität, Wissen und Wahrheit.* Berlin: Merve, 1978.
———. *The History of Sexuality.* Vol. 1, *An Introduction.* New York: Vintage, 1990.
———. "Omnes et Singulatim: Towards a Criticism of 'Political Reason.'" In *The Tanner Lectures on Human Values*, edited by Sterling M. McMurrin, 223–54. Salt Lake City: University of Utah Press, 1981.
———. *Security, Territory, Population: Lectures at the Collège de France, 1977–1978.* New York: Picador, 2007.
———. "The Subject and Power." In *Michel Foucault: Beyond Structuralism and Hermeneutics*, edited by Hubert L. Dreyfus and Paul Rabinow, 208–26. Brighton: Harvester, 1982.
Franck, Georg. *Ökonomie der Aufmerksamkeit. Ein Entwurf.* Munich: Carl Hanser, 1998.
Gärtner, Stefan. "Powerful and Dependent: Ambivalence in the Religious Leader." In *Religious Leadership and Christian Identity*, edited by Doris Nauer et al., 157–67. Münster: Lit Verlag, 2004.
———. "Staying a Pastor While Talking Like a Psychologist? A Proposal for an Integrative Model." *Christian Bioethics* 16 (2010) 48–60.
Greenwald, Carole A., et al. "A Study of the Identity of Pastoral Counselors." *American Journal of Pastoral Counseling* 7 (2004) 51–69.
Halbe, Jörn. "Chancen des Subjekts. Selbstorganisation als Leitungsaufgabe und als Praxis der Befreiung in der Kirche." *Wege zum Menschen* 56 (2004) 243–58.
Hansen Robison, Linda. "The Abuse of Power: A View of Sexual Misconduct in a Systemic Approach to Pastoral Care." *Pastoral Psychology* 52 (2004) 395–404.
Haslinger, Herbert. *Diakonie. Grundlagen für die soziale Arbeit der Kirche.* Paderborn: Ferdinand Schöningh, 2009.
Hochschild, Michael. "Was mich rettet, macht mich kaputt. Apropos einer pastoraltheologischen Neuerscheinung." *Theologie der Gegenwart* 45 (2002) 61–67.
Hoge, Dean R., and Jacqueline E. Wenger. *Evolving Visions of the Priesthood: Changes from Vatican II to the Turn of the New Century.* Collegeville, MN: Liturgical, 2003.
Hübenthal, Christoph. "Macht. Typologische und legitimationstheoretische Anmerkungen." In *Macht und Ohnmacht. Konzeptionelle und kontextuelle Erkundungen*, edited by Werner Veith and Christoph Hübenthal, 35–50. Münster: Aschendorff, 2005.
Jähnichen, Traugott. "Was macht Kirche mit Macht—was macht Macht mit Kirche?" *Wege zum Menschen* 63 (2011) 135–46.
Janowski, Gudrun. "Theologia Gubernationis—Leitung und Macht. Eine pastoralpsychologisch orientierte Reflexion." In *Gottes Profis? Re-Visionen des Pfarramts*, edited by Thorsten Peters et al., 75–105. Wuppertal: Foedus, 2004.
Kämpfer, Horst. "Macht. Bewegungen im sozialen und psychischen Raum." *Pastoraltheologie* 99 (2010) 272–87.
Karle, Isolde. *Der Pfarrberuf als Profession. Eine Berufstheorie im Kontext der modernen Gesellschaft.* Freiburg im Breisgau: Kreuz, 2008.

Karrer, Leo. "Seelsorger und Seelsorgerinnen im Schmelztiegel vieler Herausforderungen." *Theologisch-praktische Quartalschrift* 153 (2005) 240–48.

Klessmann, Michael. *Pfarrbilder im Wandel. Ein Beruf im Umbruch.* Neukirchen-Vluyn: Neukirchener, 2001.

Körver, Sjaak. "Conflicten in de context van het pastoraat: Een praktisch-theologische en pastorale reflectie." In *Ga nu allen in vrede! Omgaan met macht en conflicten in pastorale contexten*, edited by Annemie Dillen and Didier Pollefeyt, 33–53. Leuven: Davidsfonds, 2010.

Luther, Henning. *Religion und Alltag. Bausteine zu einer Praktischen Theologie des Subjekts.* Stuttgart: Radius, 1992.

Neuger, Christie C. "Power and Difference in Pastoral Theology." In *Pastoral Care and Counseling: Redefining the Paradigms*, edited by Nancy J. Ramsay, 65–85. Nashville: Abingdon Press, 2004.

Nolte, Kristina. *Der Kampf um Aufmerksamkeit. Wie Medien, Wirtschaft und Politik um eine knappe Ressource ringen.* Frankfurt am Main: Campus, 2005.

Pattison, Stephen. *A Critique of Pastoral Care.* London: SCM, 2000.

Petter, Karin. "Leiblichkeit als Machtinstrument im Wellness-Diskurs." In *Macht und Ohnmacht. Konzeptionelle und kontextuelle Erkundungen*, edited by Werner Veith and Christoph Hübenthal, 189–202. Münster: Aschendorff, 2005.

Pollefeyt, Didier. "Intimiteit in de pastoraal: Ethische kanttekeningen bij het gebruik van macht binnen de pastorale begeleiding." *Collationes* 28 (1998) 227–45.

Pott, Martin. *Kundenorientierung in Pastoral und Caritas? Anstöße zum kirchlichen Handeln im Kontext der Marktgesellschaft.* Münster: Lit Verlag, 2001.

Remmelzwaal, Albert J. *Actief en afhankelijk: Een praktijktheorie voor leiderschap in kerkelijke gemeenten.* Delft: Eburon, 2003.

Rendle, Gilbert R. "Reclaiming Professional Jurisdiction: The Re-emergence of the Theological Task of Ministry." *Theology Today* 59 (2002) 408–20.

Reuter, Ingo. "Seelsorge als eingeräumte Zeit. Zum pastoraltheologischen Spezifikum seelsorglichen Handelns in einer zeitökonomisierten Gesellschaft." *Praktische Theologie* 36 (2001) 279–88.

Reuter, Wolfgang. "Der heilsame Blick aufs Fragment. Pastoralästhetische Reflexion aus der Perspektive der Psychoanalyse." In *Pastoralästhetik. Die Kunst der Wahrnehmung und Gestaltung in Glaube und Kirche*, edited by Walter Fürst, 265–77. Freiburg im Breisgau: Herder, 2002.

Sander, Hans-Joachim. "Gott im Zeichen der Macht—ein Diskurs über die Moderne hinaus. Theologie nach Foucault." In *Gottes und des Menschen Tod? Die Theologie vor der Herausforderung Michel Foucaults*, edited by Christian Bauer and Michael Hölzl, 105–25. Mainz: Grünewald, 2003.

Schilderman, Hans. *Religion as a Profession.* Leiden: Brill, 2005.

Schlamelcher, Jens. "Ökonomisierung der Kirchen?" In *Paradoxien kirchlicher Organisation. Niklas Luhmanns frühe Kirchensoziologie und die aktuelle Reform der evangelischen Kirche*, edited by Jan Hermelink and Gerhard Wegner, 145–77. Würzburg: Ergon, 2008.

———. "Unternehmen Kirche? Neoliberale Diskurse in den deutschen Großkirchen." In *Der neoliberale Markt-Diskurs. Ursprünge, Geschichte, Wirkungen*, edited by Walter O. Ötsch and Claus Thomasberger, 213–56. Marburg: Metropolis, 2009.

Schmälzle, Udo F. "Monetarisierung von Religion und Kirche. Eine Herausforderung für die Praktische Theologie?" *Pastoraltheologische Informationen* 26 (2006) 262–81.

PART 1—Fundamental Philosophical and Theological Reflections

———. "Theologie und Qualitätsmanagement. Überlegungen zu einer pastoralästhetischen Verhältnisbestimmung." In *Dem Glauben Gestalt geben. Festschrift für Walter Fürst*, edited by Ulrich Feeser-Lichterfeld and Reinhard Feiter, 75–85. Berlin: Lit Verlag, 2006.

Sennett, Richard. *The Corrosion of Character: The Personal Consequences of Work in the New Capitalism*. New York: Norton, 1998.

Steck, Wolfgang. *Praktische Theologie I. Horizonte der Religion; Konturen des neuzeitlichen Christentums; Strukturen der religiösen Lebenswelt*. Stuttgart: Kohlhammer, 2000.

Steinkamp, Hermann. *Die sanfte Macht der Hirten. Die Bedeutung Michel Foucaults für die Praktische Theologie*. Mainz: Grünewald, 1999.

Stenger, Hermann. "Führen und Leiten zu allen Zeiten. Vom Wandel der Machtausübung in der katholischen Kirche." *Theologisch-praktische Quartalschrift* 157 (2009) 18–26.

Stortz, Martha E. *PastorPower. Macht im geistlichen Amt*. Stuttgart: Kohlhammer, 1995.

Surzykiewicz, Janusz. "Rezeption ökonomischer Führungstheorien in der Seelsorgepraxis." In *Führung. Macht. Sinn. Ethos und Ethik für Entscheider in Wirtschaft, Gesellschaft und Kirche*, edited by Uto Meier and Bernhard Sill, 560–73. Regensburg: Friedrich Pustet, 2010.

Vosman, Frans. "Macht en geweld in het pastoraat: Een bijdrage aan theorievorming over normatieve professionaliteit." *Praktische Humanistiek* 8 (1999) 33–49.

Wittrahm, Andreas. *Seelsorge, Pastoralpsychologie und Postmoderne. Eine pastoralpsychologische Grundlegung lebensfördernder Begegnungen angesichts radikaler postmoderner Pluralität*. Stuttgart: Kohlhammer, 2001.

Zulehner, Paul M. *Priester im Modernisierungsstress. Forschungsbericht der Studie Priester 2000*. Ostfildern: Schwabenverlag, 2001.

PART 2

Power and Interculturality

4

Self-Affirming Prejudice and the Abuse of Pastoral Power

Carrie Doehring

> If the other is only appreciated because he or she displays certain characteristics, attributes, or qualities whereby they become interesting for me "to learn from," and because in so doing they confirm and reinforce my identity, then, according to Levinas, we end up in one or the other form of (philosophical-ideological or religious) ethnocentrism and even racism.[1]

Professor Eloise Sangren teaches pastoral care and theology at a university-based seminary with a doctoral program. She is well known in her field of research. Several students want to be her teaching assistant next year. Those who get the chance to work with her will receive detailed letters of reference when they apply for pastoral and faculty positions. She must choose one from among these equally qualified, eager applicants. She finds herself drawn to a young woman who reminds her of herself at that age. Should she think further about her choice, perhaps by talking this over with a colleague?

---

1. Burggraeve, "Alterity Makes the Difference," 232.

PART 2—Power and Interculturality

> *Chaplain Daniel Johnson is part of a teaching team of pastors in a hospital-based clinical pastoral education (CPE) program. He is supervising Seung Lee, a young Korean-American woman who uses Buddhist practices. She brings verbatim accounts of spiritual care conversation with many periods of silence. He confers with the other supervisors about whether her quiet demeanor and accent are inhibiting her as well as patients from getting into conversations. He is frustrated that she seems to agree with everything he says without challenging him. In his training, an important learning component of CPE was the weekly interpersonal groups where conflict was encouraged as a way for students to learn more about themselves and group process. He wants Seung to be more assertive with patients and also with him.*

> *Karen McKenzie is a pastor at Evergreen Presbyterian Church in Aspen, Colorado, an upscale ski resort town in the Rocky Mountains. A member of the young adult group, Sally, has asked to speak with her about a work-related problem with her boss, Mr. Townsend, a prominent real estate agent in Aspen. When they get together Sally tearfully describes how her boss blames her for scheduling and paperwork problems that are his responsibility. Once or twice a week he calls her into his office, shuts the door, and berates her. These tirades seem to be fueled by the alcohol she smells on his breath. These outbursts remind Sally of college experiences with a boyfriend who would become intoxicated at parties and then explode in the car afterwards, accusing Sally of flirting with other men.*
>
> *Sally tells Pastor McKenzie that she prays each day that her boss will realize he has a problem with alcohol and get help. She wants to be able to forgive him, knowing that he is under a lot of stress because of the economic recession and the stagnant real estate market. If she quit her job she would likely have to leave Aspen, given the scarcity of jobs that pay a living wage.*
>
> *Hearing about Sally's work experience, Pastor McKenzie feels angry at Sally's boss for making her life miserable. She does not want Sally to put up with her boss's behavior, which she sees as abusive. She is troubled that Sally wants God to help her forgive her boss and that she may be using prayer as a way to endure abuse.*

AT FIRST GLANCE, THESE scenarios portray a teacher, chaplain supervisor, and pastor trying to be helpful. There is no overt abuse of power involving coercion, nor is there flagrant transgression of professional codes of conduct. Rather, these scenarios depict the potential for a subtle abuse of power arising from the well-intentioned wish of teachers, supervisors, and pastors that their students and congregants become like them. This tendency to favor those whose attitudes, values, and beliefs are similar to one's own, to devalue those who are different, and to use one's influence to change others into one's own image are all aspects of self-affirming prejudice.

The purpose of this chapter is to increase awareness of the insidious dynamics of self-affirming prejudice as a potential abuse of pastoral power, understand these dynamics theologically and psychologically, claim core values that reflect existential and religious beliefs, and find ways to put these values into practice in order to counteract self-affirming prejudice in helping relationships. I will elaborate the dynamics of self-affirming prejudice using process theology, social psychological research on prejudice, and intercultural approaches to spiritual care that value alterity, defined as "the irreducible uniqueness of the other."[2] After briefly outlining the concepts or research from these three theoretical perspectives, I will illustrate how these perspectives help me understand self-affirming prejudice.

Before proceeding, I would like to pause in order to describe my context. I teach in a theologically progressive graduate school of theology in the United States that values social justice. Process theology is one of the theological perspectives taught here. It uses a systems perspective that sees all of life, including God, as relationally interconnected. Process theology is a relational theology: hence the term process-relational. Process-relational theology is progressive in its definition of power as a mutual interchange of influence: the ebb and flow of agential and receptive power. Briefly described, agential power guides and influences while receptive power takes in and receives. I argue that the agential power of those in teaching, supervisory, and pastoral roles is usually inflated by social and professional privileges, making it more likely that the pastor's agential power will be unintentionally used in harmful ways to make the care receiver into the pastor's own image.

I highlight the context in which I teach in order to describe how process theology is relevant and meaningful in a progressive theological community, which is oriented around social justice. I encourage readers with more traditional theologies of God's power to use my description of the pastoral relational aspects of power within their theologies. I would not want readers to reject outright my process-relational descriptions of self-affirming prejudice because of theological differences about how God's power is understood. I realize that such theological differences can easily

---

2. Burggraeve, "Alterity Makes the Difference," 232.

become a distracting stumbling block: hence my efforts at the outset to encourage readers to take what is useful and adapt it to their theology.

Process-relational theology works well with social psychological perspectives on how prejudice arises from human inclinations to see oneself in terms of ingroups and outgroups. Social psychological research demonstrates how religion contributes to and counteracts self-affirming prejudice. These theological and psychological perspectives on self-affirming prejudice provide ways to assess the life-giving and life-limiting qualities of helping relationships and also to articulate values of human dignity and social justice that can be put into practice in order to counteract insidious abuses of power. If teachers, supervisors, and pastors want to enact core values that counteract prejudice, they will need to assume responsibility for maintaining an "other affirming" intertwining of agential and receptive power that creates a relationship of trust, such that a multilayered sense of otherness (intrapsychic, interpersonal, spiritual, and cultural) emerges and is received.

Process theology, along with social psychology, are helpful conversation partners for intercultural spiritual care, which pays attention to religious and social differences within multi-faith settings. After describing this intercultural approach to care, I will suggest and illustrate strategies for monitoring and counteracting self-affirming prejudice in helping relationships using the opening vignettes.

While these three theoretical perspectives—process theology, social psychology, and intercultural spiritual care—are relevant in my context of teaching and spiritual care, they may be less relevant for readers using more traditional or orthodox theologies. I hope that readers will use my vignettes and reflections to help them think about similarities and differences within various contexts of teaching and care-giving, and that readers will feel free to use whatever is relevant to their contexts.

A PROCESS-RELATIONAL UNDERSTANDING OF POWER

From a process-relational perspective the world is "an incredibly vast network of interlocked events. This network is the dynamic and relational web of life into which we are born and in which we live out our lives—for better or worse."[3] A process-relational understanding of existence combines "the

---

3. Loomer, "Committing Yourself," 257.

ultimacy of process with the primacy of relationships."[4] All of life is seen as interconnected in an organic process of becoming. Everything is constituted through its relationships with everything else.

These relationships are energized by power, defined as an interchange of influence within relational webs: an intertwining of agential and receptive power.[5] Agential power influences, guides, and shapes, while receptive power receives, takes in, and is influenced, guided, and shaped. This bimodal understanding of power can be contrasted with traditional views of unilateral agential power that are part of a hierarchically ordered worldview where power is synonymous with the control and force people use to have power over others.[6] Here power is seen as an individual attribute rather than a quality of relationships. It is located in the person who is in control or in charge.

> As long as one's size and sense of worth are measured by the strength of one's capacity to influence others (and this influence always takes the form of shaping the other in our image), as long as power is associated with the sense of initiative and aggressiveness, and passivity is indicative of weakness or a corresponding lack of power, then the natural and inevitable inequalities in life become wider and deeper.[7]

Within this hierarchical worldview power appears to be unilateral, given inequalities within systems of privilege. When competition is valued, then unilateral power will be valued. People exerting such power are seen as strong, while those without this kind of force are seen as weak.

Pastoral relationships participate in this web of life when there is role-appropriate intertwining of receptive and agential power. When this kind of role-appropriate mutuality is valued, then teachers, supervisors, and pastors will take responsibility for monitoring the ways that their role and social advantages inflate agential power. In order to counteract systemic tendencies to use inflated agential power in abusive ways, pastors must be able to assume intercultural responsibility for putting the other first. Before

---

4. Loomer, "Process Theology," 245.

5. "The principles of relational power mean that influencing and being influenced are so relationally intertwined that the effort to isolate them as independent factors would constitute an illustration of with one or both of Whitehead's famous two fallacies: that of simple location or that of misplaced concreteness" (Loomer, "Two Conceptions of Power," 22).

6. Magyar et al., "Sacrilege."

7. Loomer, "Two Conceptions of Power," 11.

elaborating this intercultural approach, I will review psychological understandings of self-affirming prejudice and religion, commenting on how this research can be interpreted and used within a process-relational worldview.

SELF-AFFIRMING PREJUDICE

Social psychologists have demonstrated how people often use social categories to divide people into two basic social groups: ingroups, of which they are a part, and outgroups, of those identified as different from them. People gain a sense of belonging when they see themselves as part of an ingroup, with its familiar system of roles, rules, norms, values, and beliefs.[8] These social calculations are done using prejudgments or stereotypes linked with aspects of peoples' appearance and identity, like gender and race. Prejudice can affirm one's own group (*self-affirming prejudice* or ingroup favoritism), express hostility or hatred towards a targeted group (*hate prejudice*), or protect one's group from threats (*threat prejudice*).[9]

How does religion contribute to or counteract prejudice? Religion is related to prejudice in a variety of life enhancing, life limiting, and destructive ways. While many social psychologists in the past focused on the ways religion contributes to, rather than counteracts prejudice, "the critical question isn't *whether* religion and spirituality are good or bad [when it comes to prejudice], but *when, how,* and *why* they take constructive or destructive forms."[10] Teachers, supervisors, and pastors are not usually guilty of

---

8. Tajfel and Turner, "The Social Identity Theory of Intergroup Behavior." Cabezón has a pithy description of the ways scholars of religious studies function as an ingroup: "We construct our sense of identity—our uniqueness and our otherness vis-a-vis religion in general, and non-Christian religions in particular—by appealing, for example, to notions like criticality/criticism, theoretical sophistication, methodological rigor (our ability to contextualize, to quantify, etc.), and the ability to be self-reflective and to expose our biases. These are some of the features of the intellectual program that defines us—the traits that we presume to possess and that religion, the religious, and especially the alter-religions/religious lack [as outgroups] . . . What is worrisome is that in creating a sense of identity around these core attributes, we usually do so in an uncritical way that simply presumes that we possess these attributes *in toto* and that they do not. Our sense of identity is therefore fashioned at the expense of the Other, through an implicit denigration of the Other, and specifically through a dogmatic (albeit often implicit) denial of the fact that criticality, theory, and self-awareness are also concerns for religion(s) in general, and for non-Christian religions in particular"(Cabezón, "The Discipline and Its Other," 27–30).

9. Brewer, "The Social Psychology of Intergroup Relations."

10. Pargament et al., "Envisioning an Integrated Paradigm."

abusing their power by using religion to justify hate or threat prejudice.[11] Blatant abuse of pastoral power involving religiously linked prejudice is often fuelled by right-wing authoritarianism. As such, it is easy to see how fear-based and hostility-based prejudice uses religion to justify unilateral agential power directed towards outgroups. Self-affirming prejudice is a less obvious and more insidious prejudice. It often involves affirmation of one's ingroup rather than identifying others as part of outgroups through the use of stereotypes. It is often a form of automatic prejudice that shapes relational dynamics outside of awareness.

Self-affirming prejudice, or ingroup bias and favoritism, is defined as the tendency to over-evaluate or favor those whose attitudes, values, and beliefs are similar to one's own. When people invest in social categories meaningful to them—as, for example, when pastors identify themselves as progressive Roman Catholics committed to social justice—they tend to attribute human essence to those who are similar.[12] Conversely, they perceive those in outgroups—in this case, Roman Catholics who reject social justice agendas—as having a less human essence. These dynamics operate in subtle and often unconscious ways.

Social psychologists have recently started using neuroimaging to understand the specific brain mechanisms of unconscious and automatic activation of prejudice, focusing on the amygdala, a part of the brain that responds to the emotional intensity of a stimulus.[13] For example, when Caucasian research participants are shown a series of faces for brief time periods (30 msec) that only allow for subliminal processing, the amygdala is more active when black rather than white faces are shown. When participants have more time (525 msec) to process what they are seeing, their prefrontal cortex becomes active, suggesting that higher-order cog-

---

11. That said, pastors endorsing right-wing authoritarianism will be more likely to believe that outgroups threaten their ingroup's way of life, as noted by Duckitt, "Differential Effects of Right Wing Authoritarianism and Social Dominance Orientation." Pastors with high ingroup identity and right-wing authoritarian attitudes are susceptible to experiencing symbolic threat to their systems of meaning, as described by Stephan, Ybarro, and Morrison, "Intergroup Threat Theory." As terror management theorists propose, the more an ingroup uses their religious worldview and values to ward off their terror of death, the more aggressively they will challenge outgroups that threaten their world views, sometimes going so far as to experience such groups as evil. This dynamic is described by Greenberg et al., "How Our Dreams of Death Transcendence Breed Prejudice."

12. Demoulin et al., "The Role of Ingroup Identification in Infra-Humanization."

13. Amodio and Lieberman, "Pictures in Our Heads."

nitive processing is engaged. In other words, they become aware of their prejudgments and can think about them.

Guilt can play a positive role in motivating people to counteract prejudice. In a complex study,[14] research participants were told that their neurological responses to a multiracial series of faces were "anti-Black." Those who reported feeling guilty about these responses were subsequently more likely to go out of their way to talk with a Black member of the research team. The authors speculated that guilt is a complex social emotion that can play a dynamic role in motivating people to counteract prejudice.

Neuroimaging research suggests that the more the amygdala is activated by an intensely charged stimulus, the more self-affirming prejudice will shape power dynamics, often in unconscious ways. Pastors who track their internal reactions to relational dynamics are more able to be aware of emotionally charged needs that others become like them. Similar to the research participants who went out of their way to counteract prejudice because their values made them feel guilty about being prejudiced, pastors can think through their beliefs and values about self-affirming prejudice and become intrinsically motivated to counteract such prejudice. They will not be able to eliminate self-affirming prejudice because of the ways they automatically use social categories and react in emotionally charged ways. They will be able to counteract these urges if they learn to recognize them, think through what values they want to enact, and in this process become intrinsically motivated[15] to put these values into practice in how they relate to others.

---

14. Amodio et al., "A Dynamic Model of Guilt Implications."

15. Intrinsic motivation comes from within people who want to live out their egalitarian or humanitarian values; extrinsic motivation comes from the desire to conform to societal expectations by not appearing prejudiced. In one research study, those with high internal motivation to live out egalitarian values showed very little stereotype activation compared with those who lacked such values and goals. See Moskowitz et al., "Preconscious Control of Stereotype Activation." Devine, Brodish, and Vance describe such people as *Strategics* in that they are most concerned with using strategies that conceal prejudice. *Strivers* are internally motivated people who strive to overcome prejudice and accumulate skills that help them continuously live out their humanitarian values. See Devine et al., "Self-Regulatory Processes in Interracial Interactions."

Illustrating the Dynamics of Self-Affirming Prejudice

When Professor Sangren considers the students who have applied to be her teaching assistant, she is drawn to a young woman who reminds her of herself when she was a graduate student. These memories are emotionally charged because she struggled to find a member of the all-male faculty willing to advise her. Even though it is more of an even playing field now for men and women in graduate studies, her memories may create social categories: ingroups of young women students and outgroups of male faculty and students. While seeing herself as an ally of women students could have benefits, the liability is that she may impose values and meanings on female students that are as limiting as the imposition of patriarchal values that stifled her as a graduate student.

CPE supervisor Chaplain Johnson becomes agitated when he perceives Seung as rejecting the kind of formation he experienced in CPE where intense interpersonal group process encouraged confrontation. He would never consciously describe Seung as having a lesser human essence. However, in his emotionally charged reactions, he may perceive her as limited in terms of the core human capacities that he values: namely, self-actualization through confrontation. If he is conscious of these dynamics and wants to counteract prejudice because it goes against his core values, he will need to think carefully about the goals of supervision and the process of reaching these goals. If he were to use the intercultural approach I describe in the next section, he would be likely to reconsider his cherished values of growth through self-assertion and confrontation. Is he imposing these values on Seung? If he were to value Seung for herself, and appreciate the mystery of who she is, might they together construct goals and a process of change that honors this mystery?

As an older female minister, Pastor McKenzie has seen and experienced sexual harassment and the ways women, in her assessment, sometimes use religion in life-limiting theological and psychological ways to cope with abuse. These are emotionally charged issues for her. Much as she wants to empower Sally, she will be tempted to use power in unilateral ways, especially if she sees Sally as a younger version of herself. She may even see women like Sally as having a less than human female essence when they use religion to endure abuse. While her pastoral care focus is on Sally, her reactions to Sally's boss may also get in the way of pastoral care if she experiences hate prejudice towards him, seeing him only in terms of his alcohol abuse and bullying behavior. Her emotionally charged reactions

PART 2—Power and Interculturality

will activate prejudice, which may in turn tempt her to use agential power in unilateral ways to try and achieve justice for Sally. If she is aware of these dynamics, Pastor McKenzie can consider more carefully how to monitor prejudice and live out values of justice in the ways she relates to Sally and her boss.

IDENTIFYING VALUES THAT MOTIVATE PASTORS TO COUNTERACT PREJUDICE

Process-relational theology provides a dynamic systemic way of understanding power dynamics in helping and mentoring relationships that complements psychological understandings of both the problem of prejudice and strategies for counteracting self-affirming prejudice. This theological approach also helps pastors to articulate values about relational justice and suggests ways to monitor power dynamics in order to counteract prejudice. What values might come to light in this theological and psychological exploration of self-affirming prejudice? Process theologian Bernard Loomer says that the exercise of power must operate with an appreciation for each person's uniqueness ("the conditioning contexts, histories, psychological dynamics and relationships, which largely determine what we most concretely are"). He goes on to say that:

> To do otherwise is to relate to each other inadequately in terms of abstract classes, or stereotypes, or groups looked at in a cross-sectional manner without reference to their peculiar histories. In this fashion we fail to deal with the inexhaustible and variegated richness, the confusing complexity, and the omnipresent and intertwined ambiguities present in the concreteness of individual and group life . . . Power, to be creative and not destructive, must be inextricably related to the ambiguous, contradictory, and baffling character of concrete existence.[16]

In this chapter I use a process-relational understanding of power to illustrate how to construct a theological rationale for valuing alterity and social justice, which motivates pastors to identify and counteract self-affirming prejudice. Ideally, pastors will want to construct theological values that fit their beliefs and practices. They may find that process-relational theology is congruent with their belief system, or they may wish to construct

---

16. Loomer, "Two Conceptions of Power," 24–25.

a theological understanding that is more relevant and meaningful within their worldview and beliefs.

I want to be clear that I am not proposing a universally true process-relational theology of self-affirming prejudice that is applicable to all religious traditions and faith perspectives. While this process-relational theology can be translated into Christian, Jewish, and non-theistic traditions like Buddhism, it is presented here as a contextual theology for those with a quest orientation to religious beliefs that espouses conditional rather than absolute views of religious truth.[17] Those with more traditional theistic theologies who view religious truth as absolute may agree with my psychological description of self-affirming prejudice, but will likely want to support and elaborate this psychological understanding using more traditional theologies, especially those involving an all-powerful theism. As I noted at the outset, the purpose of this chapter is to increase awareness of the insidious dynamics of self-affirming prejudice, understand these dynamics theologically and psychologically, claim core values that reflect existential and religious beliefs, and find ways to put these values into practice in order to counteract self-affirming prejudice in helping relationships. Readers are encouraged to find theologically meaningful ways of understanding and counteracting self-affirming prejudice. I use process-relational theology as one way among many to understand self-affirming prejudice. In the next section I offer an intercultural approach to spiritual care that counteracts self-affirming prejudice and abuses of pastoral power.

INTERCULTURAL SPIRITUAL CARE

Intercultural care takes into account the multilayered relationships between persons, which include the various familial, organizational, and cultural systems in which they are embedded. In its most literal sense, intercultural

---

17. There is considerable psychological research on the relationships between psychological attitudes towards religious truth, like the quest orientation, and a fundamentalist religious orientation. A major finding is that when right wing authoritarianism (RWA is defined as submission, aggression, and conventionalism in response to authorities) is part of a fundamentalist orientation, this orientation correlates positively with various kinds of prejudice. See Altemeyer and Hunsberger, "Authoritarianism, Religious Fundamentalism, Quest, and Prejudice"; Altemeyer, "Why Do Religious Fundamentalists Tend to Be Prejudiced?"; McCleary et al., "Meta-Analysis of Correlational Relationships between Perspectives of Truth in Religion and Major Psychological Constructs." Fundamentalism without RWA usually is not correlated with prejudice. Quest is usually negatively correlated with prejudice.

care is a term used to describe helping relationships between those from different countries. In a broader sense, it can be used to describe the way all helping relationships negotiate power dynamics that arise from various kinds of differences. I prefer the term intercultural rather than multicultural or cross cultural because of its emphasis on relational dynamics that have to do with power and alterity or radical otherness. The prefix "multi" in the term multicultural usually suggests a tolerant co-existence of many or diverse cultures without attention to power dynamics that afford or deny social privilege.[18]

In this chapter I sketch an intercultural approach to spiritual care that draws upon process-relational theology and the relational ethics of Emmanuel Levinas.[19] I will rely on the writing of Roger Burggraeve who lucidly details Levinas's ethic of responsibility toward the other, a term used to describe the "insurmountable irreducibility of alterity."[20] Levinas underlines the "natural" way that the ego survives by continually integrating "the other into its project of existing as a function, means, or meaning."[21] Human beings are culturally conditioned to use agential power to serve the interests of the ego and not the other. This propensity toward self-interest and self-affirmation seems to be part of the fabric of life, especially when life is a seen as a matter of survival. In this dog-eat-dog relational system, the fittest are those who enlist agential power in order to survive.[22]

Levinas proposes a different way of relating: putting the other first by "holding back"[23] or restraining self-interest and all of the automatic ways we put ourselves first. In order to counteract the value of survival so embedded in hierarchical relational systems, one must receive the other unconditionally. Receiving others unconditionally is radically countercultural. It is:

---

18. For an elaboration of the nuanced meanings of intercultural, multicultural, and cross cultural, see Lartey, *In Living Color*.

19. For an elaboration of how Levinas's relational ethics radically changes understandings of the client and the process of psychotherapy, see Dueck and Parsons, "Ethics, Alterity, and Psychotherapy."

20. Burggraeve, "Violence and the Vulnerable Face of the Other," 30.

21. Ibid.

22. Human beings clearly have the capacity to be empathic. See, for example, discussions about neuroscience research on mirror neurons that are part of empathy, summarized by Hogue, "Brain Matters." Levinas helps us appreciate how easily self-interest dominates, eclipsing empathy, especially when people are using social categories to align themselves with ingroups and experience outgroups as threats.

23. Burggraeve, "Violence and the Vulnerable Face of the Other," 32.

> ... not at all a self-evident, "natural" idea that would emerge spontaneously in our everyday struggles. It is anything but self-evident. On the contrary, it establishes an "inverted order," an *Umwertung aller Werte* [a revaluation of all values], for it is possible only as a radical transgression of our "ordinary striving" ... [24]

Process-relational theology can be used to understand what Levinas is saying about the quality of other-oriented relationships. Self-interest and survival automatically inflate agential power and eclipse receptive power. We have become accustomed to our relationships being infused and limited by these survivalist values. When we put the other first unconditionally we invert this seemingly natural way of relating. A new way of relating opens up: relational mutuality and reciprocity that is not possible when survival is the be all and end all of life. According to Levinas, we choose life when we choose unconditional receptivity that fosters webs of life shaped by reciprocity and mutuality. We choose death when we opt for the survival of the fittest, a value that fosters relational webs where agential power dominates.

How is putting the self first and valuing survival of the fittest destructive? Is survival not the most basic requirement of life? When we put ourselves first we "reduce the other to the same"; this relational dynamic fosters various kinds of moral evil, which Burggraeve lists in ascending order starting with self-affirmation/other disregard, progressing to tyranny, and escalating to murder and racism.[25] In a process-relational worldview, these kinds of evil are part of relational webs where power is used in unilateral ways that dehumanize others. James Poling writes eloquently about such relational webs: "The construction of evil systems [personal, social, and religious] requires the cooperation of many people in many ways through countless decisions to ignore the possible consequences for those who are vulnerable."[26] Similarly, Catherine Keller states:

> When we misuse the power that flows between us, when in our need and greed we collectively warp the very channels of that energy, the abuse of power becomes a disease that perpetuates itself "unto the seventh generation" ... The violative influence infects the whole system: interpersonal, intrapersonal, transpersonal.[27]

---

24. Ibid., 35.
25. Ibid., 35–37.
26. Poling, *Deliver Us from Evil*, 135.
27. Keller, *On the Mystery*, 80.

Levinas invokes the commandment "Thou shalt not kill" in order to cast in high relief the choice between life (putting the other first) and death (putting the self first). This radical imperative is meant to stop us in our tracks and make us reconsider every minute choice we make in the course of our daily lives. Within interconnected relational webs, putting the other first within one relational web may well generate ripple effects that seem denying alterity within other relationships. Choosing life by putting the other first is complex and ambiguous, especially when "evil is a chameleon that maintains itself by remaining intertwined with the good and masking itself as good."[28]

How can this radical ethic of putting the other first be practiced within a process-relational worldview that values mutuality and the intertwining of agential and receptive power? At first glance, it may seem that Levinas is advocating that teacher, supervisors, and pastors abdicate agential power in favor of receptive power. This is problematic for those in professional roles who need to use agential power in order to monitor contracts of care and practice within professional ethical codes. When there is role appropriate intertwining of agential and receptive power within asymmetrical helping relationships, those in positions of trust will use agential power to monitor power dynamics. They will shift into receptive power in order to receive the other, not to meet their own needs. As they move with the other in a dance where agential and receptive power is shared, this role appropriate mutuality will be oriented toward putting the other first.

Putting the other first in intercultural care begins with monitoring the ways that social privileges shape religiously oriented helping relationships, making it insidiously easy for teachers, supervisors, and pastors to impose their religious or spiritual beliefs and values on those seeking care. For example, when Christians do not think critically about how they are comparing their tradition to others, they risk subsuming the other's idiosyncratic values, beliefs, and spiritual practices within their own. Many comparative approaches to religion used by Christians search for similarities with various religions of the world. This search for similarities replicates the historical ways that Christians in various contexts have interpreted religions of the world through the lens of Christianity. Think, for example, of the frequently used metaphor that all religions of the world are like separate paths culminating in the same mountaintop experience of a singular transcendent reality, or the metaphor of sight-impaired persons clustered around an

---

28. Poling, *Deliver Us from Evil*, 119.

elephant, each declaring the part they touch as representing the whole. The mountain top and elephant represent a singular transcendent being.[29] The search for similarities is a search for one God who, historically, has been the Christian God found lurking in what is thought to be the deep grammar at the core of all religions.[30]

Searching for similarities is, in fact, a way of obliterating alterity; as such, it is at odds with the basic premise of intercultural spiritual care that puts the other first. "No interreligious encounter and learning is possible without a fundamental ethical respect for the irreducible and unique alterity of the other that transcends all belonging to a 'reducing genre' or kind."[31] A process-relational understanding of power abuses in spiritual care relationships takes into account the broader cultural context of postcolonialism, which may at first seem like a distal rather than proximal context for understanding pastoral abuses of power. A process-relational worldview, with its appreciation for parallel processes between helping relationships and larger cultural systems of privilege, helps us appreciate echoes of colonialism in religiously self-affirming prejudice: "If we repress our colonial and neocolonial histories, they will come back to haunt us all the more."[32]

In the second vignette, the supervisor is certainly not blatantly guilty of wanting Seung as a Buddhist to emulate Christian practices. In fact, his initial calling to chaplaincy was shaped by a rejection of classical approaches to Christian pastoral care that sought to save souls by converting others to Christian beliefs. As a chaplain-in-training he embraced a clinical approach to pastoral care that emulated the person-centered unconditional acceptance of psychotherapist Carl Rogers. His experience of interpersonal group process was part of his self-actualization that left behind the life-limiting moralism he associated with classical pastoral care. Ironically, with Seung he risks becoming a missionary for the kind of CPE transformative

---

29. Prothero, *God Is Not One*.

30. Historian of religion Bruce Lincoln describes how minimalist definitions of religion have been used as a lens to understand all religions of the world. He builds upon the radical critique of Geertz's definition of religion made by Asad (See Asad, *Genealogies of Religion*.) "Geertz unwittingly normalized features of his own (necessarily parochial) cultural/religious background . . . Geertz's error, [Asad] argues, was not simply the product of some individual failing, but a specific manifestation of problems inherent to the project," as Lincoln notes. See Lincoln, *Holy Terrors*, 1.

31. Burggraeve, "Alterity Makes the Difference," 237.

32. Rieger, "Theology and Mission between Neocolonialism and Postcolonialism," 202.

process and values that "saved" him. How can he put Seung first and appreciate what is unique and idiosyncratic about her beliefs, values, and practices?

Besides restraining the impulse to search for similarities, teachers, supervisors, and pastors need to restrain the impulse to put the self first in how they use knowledge. Given the ways that their professional status inflates legitimate, expert, information, and reference power,[33] they need to consider whether knowledge is being used in the service of self or the other. Levinas highlights the alliance of rationalism with social and professional privilege when he describes "the political character of all logical rationalism" as an "alliance of logic with politics."[34] The more that agential power is inflated by social and professional privilege, the greater the danger of knowledge being used in ways that eclipse the mystery of the other.[35] Agential abuse of psychological and theological knowledge "will no longer leave the other in its otherness but always include it in its whole . . . From this stems the inability to recognize the other person as other person, as outside all calculation, as neighbor, as first come."[36]

Agential power is necessary in order to negotiate the parameters of helping relationships that put the other first in ways that protect the other from harm. Receptive power on its own is dangerous when those in helping

---

33. French and Raven, "The Bases of Social Power." French and Raven define social power as the ability to influence another person in a given setting.

34. Levinas, *Otherwise Than Being*, 171.

35. For example, envisioning empathy as standing in the other's shoes and seeing the world from the other's perspective is problematic because of the impossibility of leaving our own perspective behind. As Iris Marion Young notes, "When this rough and ready appeal to look at issues from the point of view of others is systematized into a moral theory, however, problems may arise. In her elaboration and revision of Habermas's theory of communicative ethics, Seyla Benhabib performs one such systematization. She conceptualizes moral respect as a relation of symmetry between self and other, and thinks of moral reciprocity as entailing that the perspectives of self and other are reversible. I agree with Benhabib's overall project of elaborating a communicative ethics that recognizes difference and particularity. I argue in this essay, however, that identifying moral respect with a reversibility and symmetry of perspectives impedes that project. It is neither possible nor morally desirable for persons engaged in moral interaction to adopt one another's standpoint. I develop a concept of asymmetrical reciprocity as an alternative to this notion of symmetrical reciprocity developed by Benhabib. A communicative ethics should develop an account of the non-substitutable relation of moral subjects. Each participant in a communication situation is distinguished by a particular history and social position that makes their relation asymmetrical." (Young, "Asymmetrical Reciprocity," 340–41.)

36. Levinas, "The Temptation of Temptation," 35.

roles neglect their professional responsibility for monitoring the contract of care and assessing various kinds of risks. In order for trust to grow within helping and mentoring relationships, agential and receptive power need to be intertwined, sometimes in seemingly paradoxical ways:[37]

> The other stands in a position over me because the other is that person who pulls me out of myself, which effects transcendence. The other stands above me as the only one who offers an alternative to dwelling within the labyrinthine circuits of my own interiority.[38]

This paradoxical intertwining of agential and receptive power allows those in helping relationships to enter into the experience of the immediacy of the "strangeness of the Other, his irreducibility to the I, to my thoughts and possessions,"[39] such that "the absolutely foreign [aspects of those seeking care] can instruct us."[40]

> It is in this moment that the other is, or can be, before me in and of herself. Levinas describes this moment as coming into contact with the *face of the other* . . . The face is a living, naked presence . . . This immediate moment of coming into contact with the face is a moment of transcendence, a kind of deliverance, if you will, from the ordinary structures of being.[41]

How can those in helping relationships emulate this other affirming intertwining of agential and receptive power that creates a relationship of trust, such that a multilayered sense of otherness (intrapsychic, interpersonal, spiritual, and cultural) comes into being and is received?

---

37. "Optimal relational trust encompasses a dynamic bimodal exchange of influence; we participate in optimal relational trust not only by receiving trust, but also through offering and building trust. As pastoral providers we must learn not only to become, in the words of Karen Lebacqz, 'trustworthy trustees,' but also to become humble and courageous in offering and developing trust as we participate in the work of the covenant: doing justice and loving mercy." (Morgan, "Burdens of Disclosure," 174.)

38. Diedrich et al., "A Dialogue between the Thought of Joan Tronto and Emmanuel Levinas," 50.

39. Levinas, *Totality and Infinity*, 143.

40. Levinas, *Otherwise Than Being, or Beyond Essence*, 207.

41. Levinas, "The Temptation of Temptation," 42–43. "The face of the other is the discrete but imperative word that affects me and appeals to me neither to use force nor to misuse, violate, totalize, hate or destroy the other: 'Thou shalt not kill.'" (Boileau, "The Wisdom of Love," 18.)

What does this look like in the practice of care? I would like to suggest several strategies.

STRATEGIES

In order to counteract this insidious tendency toward self-affirming prejudice, pastors need to become more conscious of how their values shape their judgments of others. Two strategies help pastors monitor self-affirming prejudice. First, pastors can reflect on the values formed in the relational matrices of their childhood, young adulthood, and adulthood in order to monitor embedded values from childhood that may still influence their judgment of others. Clarifying values will help them become conscious of when they are imposing their embedded values on others. The second strategy is to pay attention to jarring moments when their values seem to clash with the values of others. The emotional charge of these jarring moments signals that something is going on below the surface: values held dear seem to be threatened. Recognizing emotionally charged moments when values seem to clash with the other's gives pastors a choice: they can either respond in automatic ways by imposing their values on others, or they can intentionally hold back on using agential power and put the other first.

What if Pastor McKenzie were to go through this self-reflective process as soon as she realized that her sense of urgency to intervene was emotionally charged? She could reflect on childhood values that made her feel responsible for the suffering in her parents' conflicted marriage. She might remember her childhood experience of worshipping together as a family and praying that the appearance of family solidarity at church would change the family dynamics at home, where her parents fought in demeaning ways that left everyone miserable. She might remember looking at Jesus on the cross and Mary sorrowing beside him, and thinking that if God could make her good enough, it might restore peace at home. As a young adult she rejected these childhood hopes, realizing that her parents were responsible for doing something about their relationship; this was not her or even God's responsibility. At this stage in her life, she was angry that her childhood beliefs made her carry the emotional burden of worrying about her family. These experiences shaped her feminist beliefs and her calling to ministry.

Now, listening to Sally, she imagines that Sally is trying to cope in the same way she did as a child. This interpretation is emotionally charged for Pastor McKenzie, who wants Sally to reject this way of coping and stand up for herself. By exploring the ways Sally's story reminds her of her childhood beliefs, values, and practices, Pastor McKenzie will be more able to put Sally first and see Sally for who she is.

Chaplain Johnson could benefit from the same exploration. Raised in a strict Lutheran home, he internalized a life-limiting moral way of understanding suffering as a consequence of personal sin. He went to a denominational college in order to prepare for ministry, having experienced a call during an intense church retreat as a teenager. At college his difficulties with anxiety increased, and he was referred to a compassionate psychiatrist. Medication and psychotherapy helped Chaplain Johnson experience a sense of God's goodness and forgiveness. His first CPE supervisor became his mentor. Chaplain Johnson found the interpersonal group process, especially the freedom to get in touch with anger and express it in constructive ways, very liberating.

Now he finds it jarring when Seung sits quietly at the beginning of their supervision time. He remembers how hard it was for him to be in charge of his own supervision when he was first an intern. Remembering his own journey makes him realize how different his vocational development is from Seung Lee's. This jarring moment signals that he is expecting her to be like him. If he can pay attention to this moment, sit with it, and not impose his own values on Seung, he may be able to find ways to put her first. He could try to use his own spiritual practices to hold back from using his agential power. He might, for example, center himself through prayer in order to be fully present in the moment to whatever may emerge. Putting Seung first could be very unsettling, especially if he has developed a ritualized way of doing supervision that interns quickly pick up, as they emulate his goals and the supervisory process he values. Such reflections may lead Chaplain Johnson to realize that Seung is not actually being passive and accommodating. By putting her first and having her take the lead, Chaplain Johnson can receive the gift of not knowing what will unfold.

> Through pastoral encounter with others, participants will experience the paradox of familiarity and otherness which situates them within, and draws them beyond, the present and immediate. Can we regard authentic pastoral practice, therefore, as that which draws us into encounter with the "Other," towards a deeper

understanding of our own identity-in-relation? The process of going beyond the situated and concrete in the encounter with the Other may also serve as a metaphor for the human experience of the transcendent. It speaks of an encounter with transcendence and authentic faith occurring at the very point of loss of certainty and self-possession: divine activity and presence encountered in the mystery of alterity.[42]

CONCLUSION

Process-relational theology, with its distinctions between unilateral individual power and mutual relational power, provides a psycho-systems way of understanding self-affirming prejudice. The relational ethics of Levinas puts in place an ethical framework for plumbing the life-limiting and destructive potential of self-affirming prejudice within hierarchal relational systems that value individual survival and control. In order to counteract self-affirming prejudice and the inevitable inflation of pastoral power through social and organizational privileges, teachers, chaplains, supervisors, and pastors can enact Levinas's ethic of putting the other first. Equipped with strategies for identifying and exploring moments that are emotionally charged and jarring for them, they will be ready to encounter alterity. After ensuring that an appropriate contract of mentoring, supervision, or pastoral care is in place, these intrepid teachers, chaplains, and pastors can enter into the unknown of receiving the mystery of the other. The stage is set and the curtain rises. When the other senses that his or her alterity will be honored and valued, then the other will go first and a dance will unfold.

BIBLIOGRAPHY

Altemeyer, Bob. "Why Do Religious Fundamentalists Tend to Be Prejudiced?" *Journal for the Psychology of Religion* 13 (2003) 17–28.
Altemeyer, Bob, and Bruce Hunsberger. "Authoritarianism, Religious Fundamentalism, Quest, and Prejudice." *International Journal for the Psychology of Religion* 2 (1992) 113–33.
Amodio, David M., and Matthew D. Lieberman. "Pictures in Our Heads: Contributions of Fmri to the Study of Prejudice and Stereotyping." In *Handbook of Prejudice, Stereotyping, and Discrimination*, edited by Todd D. Nelson, 347–65. New York: Psychological Press, 2009.

42. Graham, *Transforming Practice*, 206–7.

Amodio, David M., Patricia G. Devine, and Eddie Harmon-Jones. "A Dynamic Model of Guilt Implications for Motivation and Self-Regulation in the Context of Prejudice." *Psychological Science* 18 (2007) 524–30.

Asad, Talal. *Genealogies of Religion: Discipline and Reasons of Power in Christianity and Islam*. Baltimore: Johns Hopkins University Press, 1993.

Boileau, David. "Preface." In *The Wisdom of Love in the Service of Love: Emmanuel Levinas on Justice, Peace and Human Rights*, edited by Roger Burggraeve and Jeffrey Bloechl. Marquette Studies in Philosophy 29, 17–19. Milwaukee: Marquette University Press, 2002.

Brewer, Marilynn B. "The Social Psychology of Intergroup Relations: Social Categorization, Ingroup Bias, and Outgroup Prejudice." In *Social Psychology: Handbook of Basic Principles*, edited by Arie W. Kruglanski and E. Tory Higgins, 695–715. New York: Guilford, 2007.

Burggraeve, Roger. "Alterity Makes the Difference: Ethical and Metaphysical Conditions for Authentic Interreligious Dialogue and Learning." In *Interreligious Learning*, edited by Didier Pollefeyt, 231–56. Dudley, MA: Peeters, 2007.

———. "Violence and the Vulnerable Face of the Other: The Vision of Emmanuel Levinas on Moral Evil and Our Responsibility." *Journal of Social Philosophy* 30 (1999) 29–45.

Cabezón, José Ignacio. "The Discipline and Its Other: The Dialectic of Alterity in the Study of Religion." *Journal of the American Academy of Religion* 74 (2006) 21–38.

Demoulin, Stephanie, et al. "The Role of Ingroup Identification in Infra-Humanization." *International Journal for the Psychology of Religion* 44 (2009) 4–11.

Devine, Patricia G., et al. "Self-Regulatory Processes in Interracial Interactions: The Role of Internal and External Motivation to Respond without Prejudice." In *Social Motivation: Conscious and Unconscious Processes*, edited by Joseph P. Forgas et al., 249–73. New York: Cambridge University Press, 2005.

Diedrich, W. Wolf, et al. "A Dialogue between the Thoughts of Joan Tronto and Emmanuel Levinas." *Ethical Perspectives: Journal of the European Ethics Network* 13 (2006) 33–61.

Duckitt, John. "Differential Effects of Right Wing Authoritarianism and Social Dominance Orientation on Outgroup Attitudes and Their Mediation by Threat from Competitiveness Outgroups." *Personality and Social Psychology Bulletin* 32 (2006) 684–96.

Dueck, Alvin, and Thomas D. Parsons. "Ethics, Alterity, and Psychotherapy: A Levinasian Perspective." *Pastoral Psychology* 55 (2007) 271–82.

French, John R. P., Jr., and Bertram H. Raven. "The Bases of Social Power." In *Studies in Social Power*, edited by Dorwin Cartwright, 150–67. Ann Arbor, MI: Institute for Social Research, 1959.

Graham, Elaine. *Transforming Practice: Pastoral Theology in an Age of Uncertainty*. New York: Mowbray, 1996.

Greenberg, Jeff, et al. "How Our Dreams of Death Transcendence Breed Prejudice, Stereotyping, and Conflict: Terror Management Theory." In *Handbook of Prejudice, Stereotyping, and Discrimination*, edited by Todd D. Nelson, 309–32. New York: Psychological Press, 2009.

Hogue, David. "Brain Matters: Neuroscience, Empathy, and Pastoral Theology." *Journal of Pastoral Theology* 20 (2010) 25–55.

Keller, Catherine. *On the Mystery: Discerning Divinity in Process*. Minneapolis: Fortress Press, 2008.

PART 2—Power and Interculturality

Lartey, Emmanuel Y. *In Living Color: An Intercultural Approach to Pastoral Care and Counseling*. London: Jessica Kingsley, 2003.

Levinas, Emmanuel. *Otherwise Than Being or Beyond Essence*. Translated by Alphonso Lingis. The Hague: Martinus Nijhoff, 1981.

———. "The Temptation of Temptation." Translated by Annette Aronowicz. In *Nine Talmudic Readings*, edited by Emmanuel Levinas, 30–50. Bloomington: Indiana University Press, 1990.

———. *Totality and Infinity: An Essay on Exteriority*. Translated by Alphonso Lingis. Pittsburgh: Duquesne University Press, 1991.

Lincoln, Bruce. *Holy Terrors: Thinking About Religion after September 11*. Chicago: University of Chicago Press, 2008.

Loomer, Bernard M. "On Committing Yourself to a Relationship." *Process Studies* 16 (1987) 255–63.

———. "Process Theology: Origins, Strengths, Weaknesses." *Process Studies* 16 (1987) 245–54.

———. "Two Conceptions of Power." *Process Studies* 6 (1976) 5–32.

Magyar, Gina M., et al. "Sacrilege: A Study of Sacred Loss and Desecration and Their Implications for Health and Well-Being in a Community Sample." *Journal for the Scientific Study of Religion* 44 (2005) 59–78.

McCleary, Daniel F., et al. "Meta-Analysis of Correlational Relationships between Perspectives of Truth in Religion and Major Psychological Constructs." *Psychology of Religion and Spirituality* 3 (2011) 163–80.

Morgan, Virginia R. "Burdens of Disclosure: A Pastoral Theology of Confidentiality." PhD diss., Iliff School of Theology and University of Denver, 2010.

Moskowitz, Gorden. B., et al. "Preconscious Control of Stereotype Activation through Chronic Egalitarian Goals." *Journal of Personality and Social Psychology* 77 (1999) 167–84.

Pargament, Kenneth I., et al. "Envisioning an Integrative Paradigm for the Psychology of Religion and Spirituality: An Introduction to the American Psychological Assocation Handbook of Psychology, Religion and Spirituality." In *American Psychological Association Handbook of Psychology, Religion and Spirituality*, Vol. 1, edited by Kenneth I. Pargament et al., 3–19. Washington: APA, 2013.

Poling, James N. *Deliver Us from Evil: Resisting Racial and Gender Oppression*. Minneapolis: Fortress Press, 1996.

Prothero, Stephen. *God Is Not One: The Eight Rival Religions That Run the World and Why Their Differences Matter*. New York: HarperOne, 2010.

Rieger, Joerg. "Theology and Mission between Neocolonialism and Postcolonialism." *Mission Studies* 21 (2004) 201–27.

Stephan, Walter G., et al. "Intergroup Threat Theory." In *Handbook of Prejudice, Stereotyping, and Discrimination*, edited by Todd D. Nelson, 43–59. New York: Psychological Press, 2009.

Tajfel, Henri, and John C. Turner. "The Social Identity Theory of Intergroup Behavior." In *Psychology of Intergroup Relations*, edited by Stephen Worchel and William G. Austin, 7–24. Chicago: Nelson-Hall, 1986.

Young, Iris Marion. "Asymmetrical Reciprocity: On Moral Respect, Wonder and Enlarged Thought." *Constellations* 3 (1997) 340–63.

5

"When I Am Weak, Then I Am Strong"
An African Christian Reflection on the Ambiguities, Paradoxes, and Challenges of Pastoral Power

Emmanuel Lartey

"Power is not a substance. Neither is it a mysterious property whose origin must be delved into. Power is only a certain type of relation between individuals."[1]

"Power is like an egg. When held too tightly it may break, or it falls and breaks when held loosely."[2]

PASTORAL CAREGIVERS ARE INEVITABLY engaged on a daily basis with issues of power and relations of power. Included in the list of pastoral caregivers whose relational work is the focus of this chapter are pastors, chaplains in different institutions, congregational leaders, pastoral counselors and pastoral psychotherapists. Pastoral caregivers are relational experts professionally seeking to promote health in personal, social, environmental relations,

---

1. Foucault, *Power*, 324.
2. Akan proverb from Ghana. See Korem and Abissath, *African Proverbs*, 94.

and ultimately in all human relationships with the divine. Power, studies of power and the exercise of power in pastoral relationships are complex and ambiguous. Pastoral caregivers live in the midst of the challenges and ambiguities of power. Pastoral caregivers work constantly in the midst of relations between persons. Pastoral caregivers are generally upright persons of integrity, especially moral because they seek and actively work for the well-being of others. They are committed to helping people, and do help them at the most crucial levels of their lives, with issues that lie in the intra-personal, the interpersonal, the communal, and the spiritual dimensions of human life.

Pastoral caregivers are very well-trained people who frequently are also engaged in the education of others to be professional helpers. They have typically spent several years studying their arts and practices. They frequently engage in Continuing Education programs, in-service workshops, retreats, seminars, and special training sessions to continue studying their areas of expertise both in theory and practice. Pastoral caregivers are in therapy for themselves and work with individual supervisors. How could they abuse or misuse power? How could these morally upright, sensitive, and thoughtful people full of the milk of human kindness and attuned to the well-being of others (parishioners, clients, and the communities they serve) go wrong?

Michel Foucault devoted a substantial portion of his philosophical reflections to the subject of power. Foucault's overriding interest lies in "subjects," in other words people as subjects and the ways in which we come to selfhood as subjects. In an essay titled *The Subject and Power*, first published in 1983, Foucault states categorically "it is not power, but the subject that is the general theme of my research."[3] Power in human terms has integrally to do with relationships. For Foucault, in essence, power describes a form of relationship between people. It is this way of considering the essence of power that is of immense value to pastoral caregivers interested in exploring the power dynamics of their day-to-day work. The following eight theses, which seem to me consistent with several of Foucault's concerns, are helpful in consideration of the challenges and ambiguities of the power relations between pastoral caregivers in different positions of authority and their parishioners, clients, and communities. These statements constitute the presuppositions upon which discussions in this chapter are based.

---

3. Foucault, *Power*, 327.

First, that power is an inevitable part of our human reality. Second, that power is a relational given. All human relations involve power in some shape or form. Third, that all relations between professional helpers and their clients are necessarily asymmetrical. This is as it is and is neither good nor bad. Fourth, that power is by nature ambivalent.[4] Foucault argues that power is an ambiguous, multivalent resource, and danger. Binary oppositional thinking does not come close to dealing with the complexities of power. Weak/strong; moral/immoral; knowledgeable/ignorant; male/female; sensitive/insensitive—these all exist to varying degrees on both sides of the pastoral caregiver/client dyad and in complex ways within the relationship between them and within the communal contexts within which pastor and parishioner engage. Fifth and closely related to the preceding point, power is both an asset (productive) and a danger.[5] Power is not all and always bad. Like a sharp knife, it is crucial when harnessed and utilized wisely in the service of the wellbeing of all. Sixth, that all persons have some power. Power exists in the least expected places as well as the obvious places. Seventh, that power is always relative. Eighth, power is embedded and often hidden in various social exchange media such as money, language, and knowledge.

Foucault writes of his seeking to study "the way a human being turns him- or herself into a subject," and how he has done this through studies of sexuality.[6] In a way akin to this, I have for all my professional life been interested in exploring how human persons become *fully functioning persons*. I have been most fascinated by how "culture," a nebulous and multi-faceted term that refers essentially to the symbolic realms of our social lives, impacts us as persons. How the social and symbolic forces at work from without us—social, contextual forces—have such an impact on our internal states, the most important motivating mechanism of our ordinary lives. In this regard, what has really riveted my attention has been how ordinary, "normal" good people can be involved in some of the most alarming forms of cruelty

---

4. Foucault, *Power*, xix. "Nothing, including the exercise of power, is evil in itself—but everything is dangerous."

5. Foucault wrote about the "productivity of power" (power relations are integral to the modern social productive apparatus, and linked to active programs for the fabricated part of the collective substance of society itself) and the "constitution of subjectivity through power relations" (the individual impact of power relations does not limit itself to pure repression but also comprises the intention to teach, to mold conduct, to instill forms of self-awareness and identities). Foucault, *Power*, xix.

6. Ibid., 327.

PART 2—Power and Interculturality

and yet appear to be just fine. How did the Jewish Holocaust happen; how did the Rwandan genocide come to be; how come there were massacres in Darfur, or Srebrenica? How do ordinary socially upright families hold such "secrets" of cruelty and abuse? In this chapter my concern is how pastoral caregivers engage in relations of power for good or ill.

Swiss Jungian psychologist Guggenbühl-Craig, in a book titled *Power in the Helping Professions*, presents compelling questions from Jungian analytical perspectives that are intriguing and compelling in the exploration of the exercise of power in therapeutic and helping institutional contexts. He asks:

> What drives a man [sic] to concern himself with the dark side of social life? What makes it possible for him to deal each day with unhappy, unfortunate, maladjusted people? What fascinates him about this dismal side of life?[7]

By analyzing and reflecting on Jung's notion of the "shadow," Guggenbühl-Craig addresses some of the paradoxes of professional helpers. He says:

> In my years of analytical work with social workers, I have noticed time and again that whenever something must be imposed by force, the conscious and unconscious motives of those involved are many-factored. An uncanny lust for power lurks in the background.[8]

In a somewhat crudely and overstated manner, he continues:

> People are the most cruel when they can use cruelty to enforce the "good." In daily life we often suffer pangs of conscience when we permit ourselves to be excessively motivated by the power drive. But these guilt feelings completely disappear from consciousness when our actions, while unconsciously motivated by a lust for power, can be consciously justified by that which is allegedly right and good.[9]

I disagree with the totalistic aspects of this statement in which "guilt feelings *completely disappear* from consciousness." This seems to me an overstatement. Nevertheless, what it points to in terms of unconscious suppression and conscious justification merits consideration in the face

7. Guggenbühl-Craig, *Power in the Helping Professions*, 28
8. Ibid., 12
9. Ibid., 23.

especially of the sexual abuse of minors by clergypersons in high ecclesial office, some of whom have sought to justify their actions in terms of the "good" of their victims, as well as other extreme acts of cruelty meted out by caregivers in the exercise of their duties "for the good of the clients."

Theological considerations would help us to recognize that no one can or does act out of exclusively pure motives. Writing to the Romans, Saint Paul grapples with this truism in his own life. "I cannot understand my own behavior. I fail to carry out the things I want to do, and find myself doing the very things I hate."[10] He goes on to say, "In fact, this seems to be the rule, that every single time I want to do good, it is something evil that comes to hand."[11] Even the most noble of deeds are based on pure and impure, great and not-so-great motivations. The more we pretend to ourselves that we are operating exclusively from selfless motives, the more influential our "power shadow" becomes, until it finally betrays us into making some very questionable decisions. Guggenbühl-Craig again:

> C.G. Jung repeatedly pointed out that, whenever a bright psychic content becomes lodged in the consciousness, its opposite is constellated in the unconscious and tries to do harm from that vantage point.[12]

In line with his views on the unconscious, Jung postulated three aspects of the shadow, namely (1) the personal (2) the collective, and (3) the archetypal. There is for Jung, a "personal shadow" that embraces images, fantasies, drives and experiences that have had to be repressed for personal reasons in the course of an individual's personal development. According to Guggenbühl-Craig, "the modern western European's personal shadow often includes certain sexual perversions and a great deal of repressed aggression."[13] Jung's conceptualization of a collective unconscious includes the notion of a "collective shadow" that contains the "dark other side of the collective ideal," and that "tries to demolish collective ideals."[14] Further, there is the "archetypal shadow," which for Jung would approximate "evil," the absence of good, and which for Guggenbühl-Craig "in the course of history has been represented by such symbols as the Devil, or the alche-

---

10. Rom 7:15 Jerusalem Bible.
11. Rom 7:21 Jerusalem Bible.
12. Guggenbühl-Craig, *Power in the Helping Professions*, 38.
13. Ibid., 96.
14. Ibid.

mists '*sol niger* (black sun)."' He continues, "many of the more frightful gods and goddesses in religious history are symbols of this archetypal shadow: Shiva, Loki, Beelzebub." Considering Jungian discourse on *archetypes*, it is my contention that Jung's notions of archetypes could refer to cultural-symbolic as well as spiritual-relational dimensions of transpersonal human experience.

In this essay therefore, drawing on Jungian considerations, I should like to explore four levels of the relations of power at which pastoral caregivers are involved. These are (1) *personal power relations* (2) *collective power relations* (3) *cultural power relations*, and a fourth that arises out of the spiritual/theological or pneumatological dimensions of the practice of pastoral caregivers (4) *spiritual power relations*.

I should like to emphasize that these levels are interconnected and interpenetrating realities. For example, recognized social ills such as racism, sexism, classism, heterosexism, able-bodyism, et cetera reside at all these levels and may operate on one or all of them simultaneously. As such, I am arguing that issues of pastoral power exist at the *personal* (intra- and interpersonal) level. Dynamics of pastoral power are manifest at the *collective* (institutional, family, neighborhood, church, school, etc.) level. Challenges of pastoral power are embedded in and occur influentially (and often most unconsciously) at the *cultural* level. This is the level of the images and symbols associated with national, institutional, religious, and ideological beliefs and institutions. *Spiritual* power issues have to do with the reality of the theological/spiritual relatedness out of which the practices of pastoral authority and power emerge. Issues of pastoral power are clearly and typically implicated on this level. Further there is a shadow side to each of these dimensions of our experience. In these discussions, I am utilizing "pastoral power" in a sense that differs from Foucault's usage of the term. For Foucault pastoral power had much to do with the adoption by governmental and other state institutions of relations that drew upon the notions of humane care introduced largely by Christian teaching. In this essay, the emphasis is upon the relations of power between pastoral caregivers and the parishioners, clients, and communities with whom they relate.

Pastoral power in the specific sense of relations between pastoral caregivers and clients operates at and needs to be analyzed along these four interacting and interpenetrating levels. When analyzing pastoral power it must be borne in mind that it is not merely a question of spiritual power. It is important that we recognize the impact of the first three upon the spiritual dimension. Moreover, it is necessary that we recognize the fact that pastoral caregivers inhabit and address the collective and the cultural dimensions of power. Also, in exploring pastoral power we must give attention to intra-personal and inter-personal power issues long before they become manifest through scandals that become public.

In the essay referred to earlier on "the Subject and Power," Foucault studied power by examining the various forms of resistance to or struggles against power. He argued that there are three main types of struggles. Firstly, he argued that people struggle "against forms of domination," especially in ethnic, social, and religious terms. Secondly, the struggle is "against forms of exploitation that separate people from what they produce"; and thirdly, there are struggles against forms of subjectivity and submission in which the struggle is against "that which ties the individual to himself and submits him to others in this way."[15] This latter form I would term struggles against *subjugation*. It is my view that each of these three forms of struggles needs to be engaged strategically at each of the *four* levels identified through Jung's analysis of our human reality, namely the personal, the collective, the cultural, and the spiritual. As a result of combining Jung's levels of our human experience with Foucault's forms of power struggle we are able to analyze power dynamics by means of a grid made up of *twelve* cells.

A MATRIX FOR THE ANALYSIS OF POWER

	Domination	**Exploitation**	**Subjugation**
Personal	Personal Domination	Personal Exploitation	Personal Subjugation
Collective	Collective Domination	Collective Exploitation	Collective Subjugation
Cultural	Cultural Domination	Cultural Exploitation	Cultural Subjugation
Spiritual	Spiritual Domination	Spiritual Exploitation	Spiritual Subjugation

15. Foucault, *Power*, 331.

PART 2—Power and Interculturality

Let us then examine pastoral power as it is operative in each of these analytical cells.

Personal "Power" Issues

> "Our deepest fear is not that we are inadequate. Our deepest fear is that we are powerful beyond measure. It is our light, not our darkness that most frightens us. We ask ourselves, 'Who am I to be brilliant, gorgeous, talented, fabulous?' Actually, who are you *not* to be? You are a child of God. Your playing small does not serve the world. There is nothing enlightened about shrinking so that other people won't feel insecure around you. We are all meant to shine, as children do. We were born to make manifest the glory of God that is within us. It's not just in some of us; it's in everyone. And as we let our own light shine, we unconsciously give other people permission to do the same. As we are liberated from our own fear, our presence automatically liberates others."[16]

As Marianne Williamson presents it, power, first of all, is crucial to wholesome living. We need to embrace our God-given inner strength. It is the life-line that can keep us going in the face of all odds. A goal of therapy is to help people draw out and draw on their personal strength to overcome what may be dragging them down. To cultivate inner personal strength is a noble, desirable, and necessary goal for any person. We speak of "empowering" people. By this token we acknowledge that each has some power that we seek to enhance and build upon, or to increase. There is no human person alive who is totally devoid of power. As such all can be "empowered." At the same time, there is the need to struggle against the shadow side of personal power, namely all forms of personal power that tend in the direction of evil. Such a struggle is inward and personal. A necessary inward struggle if the utilization of power is to serve the good of self and others. An exploration of the affirmation of personal power and the struggle against its abuse involves an examination of issues of personal domination, personal exploitation, and personal subjugation.

---

16. Williamson, *A Return to Love*, 190–91.

The Struggle against Personal Domination

Personal domination occurs when we feel personally overcome and in a constant state of "beholdeness" to others. We feel inordinately and personally bound to a person, (e.g., father, mother, boss, pastor, bishop) a group, (e.g., family, church, community, school, work) an idea, (e.g., teaching, value, expectation), or a thing (e.g., an emblem, flag, symbol). The feeling is often expressed in the words "something seems to have gotten a hold on me and I can't get free." Where personal domination exists, the sense of obligation produces extreme guilt feelings when we are unable to fulfill the requirements of our bondedness. We feel unable to think our own thoughts without feeling a sense that we are betraying someone or some cause. The struggle is a personal one. It is a struggle for selfhood, for a differentiated self that is not independent and isolated, but rather enjoys a necessary sense of freedom and selfhood in thought, feeling, and action.

To be free of personal domination is to be able to be self-directed, to listen with affirmation and respect to the "inner voice" of one's self, and to engage in acts of obedience to external and social responsibilities with a sense of inner directedness, free choice, and unobligated willingness.

The Struggle against Personal Exploitation

Personal exploitation typically occurs when our work is taken for granted, when we feel "used," when we are not given due regard or reward for our labor. We feel taken advantage of and the palpable sense of outrage is directed within. "Why do I allow myself, my skills, or my expertise to be taken so much for granted?" Such exploitation denies or truncates the necessary relationship that ought to exist between a producer and his or her product, whatever that product may be. The labor of the producer is exploited when it serves to enrich someone the producer has not freely elected for it to enrich. In the relations that existed between colonizer and the colonized, the slave and the master, personal exploitation was basic and essential. Historically, exploitative relations of power continue to exist psychologically, emotionally, and economically, long after the condition of slavery or colonization has come to a formal end. Pastoral caregivers can personally exploit their clients, parishioners, and community members.

Sexual abuse is also a form of personal exploitation where one's sexual being is the victim of "theft." One's being is taken advantage of and "used" for the satisfaction of another. This is a most pernicious form of personal exploitation in which it is not one's labor, but rather one's personal selfhood that is violated and taken from one.

The Struggle against Personal Subjection or Subjugation

Personal subjugation occurs when we know ourselves demeaned or degraded. Colonization and slavery entailed a massive and extensive exercise of personal subjugation. Subjugation is usually by force of arms, coercion, ridicule, or other means against which the colonized feels powerless—unable to successfully resist without losing their existence. This sense of degradation crushes dignity, selfhood, and creativity. The sense of powerlessness and helplessness that is enforced produces forms of servile mimicry of the oppressor by the oppressed. Among many formerly colonized people, the very nature of their personal faith bears the marks of such subjugation. Such people find no way to be creative, innovative, or to draw on their own resources. A dependency complex is what is fostered.

Pastoral caregivers and care-receivers are called upon to struggle against all forms of personal subjugation when these are directed at them. Whenever it is realized that persons, whether they be teachers, trainers, supervisors, or institutions (e.g., churches, communities or associations) are wittingly or unwittingly dominating, exploiting, or subjugating persons, we must struggle against them. We are also called to struggle against our own personal tendencies towards domination, exploitation, and subjugation of others with whom we have relations, including our parishioners, clients, and the community members we serve. It is important to constantly interrogate the necessary asymmetries of power between caregiver and care-receiver to see if there are any pastoral practices that subjugate and thus suffocate and invalidate the relationship and its therapeutic potential.

Collective Power Issues

Communities need to recognize and access the communal assets they possess. Collective assets are those powerful possessions present in communities that can be drawn upon to face challenges, win over the odds, and surmount the obstacles that lie in the path of—and often frustrate—communal well-being. We have seen members of communities devastated by disasters pull together and generate strengths that for years have lain dormant within them to successfully restore their fortunes. For instance, many analysts and commentators have commented that Japan seems to have the collective will to overcome the set back of the earthquake, tsunami, and nuclear plant catastrophe that befell her in 2011. The reason lies in the evident strength and resilience of the Japanese people. It was striking to observe on TV screens globally the collectively powerful way in which they behaved following the tragedy. Noticeable in the midst of the crisis was communal behavior characterized by *calmness* with hardly any signs of chest-beating or wild grief; *dignity*, with disciplined queues for water and groceries with not a rough word or a crude gesture; *grace*, where people bought only what they needed for the present, so everybody could get something; *order*, with no looting in shops, no honking and no overtaking on the roads; *sacrifice*, for example when as many as fifty workers stayed back to pump sea water into the Nuclear reactors; *tenderness*, as restaurants cut prices, an unguarded ATM is left alone, and the strong cared for the weak; *training*, with the old and the children helping each other, everyone seemed to know exactly what to do and they did just that. During the acute crisis, the Media showed magnificent restraint in the bulletins. No sensationalizing, only calm reportage, and, *collective conscience*, when the power went off in a store, people put things back on the shelves and left quietly. These seem to be the marks of the positive characteristics of collective power.

Power is a great and necessary ingredient in the survival and thriving of individuals and peoples. At the same time it is necessary that we engage.

The Struggle against Collective Domination

The uprisings in North Africa and the Middle East in 2011 and 2012, which became dubbed the "Arab Spring," are palpable examples of the struggle against collective domination. The struggle for independence from European colonialism on the African continent and across the globe, where European countries had dominated and seized lands and peoples for their possession and control, is another example of the collective exercise of power to overcome domination. The struggle for autonomy and self-governance on the part of churches and communities of faith established by colonials is another relevant example of this struggle. Wherever social groups have become subject to the control and domination of other groups, sometimes by virtue of numbers or of superior military weapons, we have a situation of collective domination. The maintenance of such domination requires the use of excessive or superior force, coercion, intimidation, or political manipulation. The overthrow of such dominant forces has always been costly in terms of human life and resources. The motivation for collective domination is most often economic. As such, domination prepares the way for collective exploitation.

The Struggle against Collective Exploitation

Examples of collective exploitation include situations where the labor of a people by virtue of race (e.g., Blacks), gender (e.g., women), class/caste (e.g., the "untouchables" in India), or age (e.g., children) is utilized by powerful forces and systems with no regard for due compensation. The world economic system appears to have been engineered to ensure the collective exploitation of the South by the North. Post-political independence means that many former colonial countries continue to engage in an on-going struggle for economic growth. This battle is a structural struggle against systems of economic exploitation. Whenever the possessions of a group of people are forcibly taken and utilized for the satisfaction or betterment of others, collective exploitation is operative.

The Struggle against Collective Subjugation

Closely following and related to collective exploitation is collective subjugation where the collective sense or feeling widely shared within a community is one of the loss of dignity, self-worth, and personhood. The late francophone African theologian, Englebert Mveng, referred to Africans as a people experiencing "anthropological poverty"—because African, therefore *ipso facto* "poor" in all ways. Mveng writes concerning anthropological poverty that "It consists in despoiling human beings not only of what they have, but of everything that constitutes their being and essence—their identity, history, ethnic roots, language, culture, faith, creativity, dignity, pride, ambitions, right to speak."[17] The converse is true of Caucasians—a sense of racial pride, privilege, and the power to control, dominate, define, and determine the futures of all other peoples.

---

17. Mveng, "Third World Theology," 220.

Cultural Power Issues

The symbols, artifacts, ideologies and signs of social groups are important means by which they find solidarity, cohesion, and dignity. Images and ideologies have power. Privilege and social prestige is often accorded to persons and groups in terms of their cultural power. Examples of cultural power include facility in dominant languages; skill in the production of high art (vs. low art); race—the privilege of whiteness; heritage, counted in terms of historical legacy; and membership of preferred or respected ecclesial denomination.

The Struggle against Cultural Domination

This entails the struggle against the use of symbols to portray and convey dominance, power- over, and superiority. There are conflicts among African Christians as to the significance and utility of various aspects of historic African culture. Whereas features of European culture presented as "Christian" (e.g., the Christmas tree, the tiered wedding cake) are deemed acceptable, forms and features of historical African culture (e.g., the pouring of libation in prayer, traditional dress) are considered pagan and evil and so not acceptable. A notable Ghanaian scholar and musicologist, the late Dr Ephraim Amu, was denied ordination by the Presbyterian Church to which he belonged—founded by the Basel Mission, because he preferred to dress in African historical attire—using the sacred hand woven cloth—instead of in European suits.[18] Dr Amu composed the National song along with several other choral pieces that are considered classic Ghanaian traditional music.

---

18. Fred Agyemang writing of Dr. Ephraim Amu quotes the then (1932) moderator of the Presbyterian Church of Ghana's response to Amu's request to wear African attire in the pulpit: "Since our mentors the Basel missionaries came here in 1828 they did not allow their teachers and ministers to wear native attire in public. It is never done. A church worker—teacher, catechist, or minister—should always appear modestly as a servant of God." Agyemang explains: "This invariably meant a European black woolen or alpaca coat and trousers, black shoes, white shirt and black tie and black hat. At any rate, to them, any modest European dress was preferable to African attire." Agyemang, *Amu the African*, 75. Sadly this remains the requirement to this day in Ghana.

PART 2—Power and Interculturality

The Struggle against Cultural Exploitation

This entails the struggle against the use of political, economic, and other coercive means to extract material and cultural wealth, historic symbols of heritage such as artifacts, *objets d'art*, et cetera from others without regard for their rights. Museums in Europe and North America are replete with artifacts that originate from Egypt and other parts of the world. These objects continue to be kept in spite of protests from their countries of origin. The paternalistic excuses given continue to be "better resources for the preservation of these world heritage objects."

The Struggle against Cultural Subjugation

The struggle against cultural subjugation is the struggle for the dignity of a people—such that their cherished values and traditions are not ripped from them and replaced by those of another people. When Westerners have encountered other forms of socialization processes for the young in traditional societies, by and large the proponents of Western education have suppressed, denigrated, ridiculed, or else ignore these processes and have imposed their own as superior, or else have been exclusively able to deliver on "civilization." Frequently, local languages have been learned, written, and used to communicate by many Western educators. However, in spite of this apparent recognition of a people's culture, the preferred values that have been transmitted have been the Western European values. To that extent, local cultures and customs have been undermined through the use of local languages.

Spiritual/Archetypal Power Issues

According to Jung, archetypes are innate, universal, psychic dispositions that form the substrate from which the basic symbols or representations of unconscious experience emerge.

Examples would include Mother, Father, Child, Redeemer, Lord, Lady, Doctor-patient, Master-Servant, Black-white, Teacher-student, The Hero, The Devil, the Mascot. These universal symbols play out in the narratives and ideologies of different cultures.

The Struggle against Spiritual Domination

Spiritual domination typically occurs when people are overwhelmed by a pastor's spiritual expertise or authority. They are held in thrall of the pastor and find themselves unable to function spiritually in the absence of the pastor. The "expert" pastor who introjects such feelings of superiority and indispensability then often goes on to actually significantly disempower individuals and communities. Many persons of faith wittingly or unwittingly collude with their own spiritual domination through acquiescing in the face of the abuse of such power. In several situations, the parishioners see the pastor as vicariously representing them in all things before the divine presence. Their wish is that the pastor be "spiritual" on their behalf so that they do not need themselves to undergo the rigors and disciplines of their faith. So long as the pastor prays for them they do not need to pray. This soon leads to a complete abdication of their own spiritual agency and to a spiritual domination by the pastor.

The Struggle against Spiritual Exploitation

Spiritual exploitation occurs when "spiritual work" is taken for granted. When pastors are never adequately compensated for their time, efforts, energy, use of knowledge, teaching, counseling, or other skills for which other professionals would be paid. All work that is considered "pastoral" in such a mindset is voluntary. Spiritual work is by virtue of it being "spiritual," not to be "paid for."

In this way, churches and other religious organizations get away with massive exploitation of the spiritual resources, not only of the ordained, but also of others in positions of leadership and service.

The Struggle against Spiritual Subjugation

Spiritual subjugation has occurred on a massive level in the encounter of Western Christianity with the other faiths of the world. In its encounter with African religion for example, Christianity engaged in a huge exercise of spiritual subjugation, where the religious beliefs and practices of an illustrious people were denigrated with pejorative terms such as "folk" superstition, traditional, magical, animistic, fetishistic, et cetera. Characteristics that all religious traditions share in a measure become seen as the total

PART 2—Power and Interculturality

picture of these "other religions." This reductionism serves the purpose of discrediting the other religious traditions and elevating one's own as being exclusively true or else solely capable of delivering anything of salvific value.

All of these levels of human encounter and spheres of struggle for power intersect and interpenetrate. Any exploration of the ambiguities of power needs to examine each of them as well as how they may be mutually interacting in a given situation.

At this juncture, I wish to engage in a brief exposition of a traditional African community's structures of and exercise of power that may help to illuminate our discussion and offer some intriguing thoughts on the challenges of power relations for our consideration.

RULERSHIP IN AN AFRICAN HISTORICAL COMMUNITY

As an example of an ancient African people who sought to harness necessary power within their rulers whilst curtailing excesses, the Asante offer us a worthwhile example. Known historically for their powerful, effective, and proud leadership style, the Asantes had developed, well before the arrival of Europeans, a system of governance that was personally, collectively, culturally, and spiritually powerful. Renowned sociologist, historian, and later politician, Professor Kofi Busia, wrote about *The Position of the Chief in the Modern Political system of Ashanti*.[19] Researching in the early 1940s, Busia writes,

> The chief was bound by oath to consult the elders on all matters, and to obey their advice. The government thus consisted of the chief and the elders. They met regularly, for it was the duty of every elder to visit the chief every morning. In this way the elders met informally to discuss the business of the day and other affairs of State.[20]

The proud, stalwart Asante male monarch was dependent upon a woman ruler:

> The queen-mother is described as the "mother" of the chief. She is more often his sister, but constitutionally she is regarded as the chief's mother, hence her title, Ɔhemmaa (female monarch), is usually translated queen-mother. She is expected to advise the

19. Busia, *The Position of the Chief in the Modern Political System of Ashanti.*
20. Ibid., 14.

chief about his conduct. She may scold and reprove him in a way none of his councilors can. . . . When a chief's stool (i.e., *throne*) becomes vacant, it is from the queen-mother that the elders ask for a man to fill the vacant stool.[21]

In fact, says Busia, "it is a common belief that in the olden days it was women who were chiefs. The traditional histories of Wenchi, Mampong, Juaben, and other divisions in Ashanti tell of women who were chiefs."[22]

Ultimately, the chief's role remained subject to the will of the people.

> The Ashanti had a constitutional practice which ensured that the will of the people was given consideration. They had ultimately the constitutional right to destool a chief. As the fundamental principle was that only those who elected a chief could destool him, a destoolment required the consent of the elders. Sometimes they (i.e., the elders) initiated a destoolment themselves when, for example, a chief repeatedly rejected their advice, or when he broke a taboo, or committed a sacrilegious act.[23]

Chiefs were destooled for, among other things, drunkenness, being a glutton, dealing in charms and noxious medicines, an abusive tongue, for not following the advice of his elders, and for cruelty. Busia concludes,

> The efficiency of the system depended on the chief acting with the concurrence and advice of his elders, on an effective popular control of both the chief and his elders, so that they discovered and realized the will of the people in their legislative and executive functions, and finally on the adequacy of the lineage system to give representation to all the members of a tribe or residents of a territorial Division. To a large extent these conditions were satisfied in Ashanti until after 1896.[24]

CONCLUSION

In conclusion, I would like to offer four thoughts that may help to further operationalize the arguments that have been made drawing on Jung, Foucault and the Asante people of Ghana.

21. Ibid., 19 (Translation in italics mine).
22. Ibid., 20.
23. Ibid., 21.
24. Ibid., 22.

First, it is imperative that pastoral caregivers accept that, individually and collectively, we have a *shadow*. We have a power shadow. Pastoral caregivers, the church, and each congregation have a power shadow. Inevitably if we stand in the sun (i.e., seek to do right), we will cast a shadow. The truth is that we can achieve a more genuine self-acceptance, based on a more complete knowledge of who we are, if we will accept all the realities of who we are, instead of denying or pretending that such is not the case and keeping the "shadow" unconscious, thus giving it unrestrained power over us.

Second, it is crucial that we discern, or in simpler terms recognize, the power shadow that pervades all our endeavors. Such discernment must be sought on all the levels we have discussed, the personal, collective, cultural and spiritual. We must rigorously and self-critically explore each dimension for the domination, exploitation and subjugation that we are subject to and that we impose on others.

Third, all pastoral caregivers need to do what Jungian therapists refer to as *shadow work*. This entails a careful facing of the issues, especially on the socially undesirable side of things from the personal through the spiritual. We are summoned to look the shadow in the face, calling a spade a spade as well as facing the ambiguities and tensions at each level. With vigilance we need to confront and defuse negative emotions that erupt in our daily lives and challenge policies, teachings, practices, and images that demean, exploit, and/or subjugate us, and by which we wittingly and unwittingly dominate, exploit, and subjugate others. Caregivers must recognize and challenge the "projections" (myths) that color our opinions of others. Caregivers need to heal our relationships through more honest self-examination and communication. Pastoral caregivers are called upon to use creative imagination (e.g., drawing, writing, rituals, dance, movement, rhythms) to help us own our whole (total) selves—including our power shadows.

Finally, the paradoxical principle that Saint Paul learned through the "thorn in his flesh" (2 Cor 12) is instructive. True power is made manifest in weakness. Theologically, our human power lies in vulnerability. Paradoxically, it is when we are weak that we are strong. It is in our confronting the "power shadow" that is present with each of us personally, and with all of us collectively, and with us culturally—and also spiritually, that we can become helpers who truly help. The real healer is the "wounded" healer. The realization that pastors are neither "almighty" nor "powerless" lies in this principle. "For when I am weak, then I am strong"[25] suggests that I am strong—that I recognize my strength. However, my strength does not come through overt displays of power, but rather through a sober acknowledgement of my limits, errors and wrong thinking and acting. It is precisely in that recognition that my strength (power) lies.

BIBLIOGRAPHY

Agyemang, Fred. *Amu, the African: A Study in Vision and Courage*. Accra: Asempa, 1988.

Busia, Kofi A. *The Position of the Chief in the Modern Political System of Ashanti*. London: Oxford University Press, 1951.

Foucault, Michel. *Power*. Edited by James D. Faubion. Translated by Robert Hurley. New York: New Press, 1994.

Guggenbühl-Craig, Adolf. *Power in the Helping Professions*. Translated by Myron Gubitz. 1971. Newly revised reprint, Putnam, CT: Spring, 2009.

Korem, Albin K., and Mawutodzi K. Abissath, *Traditional Wisdom in African Proverbs*. Accra: Publishing Trends, 2004.

Mveng, Englebert. "Third World Theology—What Theology? What Third World? Evaluation by an African Delegate." In *Irruption of the Third World: Challenge to Theology*, edited by Virginia Fabella and Sergio Torres, 217–21. Maryknoll, NY: Orbis, 1983.

Williamson, Marianne. *A Return to Love: Reflections on the Principles of "A Course in Miracles"*. New York: HarperCollins, 1992.

25. 2 Cor 12:10 ESV.

PART 3

Power and Sexual Abuse

6

Intimacy in Pastoral Care
Ethical Notes on the Use of Power in Pastoral Guiding

Didier Pollefeyt

Charity toward others;
Dignity toward oneself;
Sincerity before God.
Such is the epigraph of the book I undertake.

—George Sand, April 15, 1847[1]

INTRODUCTION: THE PLURIFORMITY OF THE PHENOMENON OF POWER IN PASTORAL CARE

Extreme vulnerability to the phenomenon of "power" and "powerlessness" is inherent in the structure of a pastoral relationship.[2] Yet, by their very

---

1. Jurgrau, *The Story of My Life*, 54.
2. De Ridder, *De omheinde kamer*.

nature, pastoral relationships are often affected by an unequal distribution of power between the pastoral caregiver (priest or layman) and the pastoral care receiver. The caregiver has specific power because of the situation of the care receiver, who, in need of help, can be uncertain, dependant, lonely, or anxious. Yet, the simple fact that the pastoral caregiver is present as a guide presupposes that at that moment, the caregiver is more competent, stronger, and more powerful. The pastoral relationship unfolds in an atmosphere of emotional intimacy in which the vulnerable pastoral care receiver puts all his trust in the pastoral caregiver. The caregiver will even have to encourage the pastoral care receiver in order to create openness in their relationship. In principle, in a pastoral relationship, the caregiver is permitted to inquire about everything that he or she wants to know concerning the life of the care receiver as is seen to be relevant to the pastoral guidance.

In itself, this is a fully positive fact. Trust and openness in pastoral guidance are to be seen as the foundations of good progress and the successful outcome of pastoral care. However, knowledge also means power. The pastoral caregiver comes to know a great deal about the fears, desires, weaknesses, and needs of the care receiver, while at the same time revealing little of his or her own life. The pastoral relationship is therefore characterized by a rather unilateral emotional intimacy, in which reciprocity and total-existential alliances, in the form of relationships of friendship and love—at least knowingly and planned in the long term—are not immediately at issue. The inaccessibility of the pastoral caregiver's personality often increases the idealization of the caregiver by the care receiver. This is something the pastoral caregiver cannot escape. When, in order to lessen the asymmetrical use of power, the pastoral caregiver starts to digress about his or her own life, this will often give the pastoral care receiver the impression of a special preference of the caregiver for that one care receiver, which may even heighten the dependence of the latter. At times, when we see that the pastoral caregiver breaks the silence about his or her own life, this is part of a subtle or unknowing strategy in which power is increased by the pastoral caregiver, who raises in this way his or her control over the care receiver.

Nevertheless, the asymmetrical use of power in a pastoral relationship is not a problem in itself. In our present-day world, power seems to have acquired negative connotations. Moreover, power and the abuse of power have become synonyms. Yet, a large number of human relationships (parent-child, teacher-pupil, employer-employee, doctor-patient, police-civilian) are inevitably marked by asymmetry. In itself, this fact provides the foundation of every well-balanced society. When we, in this context, develop an ethical focus on situations of pastoral guidance in which this use of power takes a turn for the worse, one should not forget that this situation is only the negative aspect of a larger and positive reality, namely, the everyday practice of thousands of pastoral relationships based on dedication, earnestness, and sense of responsibility. Many pastoral caregivers today feel justifiably indignant and powerless about the often very generalizing and trite way in which the media utters insinuations about the pastoral relationship. Not completely without cause, the media aims its criticism on this topic exclusively at the church (or often, more precisely, priests), not at the world of psychotherapy, the family, the police, or the army. This again is a manifestation of certain forces within the media that not only do not report the facts of the present-day crisis in an objective way, but that also aim to provoke or even worsen the crisis. Nevertheless, we think that a purely apologetic reaction ("others are guilty of the same," "only we are accused of it," "the problem is exaggerated" etc.) is not the best possible reaction, on the contrary. It seems to us more fitting to engage with the issue in an open and constructive way, showing respect for the victims, based on trust in the strength of the Christian faith, while seeing the present-day incidents as an opportunity for growth in the church. However, then again one runs the risk that this analysis will be used and abused by certain groups of people.

Perhaps the most eye-catching and specific form of vulnerability in the pastoral relationship, when treating the abuse of power, is the physical vulnerability of the pastoral care receiver. This occurs in particular, but certainly not exclusively, when the pastoral caregiver is a man and the pastoral care receiver is a woman (the caregiver can also be a woman, the pastoral care receiver might be a man, a youngster, a child, or an older person). The physical abuse of power as a risk is, again, inherent in the pastoral setting itself. Usually, a pastoral conversation consists of an encounter between two people, in a room on their own, in which one (the pastoral caregiver) encourages the other (the pastoral care receiver) to express his or her feelings. In this conversation, the pastoral care receiver finds a listening ear, one that is not disturbed (or that does not seem to be) by fatigue, a bad mood, or antipathy. In this setting, one can never look upon the proportions of insight and involvement, interpretation and emphatic response as being a mathematical certainty, not for the care receiver, nor for the caregiver himself. It is not untoward, in this pastoral setting, that if the pastoral care receiver develops intense emotional reactions (uncertainty, sadness, anger, fear, etc.), the caregiver reacts not only as a pastoral "expert," but also as a human being, experiencing and expressing a strong feeling of commitment.

In this context, physical touching does sometimes occur in order to support the care receiver emotionally, or to ease the suffering, sadness, depression, trauma, and so forth. Nevertheless, the danger of crossing the borders of the advisable is present. After all, touching is, by definition, ambiguous. And this is not only because it is a source of inexhaustible and intense significance, but because it also forms the basis of the possible perversity of corporality as well, since touching is very "sensual." The skin is the service-hatch for the most intense human emotions, transmitting the most vast human sense faculty. The tactile sense consists of the most extended human playground, in which, in comparison with hearing and seeing, human control is reduced, and in which people are very susceptible to manipulation.

Of all the various kinds of power abuse, sexual abuse is the most shocking, as it is the most far-reaching, through which the other, in his or her most intimate and vulnerable form of physicality, can be touched and affected. Sometimes it can be brought about by insinuation, subtle compliments, or just by the way one looks at the other.

Even although physical abuse of power is the most blatant, one can never reduce it to any specific kind, contrary to reports motivated by a thirst for sensation. It can also express itself in more delicate ways, as, for instance, when a pastoral caregiver invites someone to be guided by himself or herself. It can also be hidden in attempts to interrogate the care receiver about all kinds of aspects of his or her existence, or, in more refined efforts to make all other relationships impossible. Binding the care receiver to the pastoral relationship in such a way that he or she is not permitted, nor even able, to have other friendships is another aspect of this abuse.

When we, in our contribution, focus on this specific form of abuse, it should not lead us to reduce all kinds of abuse to this specific issue. In other words, while sexual abuse of power is the issue that solicits the largest appeal to our moral responsibility, it remains, nevertheless, a part of a much more comprehensive phenomenon. As the most radical form of abuse, it allows us to make a sharper ethical analysis of the phenomenon of power as a whole. In the meantime, our analysis will be a plea to consider, not only this extreme manifestation, but to keep a wary eye on the vast amount of smaller and milder forms of inappropriate use of power, of which the more exceptional sexual abuse of power is the extreme example.

To summarize: the phenomenon of power is an extremely ambivalent and subtle theme. Power can be exercised in a positive way, whereby it helps to improve the quality of pastoral guidance. But power can also be abused through exerting it to physically or psychologically (emotionally) overcome the care receiver. In this contribution, we wish to develop an ethical model in which we will try to do justice to the complexity of the phenomenon of "power" in the context of pastoral guidance. We will offer a sketch of three recognizable interpretations of the phenomenon of power, representing three varied ethical implications, all of which contain truth in part, but which also have their own limitations. Starting from our critique of each of those three models, we will develop our own ethical interpretation of the phenomenon of power and will pose questions about the practical consequences of this ethical framework for pastoral care.

THE IMMORALITY OF POWER

In the light of the specific inherent vulnerability of pastoral guidance to the abuse of power, it should come as no surprise that outsiders, victims, and colleague-caregivers react with indignation when cases of abuse in the pastoral context come to light. Today, the pastoral relationship is often the last refuge to which people can flee with their problems. Public opinion reacts with feelings of disgust to news of situations of abuse. In this "moral anger," it becomes clear that people are not neutral beings in the anthropological sense. We do not remain indifferent when we are confronted with good and evil; we are connected to the good. In this sense, we can only perceive the ethical anger concerning these assaults as being positive. It reveals that people are capable of being concerned about evil and, despite all the comments of cultural pessimists about the collapse of values, that they are still able to discover themselves as allied to, or following the way of, the good. This anger, while seeming to be negative, expresses how people continue to associate the Christian message and the church with authenticity and concern for fellow human beings.

Nevertheless, there is a risk that people are being led by their ethical indignation to such an extent that, in their judgment of abuse of power, they are using simplistic and biased ethical schemes. We often observe how public opinion puts a major emphasis on the immorality of those who abuse their power in a pastoral relationship. This kind of approach to the issue is based on a dualistic vision of good and evil, in which the good is identified with the victim and the evil with the suspect. Theologically, this reasoning can be supported by the image of an "angry God" who is hostile to evil. The entire complexity of power and powerlessness in the pastoral relationship is reduced to the shocking and unambiguous confrontation between the almighty, the immoral pastoral caregiver, and the impotent and moral care receiver. Because of our genuine moral indignation, frequently we endorse such a representation of the actual abuse of power. Moreover, such a scheme contains a larger part of the truth concerning the abuse of power. Non punitive, public action against such caregivers in this kind of dualistic and simplistic scheme also results in others being placed in a demonic corner.

However, this unambiguous, very popular and misused scheme is unfair to the complexity of the phenomenon. The issue of the abuse of power is to be situated in a continuum and knows many degrees and variants. In this continuum, one finds the caregiver who, (indeed in a perverted way) searches for sense and humanity, or who, being troubled by solitude and the lack of human recognition and warmth, is driven to go on and look for affection from the care receiver. But one meets as well the pastoral caregiver who lies in an impudent way, who cheats and manipulates to obtain satisfaction. In this dualistic representation, the continuum is replaced by an unambiguous confrontation between a guilty suspect on the one hand and an unresisting victim on the other.

A certain kind of media in particular has a tendency to polarize these cases. In the accounts recorded by the media concerning the issue, the suspect is declared to be a horrible devil and the victim is presented as being defenseless. The right choice to stand up for the victim then leads to an oversimplified attitude toward the suspect. Those who dare to draw attention to the abusers of power in a pastoral context quickly become suspected of wanting to minimize the enormous harm done to the victim. The outcome of such an approach is often a very moralizing attitude toward the use of power, in which a clear distinction is preached between the "good" and the "bad" pastoral caregiver, or worse, in which the whole pastoral world is tarred with the same brush, rendering serene pastoral work extremely difficult.

In itself, this model could be a very attractive way of thinking. It offers a scheme that is easy to handle, an unambiguous warning, and a radical "no" to the abuse of power in the pastoral context. Its biggest advantage is that it puts the responsibility for the abuse of power in a clear and completely correct way in the hands of the pastoral caregiver. Therefore, this model is a very safe choice. It draws a clear moral line with regard to physical and emotional intimacy. These are boundaries that are never to be crossed. It is grounded on a linear point of view that the relationship between power and ethics is centered on the categories "warning" and "judgment" such as: "this is prohibited, and will result in punishment being exacted."

This is a very important and valuable step. In this contribution we try to demonstrate however, that when the approach to the phenomenon of abuse of power is restricted to this external moral condemnation, it will be inadequate in the long term when faced with efforts to prevent the abuse of power, or will even have a counterproductive function. In this moralizing approach there is neither place for the complexity and the paradox in the relationship between power and powerlessness, nor for the pluriformity of gradations and grey areas in this phenomenon. After all, power can be used to give advice, to reward, as well as to manipulate, to blackmail, to violate, et cetera.

This "demonizing" interpretation seems to be based on a pessimistic view of humanity. People are directed to the evil (abuse of power) and need an external moral code to restrain their "evil" desires. In addition, this approach often functions as a mechanism to defend oneself, for it allows the distinction between "good" and "bad" pastoral caregivers. In this way, it denies the real danger of the possible perversion of every pastoral relationship (and generally, of every human relationship) through the abuse of power. This simple scheme can allow the pastoral caregiver to situate the danger of the abuse of power outside his or herself by condemning it in others and, by reorganizing one's own identity without any spot or wrinkle.[3] When we do not identify with the bad caregiver, we allow ourselves to bring charges, filled with indignation, against the other and afterwards permit ourselves to feel at ease when closing the shop. In this article we want to emphasize that the question of dealing with power is relevant for every pastoral caregiver, in every phase of his or her vocation. In other words, it is not sufficient to rap other colleagues on the knuckles, in order to collectively recapture one's own purity.[4] The excessive types of abuse of power that are poured out by some kinds of media are nothing more than the enlarging and the end of the phenomenon that appears, as a possibility or sometimes as a reality, in every pastoral relationship. The same is to be said of society as a whole. It

---

3. Pope et al., *De seksuele gevoelens van de psychotherapeut*, 36–37.
4. Rodolfa, "The Management of Sexual Feelings in Therapy," 168.

is astonishing how a society can unleash a delusion of persecution against specific categories of wrongdoers, in order to purify its own identity by sacrificing a scapegoat. In the meantime, society remains collectively blind to the many other, so-called milder, but much more scattered forms of corruption (for example financial or sexual) affecting its structures.

A final objection to this model concerns the puritan reaction that it facilitates. It can result in every kind of physical expression in a pastoral context becoming subject to imputation. It can also lead to a witch hunt against anybody who dares to merely broach the issue. Here, a peculiar shift is to be noted: because of this exclusively moralizing attitude, not only the factual abuse of power is to be condemned, but, the very fact of mentioning the topic becomes problematic and even risky. And, the more general the moralizing attitude becomes, the less the pastoral caregiver will venture to discuss his or her struggle with power for fear that he or she will be stigmatized. Here the danger arises that we can only satisfy ourselves through an indisputable ban on intimate behavior within a pastoral context. Such a prohibition could be valuable *(confer infra)*, but, as a result, every conversation concerning the feelings of the pastoral caregiver would become impossible.

We believe that this danger is at times discernible in voices that resound in the pastoral world itself, uttered by people who are no longer willing to talk about the issue of intimate feelings, or who even suppress or neglect them. In this situation, an important principle of pastoral psychology has been forgotten: what has been suppressed will re-emerge, taking another shape, but having the same intensity as before. Acknowledging the problems and, a conscious management of the phenomenon of power will only be possible when we dare to confront our moral loathing of the abuse of power. Rather than continuing to moralize from an external perspective, we will have to enter, in every pastoral relationship, into the complex, internal relationship between power and powerlessness. In this way, the disgust for abuse of power will not be neutralized, but rather restructured and integrated in a reasonable and forward-looking concern, intended to tackle the problem. Undoubtedly, this is a frightening challenge, because it confronts us with the dark corners of our own being. In what follows, it will become clear that this approach will produce some important opportunities, but will give rise to several new risks as well.

THE AMORALITY OF POWER

In the second approach, one no longer speaks in moral terms of the "*abuse* of power," but instead, of the ethically more neutral category of the "*use* of power." Instead of a moralizing condemnation, one tries here to enter into the dynamics of the relationship between the caregiver and care receiver in order to attempt to understand the use of power from an insiders' perspective. In this model, one seeks to reconstruct the history of the use of power, while sometimes being subject to the indignation and anger of the victims. In this mode of thought, it often appears that the abusing pastoral caregiver himself is governed by factors outside of his or her own conscious (ill) will. The analysis of the development of the abuse of power shows, for example, how the use of power becomes a means of coping with one's own traumatic past,[5] to compensate for an unsatisfactory private life (solitude, frustrating, or unsatisfactory intimate private life, financial problems, conflict and divorce, et cetera). Sometimes the abuse of power can be traced back to the pedagogical dereliction of the pastoral caregiver when he was a child, to a low self-esteem that has to be compensated for by using power, et cetera.[6] Advocates of this second model will understand the sexual abuse of power as a result of the caregiver's desire to regain his childhood, or as the outcome of the need to humiliate women in order to unchain himself from a stifling relationship with his mother. In some exceptional cases, the abusing caregivers will be diagnosed as *borderline*-patients, or as people with asocial personalities who are, as a result of a defective *superego*, not able to control themselves from impulsive outbursts.

In short, in the second approach, we will suggest some a-moral, determining psychological factors that offer the possibility of comprehending the outcome of the use of power. Some social determinants will be added, as, for example the social depiction of men and women, (women are often portrayed as accessible objects), or the social depiction of the pastoral caregiver as the new guru. By using this approach, one even submits oneself to the risk-profile of the abusing pastoral caregiver. The pastoral caregiver who abuses power is frequently, but not exclusively, masculine, middle-age, apparently successful, well-educated, et cetera.

Understanding the abuse of power can often result in a certain degree of justification. In this second view, it becomes clear that the perpetrator is,

---

5. Rutter, *Er zijn grenzen*, 109.
6. Verelst, "Machtsmisbruik in therapie," 27.

to a certain degree, also a victim, and that it is very difficult to make a clear distinction between the phenomena of power and powerlessness, contrary to what was proposed in the first view. In this second scheme, it is not so much the dimension of guilt that is highlighted, but rather the tragedy and the dimension of fate, which is always present in the abuse of power. The forum where this currently occurs is not primarily the media, but rather the courts and the domain of psychotherapy.

Generally, from this perspective, the fusion of power and powerlessness is also applicable to the victim of abuse. The courts are very familiar with this scenario. A lawyer tries to reduce the responsibility of his client, the perpetrator, by focusing on the features and characteristics of the victim. In the context of the abuse of power in a pastoral relationship, what is often demonstrated is, contrary to the thinking of the first scheme, the powerlessness of the pastoral caregiver and the power of the care receiver. Sometimes it is argued that the responsibility for the use of power in a pastoral relationship is to be divided between the caregiver and the care receiver.

This scheme also contains part of the truth. Sometimes, the pastoral care receiver assumes part of the power in the pastoral relationship. Occasionally it is the pastoral care receiver who suffocates the pastoral caregiver. This can happen because of a sense of frustration due to the inequality in the distribution of power, which makes the pastoral care receiver long to remove the pastoral caregiver from the throne of power, to make him equal, or even to reduce him to a (sexual) weakling. This play, in which power is divided, can also be driven by the fear of the approaching end of the pastoral relationship, or by the fascination for the celibacy of the priest-pastoral caregiver.[7] A sort of statistical profile of the pastoral care receiver in this situation has been developed and it appears that this person will be: feminine, ten years younger than the pastoral caregiver, educated, in a crisis, et cetera. When the pastoral caregiver "fails" according to this view, he would appear to be badly trained. But this does not make him completely guilty, or implicate his having acted in bad faith.

This second strategy of deculpabilization is not that exceptional at all and is sometimes used as an argument to conceal complaints. "Is it true that the pastoral care receiver pretends? Is this not, only some exaggeration of a twisted mind?" The complaint of the abuse of power is then described as a "congenital" inclination women have to invent such things,

---

7. Ibid., 33–37.

ascribing these acts to innocent men, or to the imagination of children. This strategy corresponds to the general cultural tendency to blame the victims over and over again (the process of "*blaming the victims*"). When an attractively dressed woman has been raped, then she "has deserved it." The seduction-hypothesis has often been successful in the pastoral context as well. One then says that women use their bodies and helplessness in order to receive affection from the pastoral caregiver. This train of thought makes the masculine pastoral caregiver a victim of the manipulation of the female pastoral care receiver, which is a new edition of the old story of women asking to be raped.

This leads to a profound critique on the second view. This model shows us how the abuse of power is a complex reality, which makes clear that there is always some kind of unwillingness and impotence on the part of the pastoral caregiver to take a serious look at his deontological code and his mission. The pastoral caregiver always runs the risk of falling into de-ethization, in which it becomes impossible to talk of ethical categories about power and powerlessness. The abuse of power becomes psychologized and socialized to an extent that it becomes an amoral reality ("use of power"). In this model, human beings are mere puppets of the situation. The pessimistic concept of men has been replaced by a deterministic concept. Human beings become deplorable creatures who can no longer be called to account, meaning that humans are no longer free. Theologically, this view translates itself into a God who understands me as a good friend, a God who loves me, even when I am failing.

In contrast to this deterministic view, the Christian perspective maintains that a human being can never unthinkingly be reduced to the exponent of his biological infrastructure, his individual history, or his social context. Human liberty is the basic assumption of every Christian anthropology. In particular, the pastoral caregiver has to be aware of the fact that the responsibility for the abuse of power can never be left to the pastoral care receiver and, to that end, the pastoral caregiver himself—and not the pastoral care receiver—is responsible for the ethical content of the pastoral relationship. It is the pastoral caregiver who, by making use of his education and his experience and, as a result of a well-formed consciousness aided by the experience of a God who is concerned about good and evil, has to react in an appropriate way. This presupposes an openness in the training of pastoral caregivers to those elements that might stimulate or undermine the ethical level of pastoral relations. This is not easy, however, in the current cultural climate, with media-attention moralizing every action. Consequently, the media also bears, to a certain extent, responsibility for maintaining the issues they themselves posit.

THE MORALITY OF POWER

The use of power does not necessarily have to lead to the abuse of power. Power can be utilized in a constructive way, as for example when it is necessarily and justifiably applied in forced admissions to psychiatric institutions. The problem arises however, when the abuse of power is supported by ethical arguments.[8] The pastoral caregiver who abuses his or her power, does not call him or herself immoral, or a morally neutral and determined being, but will generally elicit *ethical* motives for the use of power. In this, one can recognize one of the paradoxes of being human: a human being wants to be good, even if he acts in an evil manner, even if he uses his power to do ill. A human being is marked with an inhumane urge toward self-justification.[9] Here we meet the subject of self-justification. We are all experts in thinking of good motives for the things we do, especially for those which are questionable and selfish.

Using this method, explicit and far-reaching physical touching in a pastoral context is often defended with the argument that problems cannot be solved solely by conversation and that a pastoral caregiver has the task to give of himself in order for the care receiver to be restored to health. For some care receivers, physical touching may indeed have a healing character.[10] Sometimes such touching offers the possibility of convincing pastoral care receivers of their beauty and desirability, of reinforcing their personal identity, of removing doubts and hesitation and, of overcoming feelings of physical incapacity, et cetera. These more "pastoral" grounds for physical touching are often combined with professional ethics, or a pastoral vocation, which demand that *everything* should be done to improve the well-being of the pastoral care receiver. Sometimes care receivers also seem to permit physical intimacy in the relationship with a pastoral caregiver. Given their need for warmth, they are the first to welcome the special attention received from the pastoral caregiver.

---

8. Pollefeyt, "Het kwaad als een verhaal," 193–211.
9. Moyaert, "De mens en zijn onmenselijke drang naar zelfrechtvaardiging," 77–100.
10. Geluk, *Waarden en ethiek in de hulpverlening*, 69–81.

In consequence, this third model begins with the statement that the *actual* attempts of some pastoral caregivers to abuse power in a pastoral relationship can be legitimated on an ethical, or even theological basis. For the moral justification of his or her deeds the pastoral caregiver appeals, for example, to personal authority ("I am sure this will work"), the self-esteem of the pastoral caregiver ("I would not call myself a pastoral caregiver if this did not work") or all sorts of rationalizations ("love can never be bad," "some contact will do her good," "in human relationships one has to follow the human body"). Some pastoral caregivers use ethical grounds as a defense, alleging in their own defense that no harm was done as the intimate bodily contact took place *outside* of the pastoral context.

The weak spot in this third model, which is unconvincing to public opinion and the courts, and is used mostly by the abusing pastoral caregiver himself, is obviously that nothing is said about the adequacy of this ethical argument itself. In fact, this scheme is usually nothing more than an "apology" or an ethical-esthetical "garnishing" of the abuse of power. In order to expose this argument as an ornament, one obviously has to presume a consensus on a number of basic values that apply to all human beings.[11] Only in relation to these basic values can it become clear how often the abuse of power is justified with pseudo-ethical arguments. It becomes evident now, why simply pointing at a moral can serve no useful purpose. On the contrary, the more one is portrayed as an immoral person, the more one attempts to convince oneself and others of one's good, so-called "moral" intentions, and, in consequence, the more the self-serving rationalization of the abuse of power and the abuse of power itself will increase. Here the vulnerability of all professional ethics becomes obvious.

POWER AND POWERLESSNESS OF MORALITY IN PASTORAL CARE

In this fourth part we develop our own view on power and powerlessness in the pastoral relationship. We try to go beyond disgust (immorality of power) and justification (morality of power) in order to do justice to power (guilt) and to do justice also to the powerlessness (faith) of the perpetrators and the victims of the pastoral caregiver's abuse of power. In our interpretation, the human capacity for fragmentation is a central theme.[12]

11. Pollefeyt, "De mensenrechten als nieuw verbond met Noach," 95–102.
12. Pollefeyt, "Gevaarlijk normaal!," 77.

PART 3—Power and Sexual Abuse

By fragmentation we understand the capacity of a human being to split himself up into several different domains (for example: carnality and emotionality, work climate, and private life), these being no longer connected to each other.

In order to illustrate this, we give the example of a thirty-five-year-old female pastoral care receiver visiting a forty-year-old, married, male pastoral caregiver. In the course of this relationship, the pastoral caregiver assents to the desire of his pastoral care receiver, who longs for human connectedness through intimate touching. The caregiver himself also, visibly enjoys the touching. In this particular pastoral caregiver's case, nothing like this had ever taken place. He is certainly not an ethically perverted being, but he reasoned that this kind of contact would have a healing effect on his pastoral care receiver. Indeed, the pastoral care receiver does not feel abused; on the contrary, because of this contact she experiences her own personality in a more authentic and intense way. Nevertheless, at a certain moment she asks the pastoral caregiver for a more integral form of intimacy, a request that the pastoral caregiver refuses. The pastoral care receiver is very upset and disappointed. She does not understand the pastoral caregiver, even though she still appreciates him as a person. She will even admit she has seduced him.

Even though in this case one cannot speak of the exploitation of the pastoral care receiver by the pastoral caregiver, only of his own possible satisfaction, we believe nevertheless that this is a case of power abuse. This is not, in a simple sense, a question of immorality; that would be an oversimplification of the ethical aspect of the case, but something more subtle and ambiguous. As in most other cases, this is an example of power and powerlessness, divided in a very complex way, between pastoral care receiver and pastoral caregiver. In the person of the pastoral caregiver, we see the fusion of pastoral care and intimate selfishness, with the direction of the pastoral relationship and power being conducted by the pastoral care receiver. Certain boundaries have been overstepped in respect to ethical reasoning and consciousness, power and powerlessness, good and evil.

Where, then, is the problem situated? The pastoral care receiver *encounters* the "pastoral care" of the caregiver as an expression of his personal devotion and affection. The caregiver, on the other hand, reasons that his intervention is one of a "purely" technical and pastoral nature. The pastoral care receiver does not consider the caregiver to have abused his power, but that he is inauthentic; having had an intimate relationship with him, she had experienced the intense pastoral and human power of intimacy, without which physical and human attention she would never have been able to find herself, or find healing for her wounds. The problem, however, is that the vital condition for this pastoral healing is precisely the non-pastoral character of the intimate relationship. In fact, this is an anthropological paradox inherent in human carnality, namely, that the "pastorally" efficient relationship and human richness seem to be dependent on the not-just-pastoral and instrumental character of an intimate relationship.[13] Christian ethics has always been very aware of this paradox. In the understanding of sexuality, human healing through intimate experiences is only possible when the intimate touching is embedded in the safe closeness of someone who experiences the contact as a total human being, and not just as physical gymnastics unrelated to interiority. Then, because the personal "devotion" in the intimate experience is put aside and the touching is reduced to a mere action in the pastoral process of healing, the core of the pastoral power of the intimate relationship is, itself, desecrated and nullified. The actual drama for the pastoral care receiver is not so much the abuse of power, but rather the process of mourning that she has to go through. We do not pretend here that it is impossible to develop mutual and sustainable intimacy between two equal partners outside of a pastoral relationship. Obviously, such intimacy is of course possible, although not before the pastoral therapy has ended, and within the boundaries of what can be called "authentic" in relation to the situation, in this case, the married status of the pastoral caregiver.[14]

In most cases, the pastoral relationship, as described in this example, will develop into an inadequate personal, reciprocal relationship between pastoral caregiver and pastoral care receiver, where the pastoral caregiver will keep on denying the anthropological paradox ("pastoral efficiency through non-pastoral inefficiency"). The price he has to pay is his authenticity. The only way the pastoral caregiver can keep denying this paradox is by using the so-called technique of fragmentation, namely of splitting himself up into different subareas, such as physicality and emotional life, work and family, and so forth. In this fragmentation, the pastoral caregiver isolates the physicality of his being and gives it a purely instrumental role, while at the same time setting up an ethical argument, namely by stressing

---

13. Burggraeve, *Zinvol seksueel leven onderweg*.

14. Gabbard, "Reconsidering the American Psychological Association's Policy on Sex with Former Patients," 331.

it as being "good" for his pastoral care receiver. Certain consequences or effects of the intimate actions are fragmented as well.

In the literature one often reads that fragmentation is a typically male characteristic. It is easier for men to think, feel, and live in a compartmentalized way, while women are not that gifted at compartmentalization. Men are more able to isolate certain parts of their life from the rest of their being, while women tend to live in a more holistic way.[15] This distinction also affects sexual life. For women, less than for men, and certainly never in an exclusive way, sexuality is expressed in coital intercourse, but has everything to do with total human presence and tenderness. This is why, when a male pastoral caregiver in a male-female relationship says that "nothing has happened" while referring to the fact that no sexual intercourse has occurred, he shows little knowledge of the female experience of sexuality. Generally, it becomes clear that what the pastoral caregiver and the pastoral care receiver might sense as suitable or unsuitable, can differ a great deal and that there is no such thing as an objective principle that can be used to judge every situation. Boundaries are not the same for all people.

In the meantime, the married pastoral caregiver in question knows very well that whoever touches a body touches the reflection of the whole person. In the Christian human concept, the body and soul are not two distinct components, but force-fields, which are constantly affecting each other because of their fundamental rootedness. The caregiver acts however as if he does not realize or recognize this. He deceives himself. He does not deepen the dynamics of these occurrences, while being aware of the fact that a more profound meaning is to be found. Actively, he deceives himself; passively he is deceived by himself, while denying the symbolism behind the interaction.[16] He intentionally or unintentionally shuts himself off from a certain part of reality, projecting that part into nothingness ("nothing has happened"), or reduces it to something else (for example, instinct). Obviously this fragmentation works up to a certain point, and, the pastoral caregiver himself is very aware of the fact that he is dividing himself. Most of the cases of power abuse in a pastoral context are not the result of ill will, but rather of this self deception: the giver reasons something in a pastoral and ethical way, while knowing the situation to be untenable. Nevertheless, he tries to convince himself of its acceptability and, as a consequence, becomes entangled in the issue. In other words, the pastoral caregiver knows

15. Marlet, *Compartimentaal denken*, 16.
16. Burggraeve, "Verbond, seksualiteit en gezin," 144–65.

that it is impossible to use intimacy in a technical way in order for it to become a mere pastoral power, but he convinces himself of the fact that this is not the case. The result is that the temporary pleasure offered to him creates a fragmentized and inauthentic existence as a kind of gigolo. The woman in the example felt this implicitly and indicated this when at the end of the pastoral guiding she stated "that something wasn't right at all."

It follows, that, starting from an ethical position, we are opposed *to* intimate touching in a pastoral context, not because intimacy and sexuality are "evil powers" we should try to restrict (instead of integrating them in a meaningful way), but because the use of intimacy and sexuality in the pastoral context irrevocably leads to a perversion of the significant anthropological and Christian dynamics of sexual intimacy itself.[17] Intimacy in the pastoral relationship is often harmful, because of the dimension of time that is intrinsically interconnected with an authentic relationship in a Christian perspective. From which perspective, touching the other in an all-embracing way, also means touching the person in his or her future. It is possible that the pastoral caregiver or the pastoral care-receiver sincerely believes that in the moment of pastoral contact he or she is giving his or herself authentically, in other words as a human being, to the other. In that moment, however, the person forgets that the perspective of "time" has to be part of the intrinsic finality of this devotion. After all, the integral/personal self-surrender demands an everlasting dedication and engagement in order to realize its inherent intentions, day by day, one's whole life long. This is something that is hard to realize within the context of the boundaries of a pastoral relationship.[18]

The abuse of power (not only physical abuse) occurs so frequently, not so much because of immorality, but rather because of a lack of authenticity. In this kind of self-deception, the pastoral caregiver deludes himself and others into believing that his use of power is ethically permissible. Consequently, a selective and manipulative contact with reality, beginning with his own needs and desires, comes into existence.

During the pastoral relationship, every pastoral caregiver goes through a process, almost comparable to the struggle the pastoral care receiver is experiencing with his or her own history of desires and failures. In cases of self deception, the pastoral caregiver is active (conscious) and passive (unconscious); he is powerful (the offender) and he is powerless (the victim).

17. Cornu, "De grote uitdaging van het kleine verschil," 45–67.
18. Burggraeve, "Zinvol seksueel leven onderweg," 335.

Using ethical arguments, he tries to legitimate his power and to justify his powerlessness at the very moment that he is abusing his power, or when he capitulates to powerlessness. In the event that this is *only* challenged by a moralizing lecture of condemnation, pastoral caregivers can be driven by a fear of rejection, and so even more strongly pushed into self deception. Therefore, a vision is needed in cases of abuse in pastoral settings that transcends condemnation, despite the horror and justification.

FURTHER IMPLICATIONS FOR THE PASTORAL CONTEXT

Betrayed trust is very damaging to every pastoral caregiver, and incompatible with the essence of Christian pastoral care. As a consequence, it is crucial to prevent cases of abuse, rather than waiting for them to appear in court.[19] Openness is therefore vital in this matter, thus it is of great importance that in pastoral training and education, the subject of power and powerlessness be discussed without bias.

Initially, this means that pastoral caregivers should communicate regularly among themselves and be aware of their own needs, desires, fantasies, and so forth. They need to ask themselves about the types of mechanisms they use to defend themselves, for example, if they are manipulative; if they are aware of their own desires, their appearance, their own ways of coping with things, et cetera. They have to be alert to their own relational bottlenecks, psychological blockages, emotional and sexual wounds, fundamental needs, innocent gestures, social prejudice, and above all, their own values. This will increase their self-knowledge, allowing them to cope with power. The presence of a reliable colleague/pastoral caregiver who is open to dialogue can be very helpful. As a consequence, the pastoral caregiver should be able to anticipate the imminent danger of overstepping boundaries. Measures to prevent this happening can thus be taken far more quickly. Sometimes it may be necessary to refer a care receiver to another caregiver and, to oblige the initial caregiver to himself seek help. Only the best pastoral caregivers dare to look in a mirror and ask for assistance. Sometimes this help can be offered in the context of existing spiritual guidance, but more often a certain kind of supervision will be needed.

It may also be useful to search for, or further invest in, intimate relationships outside of the pastoral context, relationships that are not swayed by the power game. These relationships offer opportunities for an authentic

19. Bolten, "Voorkomen is beter dan voorkomen," 364–68.

and integrated experience of intimacy. Often we see however, that pastoral caregivers are themselves unwilling to seek help, but instead flirt with the limits, using all kinds of pseudo-ethical and pseudo-pastoral justification for their behavior.

Subsequently, we want to emphasize the importance of both education and pastoral training and the need to listen to the experience of pastoral caregivers and receivers concerning the abuse of power. In so doing, it is possible to increase understanding of the issue. Well-organized discussions with colleagues in interventional group consultations could also be helpful. Expressing feelings of power and powerlessness should never result in criticism or condemnation.

Moreover, it may be necessary to talk to the pastoral care receiver. Here we need to emphasize the enormous difference between expressing feelings *about* power and powerlessness in the pastoral relationship and the actual giving in to types of power and powerlessness.

It is also important to stress the fusion of power, and the need for authenticity and responsibility. Before any physical touching, the pastoral caregiver has to ask himself the following question: "am I authentic; is this glance, this touching, transparent enough, both for myself and especially for my care receiver?" In a pastoral relationship, caregivers not only discover their potential power to reduce the other to an element in their strategy, but in their appearance in pure nakedness (Levinas), the other reveals himself or herself as an ethical "no" against every manipulation of power.[20] In his ultimate vulnerability, the other may approach the pastoral caregiver and, using his needs as power, overwhelm the pastoral caregiver. Consequently, power can only be authentic when it protects the powerlessness of the other from further wounds. This is the last and perhaps most radical type of power, namely the power of the ethical appeal, acknowledging the superiority of the inferior who, because of his history of vulnerability, approaches the pastoral caregiver "from above" with an implicit request not to be abused.

With this last remark, we encounter the true theological foundation of pastoral care itself: the connection between God and human beings. The pastoral relationship can never be seen in isolation as one pastoral caregiver facing one pastoral care receiver, but has always to be supported by a specific confession, which must be constantly rooted and in dialogue with a specific community of believers, possessing their own value system. In a

---

20. Pollefeyt, "Het kwaad van Auschwitz," 73–80.

pastoral relationship, there is no engagement without content, consequently no purely individualistic one. In this sense, pastoral care differs fundamentally from every other kind of therapy, even though both can replenish and even need each other. Both the therapist and the pastoral caregiver are concerned with the well-being and healing of their patients. On the one hand, the therapist thinks in terms of certain functional psychological concepts and strategies; the pastoral caregiver, on the other hand, strives to console the pastoral care receiver in the name of the liberating God of Jesus Christ. It is because of this, that pastoral care is such a raw and fundamental experience for Christians and for the life of the church: it is the pre-eminent place where shape is given to a God whose name is love and who liberates people from evil; not by judging, but through a compassion that is stronger than all fear and self deception and that transcends every kind of evil.

BIBLIOGRAPHY

Bolten, Mart P. "Voorkomen is beter dan voorkomen." *Tijdschrift voor psychotherapie* 13 (1987) 364–68.

Burggraeve, Roger. "Verbond, seksualiteit en gezin: Het seksuele lichaam als christelijke uitdaging." In *Gezien het gezin: Feiten en waarden*, edited by Wilfried A. Dumon et al., 144–65. Leuven: Davidsfonds, 1995.

———. *Zinvol seksueel leven onderweg: Concrete probleemvelden en belevingswijzen*. Leuven: Acco, 1992.

Cornu, Ilse. *De grote uitdaging van het kleine verschil: Antropologische en ethische perspectieven met betrekking tot een integraal opvoedingsproject voor relatiebekwaamheid en zinvolle seksualiteitsbeleving in het secundair onderwijs*. Leuven: s.n., 1994.

De Ridder, Hugo. *De omheinde kamer*. Tielt: Lannoo, 1994.

Gabbard, Glen. O. "Reconsidering the American Psychological Association's Policy on Sex with Former Patients: Is it Justifiable?" *Professional Psychology: Research and Practice* 25 (1994) 329–35.

Geluk, Hans L.C. *Waarden en ethiek in de hulpverlening: Een bundel artikelen over de rol van waarden in de psychosociale hulpverlening en de ethische aspecten van individuele, gezins-, relatie-, en gedragstherapie*. Baexem: Gamma, 1979.

Jurgrau, Thelma. *The Story of My Life: The Autobiography of George Sand. A Group Translation*, edited by Thelma Jurgrau. Albany: State University of New York Press, 1991.

Marlet, Johannes J.C. *Compartimentaal denken: Beschouwingen over dubbelleven*. Boom: Meppel, 1991.

Moyaert, Paul. "De mens en zijn onmenselijke drang naar zelfrechtvaardiging." In *Psychiatrie tussen mode en model: Liber amicorum professor G. Buyse*, edited by Guido Kongs et al., 77–100. Leuven: Peeters, 1989.

Pollefeyt, Didier. "Gevaarlijk normaal! Over Auschwitz of het kwaad rondom ons en in ons." *Groepspsychotherapie: Tijdschrift van de Nederlandse vereniging voor Groeps-Psychotherapie* 29 (1995) 72–83.

———. "Het kwaad als een verhaal: Schets van een hanteerbaar ethisch model voor geriatrische hulpverlening in confrontatie met het kwaad." In *Gerontologie en geriatrie 1996: Proceedings 19th Winter-meeting Oostende*, edited by Jean-Pierre Baeyens, 193–211. Leuven: Garant, 1997.

———. "Het kwaad van Auschwitz: Een centrale uitdaging in het joodse denken van Levinas." In *De vele gezichten van het kwaad: Meedenken in het spoor van Emmanuel Levinas*, edited by Roger Burggraeve and Luc Anckaert, 57–90. Leuven: Acco, 1996.

———. "De mensenrechten als nieuw verbond met Noach." In *Heeft de traditie van de mensenrechten nog toekomst?*, edited by Johan De Tavernier and Didier Pollefeyt, 95–102. Leuven: Acco, 1998.

Pope, Sonne, *et al. De seksuele gevoelens van de psychotherapeut: Hanteren in plaats van ontkennen.* Lisse: Swets & Zeitlinger, 1996.

Rodolfa, Emil. "The Management of Sexual Feelings in Therapy." *Professional Psychology: Research and Practice* 25 (1994) 168–72.

Rutter, Peter. *Er zijn grenzen: Sex als machtsmisbruik van hulpverleners met hun vrouwelijke pastoranten.* Utrecht: Het Spectrum, 1990.

Verelst, Lieve. "Machtsmisbruik in therapie: Seksuele contacten tussen pastor en patiënt." PhD diss., Katholieke Vlaamse Hogeschool, 1995.

7

A Wolf in Sheep's Clothing
Dealing Honestly with Pastoral Power[1]

Cristina Traina

Every relationship between pastor and congregant is sustained by two actors. Congregants' treatment of their pastors certainly raises important ethical questions about the use and abuse of power. For instance, lay people can exert considerable financial pressure on their pastors, unjustly accuse them of inappropriate behavior, or burden them with unfair amounts of work. But my focus here is the undeniable power of many kinds—social, ecclesial, and psychological, among others—that resides with the pastor. *From the pastor's vantage point*, what are the ethical challenges of pastoral power and its rewards? What does the loving, just use of power look like for the pastor who wields it within the strict boundaries of just relations?

This essay will argue for both practical and conceptual wholeness. Pastors must integrate their own experiences, and they must also embrace an integral vision of love that combines *agape*, *eros*, and *philia*.

---

[1]. The arguments in this essay are drawn largely from Traina, *Erotic Attunement*.

THE ETHICS OF POWER: FOUNDATIONS

Several important foundational assumptions underlie this argument. First, power operates in all social relations,[2] including ecclesial relations, and (as Stefan Gärtner has showed in his essay in this volume) it flows to its holders from a number of different sources. Second, pastors receive most of their pastoral power for the good of the community and from the community, either directly or indirectly.[3] Therefore pastors are obligated to use this power for the community, in its communal Christian identity; for individual members, in the context of Christian community; and for society at large, representing the church. Third, it is possible to abdicate this power only by severing all ties with one's community, and sometimes not even then. This option is not open to pastors in any case; they must accept the power they hold, even if they plan to use it to alter power relations for the better. In sum, to be a pastor is to hold pastoral power for the benefit of the ecclesial community and to be obliged to use it for that community's good. Therefore, pastors must constantly discern what particular sorts of power they hold in their settings so that they can use it thoughtfully and well, rather than inadvertently and badly.[4]

From the point of view of this responsibility, the images of both the "almighty pastor" and the "soft and gentle shepherd" are problematic: the

---

2. I agree with Michel Foucault: all participants in relationships that are in any way free are wielding some sort of power. See for instance Michel Foucault, "The Subject and Power." But I do not mean, as some critics believe Foucault implied, that the power is roughly equally distributed, or that power relations are the sole basis for social relations, crowding out moral principles except as justifications for power's exercise. And, I agree with Didier Pollefeyt that the power I am exercising in our relationship does not erase your responsibility for the power you exercise in it.

3. This is true even in denominations where ecclesiastical functionaries assign pastors: they do so for the good of the church.

4. Pastoral power is relative and sometimes very situational. In the northern hemisphere, sociological changes have weakened ecclesial influence in culture, and economic and educational changes have eroded some historical sources of pastoral authority within the church. There are also denominational differences. Catholics have recently blamed clergy sex abuse at least partly on priests' authority and on congregants' unquestioning reverence for it. On the other hand, in the United States, Protestant congregations have sometimes combined belief in the priesthood of all believers with "frontier" self-reliance, anti-intellectualism, and miserliness to eviscerate Protestant pastoral power. In addition, the pastoral charge to interpret the word of God and celebrate the sacraments often brings with it a random assortment of powers that are not strictly ecclesial and that the pastor might prefer not to exercise, from choosing hymns and paint colors to managing a multimillion dollar budget.

PART 3—Power and Sexual Abuse

first denies lay power and vocation, and the second abdicates pastoral power and vocation. But in today's climate, in which "personal relationships" between peers are the rule of social life, the "soft and gentle shepherd" harbors far more dangers for the abuse of power because it artificially equalizes pastor and congregant, disguising the power pastors inevitably hold. Ripe for strategies of denial, the gentle shepherd easily becomes a cover for wielding the denied pastoral power to the pastor's benefit.

For all of these reasons, strict equality is an inappropriate goal and an even more impossible condition for pastoral relationships.[5] Rather than eliding this power asymmetry, hiding the other aims that may be operating under the surface, pastors must learn how to deal justly and constructively with it. They must begin by honestly acknowledging both the power difference and the intense emotions and desires that can accompany it.[6] The Church is responsible for encouraging this kind of self-awareness and self-criticism. To the degree that the people of God punish or discourage such reflection, they are complicit in clerical power abuse.

OBSTACLES TO RIGHT USE OF POWER

In his essay in this volume, Didier Pollefeyt points out that pastoral sexual abuse, for example, is simply a special case of more common situations in which the pastor, often with good conscious intentions, is nonetheless practicing denial or moral self-justification. Pollefeyt believes that two related bad habits tend to sustain these errors. The first, isolation, has a psychological dimension: pastors are embarrassed to expose their vulnerabilities by raising questions of propriety with colleagues. But it also has a social dimension: in the United States, pastors take significant professional and legal risks if they do so. There are few "safe spaces" for such discussions.[7] The public in general and the Church specifically are to blame for

---

5. Ethel Spector Person argues that the fundamental power imbalance of the mother-infant relationship on which sexuality is propped may make it impossible ever fully to uproot dynamics of domination and submission from sexuality. Here, I am proposing that the same may be true of particular pastoral relationships; these two particular people will never be on equal footing with each other, even though the congregant and pastor may later have objectively equal social power. This assumption also cautions against counselors forming friendships with clients outside or after therapy. See Spector Person, "Sexuality as the Mainstay of Identity," 627.

6. See for instance Cooper-White, *Shared Wisdom*, 59.

7. Cooper-White reports that pastoral counselors and social workers she surveyed

both problems. Recalling with Pollefeyt's first paradigm of pastoral power, we may wish our pastors always to be unfailingly mature, inspiring, wise, and saintly. Our pastors realize that we do not want them to be finite, sinful, or in need of support, and they are therefore reluctant to show these sides of themselves.

Second, pastors tend to practice fragmentation: they act as if one set of feelings, meanings, purposes, and behaviors applied to their personal lives and another to their professional or pastoral lives. They then cross the boundaries between these "private" and "public" lives unknowingly or even at will, causing the kinds of abuse that Pollefeyt so perceptively describes.

This is hardly surprising. Probably no other vocation is more vulnerable to this sort of personal boundary-crossing. Pastors' communal leadership is built on a network of often-intense personal relationships formed around a common end. This common concern is not a project, a hobby, or a concrete goal, although it may include all of these, but the meaning and end of life itself. It is an inherently existential and intimate undertaking. In addition, pastors are (as we say in the United States) "on call 24/7." Whenever they appear in public—whether they are visiting congregants in the hospital, buying groceries, or attending meetings at their children's elementary schools—they are on duty, representing their congregations and denominations publicly, as are their family members, if they have partners or children. They typically live near or next to the church in a building owned, maintained, and therefore intimately known by members of their congregations: a building that often houses public administrative or meeting space, putting their home lives on display to their church members. And they are enjoined to lay the fruits of their private spiritual journeys before their congregations regularly in preaching. Given the intertwining of vocational and personal at every level from the most quotidian to the

---

counted self-awareness as the best prevention to unethical enactments in therapy (these include sexual behavior, but also offering sacraments, holding or touching, sitting close, etc.). One would expect counselors to debrief such events. Cooper-White reports that about a quarter of pastoral counselors and clinical social workers surveyed said they never discussed unethical enactments with clients at all, and no one she surveyed claimed to have "delved into his or her own intrapsychic material" to bring unconscious feelings to awareness and prevent future enactments (*Shared Wisdom*, 161–64). Given that supervisors also do not probe counselors deeply about their behavior with clients, Cooper-White worries that members of the profession fail to challenge each other to accomplish self-awareness (*Shared Wisdom*, 176–78). Most pastors are not trained in transference and countertransference. They would likely be even less aware and less vigilant against such enactments than pastoral counselors.

most intimate, it is almost impossible to maintain the psychological distinction between personal and vocational. The structure of the vocation battles against it at every moment.

This essay steps into the space created by Pollefeyt's suggestion: the cure lies not in enjoining pastors to divide their psyches more vigilantly, but in encouraging them to integrate the personal and vocational more fully. When a person's whole self is self-consciously present in a pastoral interaction, it is more difficult for a dormant or unconscious element of her life to exert itself over the interaction under cover of professional or vocational concern (and vice versa). I will draw upon dynamics in parenting, another example of easily corrupted benevolent power, to make this case. I will argue further that pastors must acknowledge, face, and embrace the desires, pleasures, and satisfactions of the pastoral vocation if they are not to be ruled by them.[8] To this end, I will argue that the self-emptying love of *agape* must be tempered by both the yearning love of *eros* and the communal friendship of *philia*.

INTEGRATING IDENTITY

What often lies at the root of pastoral abuse of power is not a failure to distinguish public from private or a failure to juggle multiple vocations. It is a failure to manage experiences and emotions that cut across the many genuine vocational identities one person holds—especially across identities in which power differentials differ greatly. I may take "the same" action or have "the same" physical sensation or emotional experience in my roles as

---

8. The conflict between personal and vocational that the preceding paragraphs imply is misleading. In contemporary Christian parlance, there is no conflict between the personal and the vocational because the vocational is already highly personal: it is "what God is calling me to do." Vocation is also communal because it is "what God is calling me to do in the Church and the world." For instance, vocation can be a calling to prayer, to the pastorate, to vowed partnership, to parenthood, to teaching, to community activism, or to all these simultaneously. Felt conflicts arise from the challenge of juggling these roles, all of which are both personal and communal, and from slippage between "vocation" and "profession." The latter has benefits: the professionalization of the pastorate, for example, involves consistent educational and ethical standards. But it has pitfalls as well: professions are social, functional, and economic categories that are not always callings. As both Pollefeyt and Gärtner point out, the professional vision of ministry often reduces the pastor to a private counselor, ignoring ecclesial and spiritual elements of the role; and professions imply a public role that is detachable from a personal or private life. So to the degree that the pastorate is professional or "public," it may seem to be in conflict with the personal or "private."

mother, partner, pastor, and teacher, but its meaning and its implications are quite different in each instance.

In order to honor the truth of these similarities while resisting the temptation to make them identities, we must embrace ambiguity, taken (as Donald Levine says) "not as a warrant for sloppy thinking but as an invitation to deal responsibly with issues of great complexity."[9] In this case, the path to an integrated, conflict-free, powerful subject may be to alter our view of subjects. We must embrace a complex, shifting, and ambiguous self that is nonetheless composed of identifiable, related, relatively stable identities.

Three related strategies may help us with these reflections. All are linked by one common observation: our bodies are the point of connection among all our social interactions and experiences. Bodies can be sources of confusion when we experience similar sensations or desires in different situations. They are complex: neurology, endocrinology, psychology, and ideologies of gender, ethnicity, sexuality, and geography come into play. But reflecting on their complexity also helps us to avoid turning these similarities into identities—a crucial skill for navigating power differentials.

Embracing "Much at Once"

In the first strategy, Mark Johnson reminds us to steer clear of reductionism. He argues that all words and concepts originate in bodily experiences so multivalent that the effort to describe them adequately overwhelms us.[10] We inevitably "make meaning" of them by selecting one or a few significant features that seem relevant to a specific situation, against a definite backdrop, driven by particular goals or worries.[11] For instance, we might call emotionally intimate conversation "romance" and meeting with troubled congregants "counseling." But then the thin strand of meaning we produce takes on the appearance of the universal and the normative, and we forget the other equally present features of the originating experiences: maybe the comfortable, non-exhilarating, friendly reassurance of intimate conversation, or the profoundly spiritual dimension of pastoral counseling.[12] We literally reject these other potential meanings when we create the labels.

9. Levine, *The Flight from Ambiguity*, 17.
10. Johnson, *The Meaning of the Body*, 83, 271.
11. Ibid., 109.
12. Ibid., 269–70.

PART 3—Power and Sexual Abuse

They are lost. This is not a problem until we encounter a situation of dissonance, as we do when emotional intimacy appears in an experience whose assigned meaning is "counseling." Suddenly an element of our egalitarian social lives has intruded into our decidedly unequal pastoral lives, threatening a pastoral boundary.

Johnson's observation suggests we should not panic at moments of such radical dissonance. Instead, we should first ask whether inherited labels actively obscure now-important dimensions of the experiences in which they originated. In the case of counseling, meaning choices that have reduced the pastoral role to detached, uninvolved professionalism and elevated romance to a basic, unquestionable source of experiential truth yield apparently mutually exclusive universal constants. If we do not return critically to the original "much-at-once," we must either deny or condemn the apparent overlap in our experience.

Second, in addition to recalling and describing the embodied "much-at-once-ness" from which the norms were extracted, we should examine the "much-at-once-ness" of the experience we are currently trying to evaluate. This is especially important when the experience seems to cross the borders of identities with very different power configurations. What emotions, sensations, associations, body memories, and images accompany pastoral care? What are the priorities and responsibilities that limit the use of power? And how are these different from the experiences of egalitarian friendship? What is the quality of instinctively knowing that a congregant has emerged into the light of a new spiritual or emotional understanding? What separates that from the equally profound moment of new understanding shared with one's partner of twenty years? How does a pastor's return of a spontaneous hug from a grieving congregant at a funeral home differ from wordlessly lying "spooned" with one's partner after he has received bitter and difficult news?

These are benevolent moments; some are sensual; they deploy power; they are not purely selfless; and they also are not equivalent. Some elements of a conversation with a congregant may remind me of intimate discussion with my partner, for instance, tempting me to see both interactions as romantic. But if I bring to mind the whole "much-at-once" of both my pastoral relationship and my partnership, I quickly see that imputing the same meaning to both ignores the complex and very different characters of the relationships. Likewise, the hugging pastor may, or may not, be misusing power with the aim of gaining a bit of human—even though the hug lowers his serotonin levels as much as it lowers those of his grieving congregant. We need the freedom to explore the full texture of experiences like these in order to have any hope of grasping their meaning and moral weight. This kind of reflection is indispensable to critical, self-critical life in community.

Embracing Multiple Images of Self

Whereas Johnson helps us interpret the harmonies and dissonances between experiences and the norms we distill from them, Gale Weiss highlights the harmonies and dissonances among the various socially formed "body images" (really images of our embodied selves, or our selves in full experience) that we hold simultaneously. For Weiss my "self" is my physical body given in experience, shaped by social interaction.

> [I]mages of the body are not discrete but form a series of overlapping identities whereby one or more aspects of that body appear to be especially salient at any given point in time. Thus, rather than view the body image as a cohesive, coherent phenomenon that operates in a fairly uniform way in our everyday existence . . . I argue . . . for a multiplicity of body images, body images that are copresent in any given individual, and which are themselves constructed through a series of corporeal exchanges that take place both within and outside of specific bodies.[13]

Behind Johnson's "much-at-once" moments stand Weiss's "many-bodies-at-once": my whiteness; my femaleness; my age; my sexual orientation; my identity as a daughter, partner, and mother; my vocation as pastor or teacher; my physical health or strength; my illness or weakness. Bodily integrity is rooted in a dynamic relation among many socially-enacted body images. At any moment, one identity or image may dominate my horizon, but the fluid coexistence of all these images guarantees a dynamic continuity through otherwise identity-jarring transitions like pregnancy, illness, death, job loss, or family dissolution.[14] Multiplicity and flexibility, not singularity, yield reliability and integrity.[15] Critical analysis of these overlapping body images helps us keep the door to the "much-at-once" propped open, reminding us that our body image and the bodily relations we enact must match the situation and cautioning us against sudden chang-

---

13. Weiss, *Body Images*, 1–2.
14. Ibid., 167.
15. Ibid., 51–53.

es of embodied identity—especially in relations with those over whom we hold power.

"Pastor" is an embodied identity entailing specific relations not just to liturgical space, but to sick rooms, confessionals, private offices, and civic gatherings. Trivial examples are the free parking pass clergy in my community receive to visit hospitals or the deference pastors wearing clerical collars receive when they enter them. Weiss argues that we should not accept such body images uncritically. They are culturally enforced, and they can clash unhelpfully, making some mutually exclusive.[16] This embodied identity of "pastor" sometimes feels incompatible with the "intimate friend," "sexual partner," or any number of other identities. Such prohibitions yield a fragmentation that is stifling, and sometimes even dangerous. Rather, identities of father and pastor (for example) are "occupied by the same person at the same point in time"[17] even if, at any given moment, one is in the foreground and the other in the background. If a person is a convergence of many social, bodily strands whose prevalence shifts with the situation, the whole person is, or should be, present in all of them, but with a clear sense of which social, bodily identities should be operating here and now and which should be sidelined. Vulnerability and power are among the most urgent factors to consider in this decision.

Together, Johnson and Weiss propose powerful tools for the critical self-awareness that must accompany the use of power. Both point out that our abstractions and images are largely so unself-conscious that they strike us as given. For instance, we inhabit body images so automatically that (like a colleague whom Weiss describes) we may deny that we have any.[18] Critical and self-critical awareness of the "much-at-once-ness" of our experiences and bodily relations will help. But we must also reflect upon them corporately to overcome parallaxes that our own histories or societies may have imposed.

Embracing Our Complex Pasts

The third image of self-integration rests on a hypothesis: Sigmund Freud's theory of "propping," which explains how new sensations, emotions, and

---

16. For examples drawn from women's reproductive lives and women's illness see Weiss, *Body Images*, 53–54, 61–63.

17. Ibid., 54.

18. Ibid., 165–67.

meanings build themselves on the foundations of existing ones, creating "much-at-once-ness" and new, simultaneous identities. The new experiences overlap with and recall the old ones, but they are not identical. This is another tool that can help us to avoid crossing wires abusively, mistaking the feel of this power-racked situation for that of a more benign one.

Jean Laplanche argues that in Freud's "Three Contributions to the Theory of Sex" the sexual drive leans, or is "propped," on a more basic drive, hunger.[19] That is, early suckling satisfies hunger by bringing in milk, but eventually a second satisfaction appears alongside the first one: the sensual pleasure of suckling itself. This experience comes into being through feeding, but is not feeding and is eventually detachable from it. Freud argues that any pleasure arising from a basic drive, in distinction from it, is by definition sexuality: sexuality comes to be in the moment a second layer of meaning or pleasure arises.[20]

Freud may have created a category both too narrow and too diffuse when he defined sexuality as *every* new pleasure that arises alongside and dissociates itself from a vital function. Propping is a useful analogy for some equally strong, but looser experiential associations. New embodied pleasures and meanings are always arising in connection with old ones, propped on them or borrowing from them, providing ample opportunity for us to confuse the two in interpretation. Nursing mothers are a good example. In Western culture, a woman's sexual enjoyment of her own breast is likely to come first in her consciousness, followed later by the pleasure of suckling an infant. In this case, the root experience is what we would call "sexual" or "genital." The new experience of suckling recalls the original sexual one in both sensation and meaning—in some ways it "feels like" sex. But, recalling Johnson and Weiss, in its much-at-once-ness and in its new, simultaneous maternal identity, breast feeding is also importantly different from sex. In sex, physical enjoyment is the goal; in breast feeding, the primary aim is feeding, and physical enjoyment is often unavoidable, but

19. Laplanche, *Life and Death in Psychoanalysis*; see in particular 8, 15–26. Laplanche is commenting on "Three Contributions to the Theory of Sex."

20. Laplanche, *Life and Death*, 17–18, 22. This is the insight behind Freud's theory of pansexuality: any drive, any part of the body can (but in a given person usually does not) become a point of such "propping" (26). In addition, the breast and the mouth that suckles it are not "the same things" in feeding as in sensual suckling, even though both may be occurring simultaneously for the infant: one gives the pleasure of food, the other the pleasure of sensuality. Thus the breast one enjoys in adult sexuality is not the same breast, exactly, that one enjoyed as younger infant feeding, or as an older infant both feeding and suckling for pleasure (Laplanche, *Life and Death*, 20).

concomitant. In sex, the pleasure is usually orgasmic and overwhelming; in breast feeding, it is usually diffuse, less intense, and (to the degree that it involves oxytocin and prolactin) helpful to the aim of feeding. In "good" sex, partners are roughly equal in power and maturity; "exchange" would be one fair way to describe their experience. In breast feeding, a powerful adult gently nurtures an infant so vulnerable that his survival and development depend on her care.

Remarkably, in breast feeding, women routinely accomplish the apparently impossible: they construct a new nurturing identity and relationship not just *next to* the compelling and extraordinary power of egalitarian genital sex, but actually *sharing* much of the same embodied foundation, and they do this in order to feed and nurture vulnerable infants who need protection from the power of full-blown adult sexuality. If it is possible to accomplish this feat of continuity-in-transformation across power difference with as visceral and often overpowering a force as sexuality, then it ought to be possible to manage the same continuity-in-transformation in pastoral relationships—not just for sexuality, but for other desires, pleasures, and drives that we first experience in more egalitarian settings.[21]

In both cases awareness of a complex multivalence can prevent personal fragmentation, drawing connections that are not identities, helping us to employ the wisdom of the full palette of our experiences while remaining alert to the ways that power relations and their purposes in this case may differ from earlier experience. This ambiguity is not sloppy in the sense of being vague or indeterminate; it is complex and must be perceptive, reflective, and critical. It also is not merely private, or it would be captive to subjective, self-justifying parallax; it has identifiable patterns and qualities and so is material for corporate reflection.

21. To continue the parallel, Freud would argue that infants are not simply inert, malleable matter. They are sexual subjects, unfolding their sexuality in way appropriate to their level of development. But Freud would also argue that responsibility for the mother-infant relationship lies with the mother, who holds the power, who is accountable for the infant's welfare, who constructs the world in which the infant finds his way. She is charged with making this a safe world, and so she fashions a new, intimate, and embodied way of caring for her infant in his appropriate need. Similarly, congregants are certainly subjects, and they bear all the moral responsibility for their actions that their maturity implies. But the final responsibility for maintaining the boundaries of the pastor-congregant relationship lies with the pastor: the person who is given power specifically to lead, nurture, feed, comfort, and challenge the congregation. The pastor, too, must fashion new, embodied ways of caring for congregants in their appropriate need that build on, recall, but differ in important and subtle ways from familiar egalitarian modes of relating.

Keeping these connections and distinctions before us is important because equality of power and wisdom is an ideal that can never be realized in the world we know. A pastoral care relationship exists because a vulnerable person, however capable in other arenas of life, lacks in some area where the pastor is presumed to possess greater wisdom. Even when the relationship empowers the congregant, he is permanently indebted and therefore less powerful in that relationship. Only if we acknowledge this asymmetry can we channel power constructively.

INTEGRATING LOVE

In addition to being complex, the pastoral relationship is typically rewarding. People become pastors not just out of self-emptying, *agapic* love for God and the Church, but because they enjoy and work well with people, they think their gifts will be well-used and well-developed in ministry, and they believe it will be a fulfilling vocation. But because they also hold significant power, we must account ethically for this hunger, satisfaction, and pleasure. Here I want to make a counter-intuitive claim: *eros*, or desiring love, is essential to productive and just relations between unequals. It acknowledges the human finitude, imperfection, aims, and projects of the lover and the beloved—the pastor and the congregant—as well as the congregant's need to be delighted in as an individual. Submerging or denying *eros* is likely to yield misuse of pastoral power through loss of "much-at-once-ness." But if we want to admit *eros* to the pastoral fold, it needs a chaperone: *philia*, the egalitarian mutual love of the committed community.

Eros as a Corrective to Agape

This formulation overturns the influential *agape*-centered ethic promoted by Anders Nygren in the last century.[22] In Nygren's famous schema, *agape* is self-sacrificial love modeled on God's self-emptying love for humanity. It is not motivated by any goodness in the beloved; spontaneous and undeserved, it arises from the giver's generosity. It flows from infinite resource toward lack or need, bestowing worth on the object of its love.

---

22. One could argue that Catholics viewed priests as the guaranteed conduits of God's grace, so what came from the priest must be a product of God's self-emptying love.

Despite questionable biblical precedent, Nygren's version of *agape* has been the ideal of pastoral love.[23] *Agape* does seem to be the most appropriate love for situations of unequal power. *Agape* is not self-interested; it aims to improve the beloved, not the lover; and it does not play favorites. It uses its power kenotically and benevolently. Only *agape* is unconditional, showering the beloved with love *in spite of* rather than *because of* her particular downfalls or strengths. Only *agape* remains constant in the moments when the beloved really is not lovable. Only *agape* is utterly profligate. Only *agape* can leave the hope of reciprocity aside and love even when reciprocity and mutuality are unlikely or impossible.[24]

To the contrary, according to Nygren, *eros* is not just a lesser love, but the antithesis of the Christian ideal. Motivated by its own selfishness and lack, it pursues value for its own improvement.[25] Nygren's *eros* is choosy and capricious. It is driven by the lover's taste for value that expresses the needs or desires of the lover to possess the goods that reside in the beloved. It is self-asserting and acquisitive. It appears to capture, rather than to call forth, others' goodness. It treats the beloved instrumentally, focusing on the beloved to the exclusion of all other goods and relationships, turning selfishly inward rather than selflessly outward, using power to overwhelm the vulnerable objects of affection. It seems chancy, worth risking in egalitarian romance, but unreliable for relations involving unequal power or large groups of people. Contemporary revivals of *eros*, although they stress the mutual benefit of *eros*'s potential affirming, egalitarian dynamism, tend to view sexual love as the paradigm of *eros* and so reinforce many of these troublesome impressions.[26]

Yet *agape* has its limits, especially for human lovers whose resources for self-emptying are finite. Flawed *agapic* love is dangerous because its distortions are denied precisely in the name of self-sacrifice. What pastor

23. Arguments that strict distinctions among *agape*, *eros*, and *philia* can be found in the New Testament and Septuagint are hard to sustain. See Barr, "Words for Love in Biblical Greek"; and Blye Howe, "Passionate Love."

24. For recent appreciations of *agape* see in particular Collins Vacek, *Love, Human and Divine*; Miller-McLemore, "Generativity, Self-Sacrifice, and the Ethics of Family Life"; and Purvis, "Mothers, Neighbors and Strangers."

25. Nygren, *Agape and Eros*, 210.

26. See among others Nakashima Brock, *Journeys by Heart*; Ellison, *Erotic Justice*; Bathurst Gilson, *Eros Breaking Free*; Heyward, *Touching Our Strength*; Isherwood, *The Power of Erotic Celibacy*; and Lorde, "Uses of the Erotic." On these developments, see, among others, Black, "The Broken Wings of *Eros*"; Blodgett, *Constructing the Erotic*; and van Schalkwyk, "Heretic but Faithful."

has never sheepishly enjoyed accolades for unhealthy, martyric overwork? In addition, *agapic* self-gift becomes dangerous and guilt-inducing for both giver and receiver when need is intense. It can set a bad example when the giver becomes grim. Allowing the "in spite of" character of *agape* to eradicate the "because of" character of *eros* can destroy the receiver's self-confidence. Perhaps the greatest danger of *agape* for pastors is that they face infinite need, but they do not possess infinite resources. Endless giving with no reward exhausts. Pastors can easily burn out and become resentful, overwhelmed by the burden of an impossible obligation to empty themselves. All of these vulnerabilities tempt pastors to abuse power by becoming abusive, demanding, or controlling; the temptation is magnified if the banner of *agape* protects them from criticism.

Rather than envisioning the often-binary *agape* and *eros* as competitors and crowning one supreme, Edward Vacek and others suggest they are interdependent.[27] To this end, we must explore *eros*'s pastoral virtues. At its best, although *eros* does include self-love and self-development through connection with the beloved, it is not exclusively a form of self-love. Because *eros* is attracted to the good in the beloved, it loves because of, not in spite of, the beloved's particular qualities. It not only appreciates them rationally, but delights in them, and that delight is an irreplaceable gift to the beloved. The direct, immediate gift of erotic delight is indispensable for pastoral relationships; it draws out qualities in a congregant that will benefit from focused affirmation and cultivation by a pastor who is genuinely committed to his welfare and that might have been invisible to him otherwise. We would be stunted if people who know us well loved us only in spite of, and not also because of, our best qualities.

Second, as Wendy Farley argues, desire is a necessary element of life. It is a constant state of being, a sensor or a compass that points us toward goods to be pursued. It is not a signal to fill ourselves up with them. We are meant to enjoy them precisely in their imperfection and temporariness. Christian *eros* does not burden the beloved with the task of being the lover's missing piece. It loves not a false, projected image, but the beloved as she really is, with all her limitations.[28] It is the appropriate love of finite beings for other finite beings, against the backdrop of God's delighted love.

---

27. Vacek, *Love, Human and Divine*, 265; see also 280–81. For a similar argument aimed at a more popular audience, see also Ferder and Heagle, *Tender Fires*, 98–99.

28. Farley, *The Wounding and Healing of Desire*, especially 13–17, 65–77; See also Traina, "Captivating Illusions."

Third, as Vacek and others point out, by creating a cycle of reciprocity, erotic love can counteract *agape*'s tendency to deplete itself. The lover becomes valuable to the beloved both by affirming the beloved's particular gifts and by exerting creative energy for the beloved's good and at his inspiration. The beloved loves the lover in response, creating a circle of erotic affirmation that awakens the lover to her own goodness and value in the eyes of the beloved.[29] We are all familiar with the workings of this dynamic in romantic relations, but it happens as well in relations of unequal power like parenting, teaching, and pastoring. These moments of affirmation recharge the batteries that the often one-sided exercise of *agape* can deplete.

Finally, even contemporary efforts to retrieve *eros* from its long Nygren exile miss two important elements of *eros* that Plato describes in his *Symposium*.[30] First, the lover's creativity is part of the essential structure of desire. The need that eros fills is not a lack in the sense of an absence. Rather, the beautiful or good is a missing catalyst that activates the lover's creative potential. In Catherine Pickstock's words, desire for the beloved delivers "an expression of [the lover's] self that was always bursting to come forth but could only do so by way of the other 'on the body of the beautiful' (Plato 1925a: 206c)."[31]

The beloved helps the lover deliver the creation with which the lover was already "pregnant" before the encounter.[32] There are endless examples in pastoral ministry. What is liturgy without a congregation, bible study without study group, or a church council without members? Few pastors' skills can be realized without creative collaboration with church members whom she loves and values. This does not mean that one can love just anything productively; the lover, the beloved, the love, and the creation must be compatible. Thus, one might say that pastors must love congregants under the aegis of a goal that is appropriate to the congregants' gifts, the congregations' good, and the pastors' virtue, because loving them under other rubrics—say, sexual pleasure—both violates congregants and thwarts pastors' creative pastoral power.

---

29. Vacek, *Love, Human and Divine*, 256–28.

30. Plato, *Symposium*.

31. Pickstock, "*Eros* and Emergence," 108. Pickstock calls this the "satisfaction" of desire, but as Costa, Sheffield, and even Diotima demonstrate, it is at most a pause, not a resting place. See Costa, "For the Love of God"; and Sheffield, *Plato's Symposium*.

32. Sheffield, *Plato's Symposium*, 86–94; on pregnancy and emergence see also Pickstock, "*Eros* and Emergence," 108–109. See also Irigaray, "Sorcerer Love."

Second, against our intuition that *eros* should be egalitarian, in the *Symposium*, *eros* always crosses power boundaries. Men seek beautiful women on whom to beget children, or beautiful boys on whom to beget virtue, or young men with beautiful minds on whom to beget philosophy, and—in an unlikely gender reversal—Diotima begets wisdom on Socrates.[33] The lover draws the like-minded, less powerful beloved into the lover's creative project and transforms him. Further, if the lover does succeed, the benefit flows beyond the lover and the beloved to others—in this case, to all of Socrates's dinner guests. But the important point is that powerful lovers reap the rewards of their love only when it truly benefits or "brings forth upon" their beloveds and, consequently, benefits the community.

Pastors' love toward congregants mirrors much of what Plato says about philosophers' love toward young men who desire knowledge and virtue. Unlike ancient philosophers, pastors do not select all their protégés. But pastors' love for their congregants does bring forth upon them creatively. Pastors teach, preach, counsel, celebrate, and even play in forms that shape their congregations in palpable, unpredictable ways.[34] The delight that accompanies their successes is not the aim of their work, but neither is it an optional luxury. Without it, burnout is likely. This cycle of desire, accomplishment, and enjoyment graces the best pastoral work. But this enjoyment has an important quality: because it arises from creativity rather than possession, it spurs pastors to further creative work for their congregations.

---

33. We would not now say that women are men's inferiors or that bringing forth a child through sex automatically benefits a woman, but this judgment would easily fit Plato's logic. In feminist interpretations of Diotima's speech there is substantial disagreement 1) over the degree to which Socrates's telling might stifle or distort an insight that represents a then-current tradition of women's wisdom and 2) over the relationships among physical, intellectual, and spiritual desire. See Irigaray, "Sorcerer Love"; Nye, "Irigaray and Diotima at Plato's Symposium"; Chanter, *Ethics of Eros*, 160–62; and Orr, "Diotima, Wittgenstein, and a Language for Liberation."

34. This model also suggests grounds for erotic collaboration on larger scales relevant for Christian community and for politics. If *eros* desires the good as catalyst for creativity, any number of lovers can pursue the same object cooperatively; for instance, all the guests at the dinner party are, at least potentially, capable of benefiting from Socrates's wisdom simultaneously. In the words of Grace Jantzen, not "violence and the victimage mechanism but creativity, desire springing from fullness rather than premised upon a lack . . . is the root of hominization and the basis of the passion for transformation." (Jantzen, "New Creations," 286, 287) Jantzen takes the thesis that common loves beget competition from René Girard.

This picture is lovely, but how Christian is it? Is it really the case that a love that imitates God has both *agapic* and erotic moments, "in spite of the evil" and "because of the good" tendencies? Christian theology is full of the cross and God's self-emptying love, but it also has a strong tradition of devoted, passionate, fierce, almost meddlesome divine care for the beloved.[35] God's love "brings forth upon" Israel's potential for goodness erotically and even jealously, as it "brings forth upon" the wisdom of the Gentiles upon whose hearts the law is written (Rom 2:14–15). Human erotic love is only analogous to divine *eros*; only God also creates the good God fiercely loves. But so is human *agape* only analogous to divine *agape*; only God can bestow grace.

If the vision passes the theological test, does it fulfill the practical test as well? Is it too susceptible to human finitude and sin? *Eros* is not its own guarantee of justice and creativity. It requires virtue. One of the most important internal protections against unintentional abuse of my power is my attunement to all the dimensions of the other's situation, strengths, and needs. Her good, not mine, must remain the focus of my erotic love for her. Linda Holler and Wendy Farley provide philosophical and theological backing for the virtue that protects this priority: my surest path to attunement with you is contemplative attunement to myself. I must be aware of my own feelings, fears, and desires. This awareness lessens the possibility that I will accidentally confuse you with me or use you to fulfill my unacknowledged needs; it also increases the probability that I will recognize and honor your true strengths.[36] As Pollefeyt and others agree, actually meeting my spiritual, social, and physical needs once I have uncovered them is an essential second step; only if my most basic human needs are fulfilled outside my congregation am I really free to meet my congregants in a pastoral role. Genuine *agapic* love could undertake the same inventories contemplatively, but it is likely to fall short of attunement by focusing on the other to the neglect of the self. Erotic love, which acknowledges my limitations and harnesses my strengths and desires to your gifts and needs, has the advantage of making a structural demand for self-evaluation.

---

35. See for example Johnson, *Quest for the Living God*, chapters 3 and 4.

36. See Farley, *Wounding and Healing of Desire*, and Holler, *Erotic Morality*. For massage therapists' presentation of this challenge, see Middlesworth, "Self-Evaluation for an Ethical Practice"; and Benjamin and Sohnen-Moe, *The Ethics of Touch*.

POWER IN COMMUNITY: PHILIA

But contemplative efforts at individual virtue are not fail-safe. Certainly a parent, pastor, teacher, or therapist is responsible for "policing" the boundaries of an unequal power relationship for the sake of the work that must be done for the less powerful partner. And conscious acceptance of inequality, desire, and satisfaction permits the powerful to name their own interests honestly rather than hiding them under the cloak of self-emptying *agape*. Still, we know that even in the best of situations, the benefits that flow to the more powerful person in this relationship—improving in her vocation, learning to know herself better, and being enriched by the other's success—disqualify her as an objective "police officer," even if they never become explicit goals of the interchange.

What can overcome the parallax that both *agape* and *eros* risk? As Edward Vacek argues, Christian love should encompass *philia* as well.[37] *Philia* has had many descriptions in the past century, drawing variously on Aristotle and the New Testament epistles, sometimes flavored strongly by the commonsense experience of educated Euro-American male friendship.[38] For our purposes here, it is the mutual love of friendship in community. Friendship is mutual because reciprocal.[39] It is love because it is dedicated to the other's good.[40] And it is communal in the sense that the friends are united by their common love for the community and for its purposes.[41] As Johnson writes of James 4:4, *philia* implies complete identification or "one souledness."[42] In the church, *philia* is a shared love of God that inspires mutual appreciation and collaboration toward common goals: word, sacrament, service, and witness.

This final quality is essential for pastoral relationships. The ecclesial context frames everything. For instance, friendships between pastors and

---

37. Vacek, *Love, Human and Divine*.

38. See for example Vacek, *Love*; Pieper, *About Love*; Lewis, *The Four Loves*; Tillich, *Love Power, and Justice*; Chanter, "Antigone's Excessive Relationship to Fetishism"; Johnson, "Friendship with the World/Friendship with God." Lewis's vision is particularly influenced by his own culture of friendship and particularly anxious to avoid homoerotic implications. All these accounts of *philia* refer implicitly to chapters 8 and 9 of Aristotle's *Nichomachean Ethics*.

39. Vacek, *Love*, 280–92.

40. Aristotle, *Ethics*, 260–61.

41. Pieper, *About Love*, 114.

42. Johnson, "Friendship," 173–74.

church members thrive in the context of the congregation and its goals. The good they wish for each other and themselves must be the good of the congregation as a whole. A friendship that endangers the congregation's good, then, transgresses *philia*. In addition, while pastors and congregants may not have identical power within the congregation, with respect to both its goals and their own devotional lives, they are on equal footing, companions on the same journey of faith. Finally, the friendships that crisscross a community of faith enrich it for all its members. The breach of a friendship or the loss of one person impoverishes the experience of community for all.[43] Thus within congregations individuals must remember that the friendships they make, sustain, wound, and repair are not their private matter. A too-exclusive friendship or a boundary violation damages the entire congregation. Rather, friendships must be maintained with the community's mission in mind in order to provide energy, resilience, and security to the whole.

Thus friendship is no light matter. It is a commitment that demands virtue. It is so intimate, demanding, and time-consuming that, as Aristotle warns, we cannot actually have very many close friends.[44] But in an ecclesial setting, friendship is also especially rewarding. As Josef Pieper argues, friends can be united by common loves ranging from automobiles through food to political causes. But in the church, the common object of their love is God. Friends love God together, affirm each other as loved by God, and wish for each other's union with God. Friendship is then the first step toward caritas, loving from God's point of view.[45]

Finally, as Chanter and Cowley insist, without friendship, there can be no community at all. Chanter reads Sophocles's *Antigone* as arguing that society must be founded on the bonds of friendship—of shared values and mutual well-wishing—not mere clan connections, which, though loyal, are unreflective. Reflecting on Benedict's XVI's *Deus Caritas Est*,[46] Cowley warns that pure *agape*—an "individualistic, nonmutual and task-oriented love"—is too generic and indifferent to found a robust social ethic—or, in our case, to found a robust congregational ethos. And solidarity certainly requires *philia*.[47]

---

43. Lewis, *Four Loves*, 92.
44. Aristotle, *Ethics*, 264.
45. Pieper, *About Love*, 117–18; see also Cowley, "Philia," 24–26.
46. Benedict XVI, *Deus Caritas Est*.
47. Cowley, "Philia," 30, 33–35.

All of this points toward the necessity of framing all love relations within the framework of love in and for community. Whether it is disinterested, kenotic *agape* or particular, creative *eros*, love needs to be tempered by what Americans like to call the "big picture": the good of the community as a whole, in God. Consequently, as Edward Vacek argues, we need love as *agape* to overcome our selfishness; love as *eros* to overcome our pessimism; and love as *philia* to correct false isolation, both as individuals and as dyads.[48] All pastoral relationships occur within this larger ecclesial context and so are inclusive and potentially expandable. They are in the end ecclesial relationships, not private relationships.

Thus as Pollefeyt and pastoral counselor Pamela Cooper-White insist, the individual practice of critical reflection on *eros* must be measured against its ecclesial context and supplemented by a communal practice of critical reflection supported by *philia*. The final important barrier to unintentional abuse of power is creation of institutional support to back up these virtues: structures of critical and self-critical accountability to others. This can include feedback from the less powerful people with whom we are in relationship. But it also means frank discussion of our desires, needs, and worries with peers. This is a trite suggestion; *of course* parents, teachers, and pastors consult about challenging and possibly compromising relations with vulnerable people. But in the United States, at least, it is often not safe to do so. One becomes professionally compromised and perhaps legally liable if one admits to failings or doubts; counselors and supervisors tend not to use even supervisory relationships for this purpose. A gaping hole in American protection against abuse of power is the lack of genuinely safe but challenging opportunities for these discussions.

Finally, pastors must be accountable to church members on ministry committees; to colleagues in clergy support groups; and to ecclesiastical superiors like bishops. Their emotional and social health, both inside and outside their congregational lives, needs frequent assessment.

Pastors who cultivate awareness of their own simultaneous, overlapping "much-at-once" experiences and identities and who balance self-gift with a genuinely self-aware erotic love in the context of dedication to the community will be neither almighty nor soft; they will be gently powerful, and they will use their power for the benefit of the Church and with its help. The challenge we face is the challenge of cultivating and sustaining this vision of ministry.

---

48. Vacek, *Love*, 308–11.

PART 3—Power and Sexual Abuse

BIBLIOGRAPHY

Aristotle. *Nicomachean Ethics*. Translated by James A. K. Thomson. Rev. ed. New York: Penguin, 1976.

Barr, James. "Words for Love in Biblical Greek." In *The Glory of Christ in the New Testament: Studies in Christology in Memory of George Bradford Caird*, edited by Lincoln D. Hurst and Nicholas T. Wright, 3–18. Oxford: Clarendon, 1987.

Benjamin, Ben E., and Cherie Sohnen-Moe. *The Ethics of Touch: The Hands-On Practitioner's Guide to Creating a Professional, Safe and Enduring Practice*. Tucson: SMA, 2005 [2003].

Benedict XVI. *Deus Caritas Est*. December 25, 2005. http://www.vatican.va/holy_father/benedict_xvi/encyclicals/documents/hf_ben-xvi_enc_20051225_deus-caritas-est_en.html.

Black, Peter. "The Broken Wings of *Eros*: Christian Ethics and the Denial of Desire." *Theological Studies* 64 (2003) 106–26.

Blodgett, Barbara. *Constructing the Erotic: Sexual Ethics and Adolescent Girls*. Cleveland: Pilgrim Press, 2002.

Brock, Rita Nakashima. *Journeys by Heart: A Christology of Erotic Power*. New York: Crossroad, 1988.

Chanter, Tina. "Antigone's Excessive Relationship to Fetishism: The Performative Politics and Rebirth of *Eros* and *Philia* from Ancient Greece to Modern South Africa." *Symposium* 11 (2007) 231–60.

———. *Ethics of Eros: Irigaray's Rewriting of the Philosophers*. New York: Routledge, 1995.

Cooper-White, Pamela. *Shared Wisdom: Use of the Self in Pastoral Care and Counseling*. Minneapolis: Fortress Press, 2004.

Costa, Mario. "For the Love of God: The Death of Desire and the Gift of Life." In *Toward a Theology of Eros: Transfiguring Passion at the Limits of Discipline*, edited by Virginia Burrus and Catherine Keller, 38–62. Transdisciplinary Theological Colloquia. New York: Fordham University Press, 2006.

Cowley, Catherine. "*Philia* and Social Ethics." *Forum Philosophicum* 14 (2009) 17–37.

Ellison, Marvin M. *Erotic Justice: A Liberating Ethic of Sexuality*. Louisville: Westminster John Knox, 1996.

Farley, Wendy. *The Wounding and Healing of Desire: Weaving Heaven and Earth*. Louisville: Westminster/John Knox, 2005.

Ferder, Fran, and John Heagle. *Tender Fires: The Spiritual Promise of Sexuality*. New York: Crossroad, 2002.

Foucault, Michel. "The Subject and Power." In *Michel Foucault: Beyond Structuralism and Hermeneutics*, edited by Hubert L. Dreyfus and Paul Rabinow, 208–26. Chicago: University of Chicago Press, 1982.

Freud, Sigmund. *The Basic Writings of Sigmund Freud*. Translated and edited by Abraham A. Brill. New York: The Modern Library, 1995 [1938].

Gilson, Anne Bathurst. *Eros Breaking Free: Interpreting Sexual Theo-Ethics*. Cleveland: Pilgrim, 1995.

Heyward, Carter. *Touching Our Strength: The Erotic as Power and the Love of God*. San Francisco: HarperSanFrancisco, 1984.

Holler, Linda. *Erotic Morality: The Role of Touch in Moral Agency*. New Brunswick, NJ: Rutgers University Press, 2002.

Howe, Mary Blye. "Passionate Love." *Mars Hill Review* 11 (1998) 53–62.

Irigaray, Luce. "Sorcerer Love: A Reading of Plato's *Symposium*, Diotima's Speech." Translated by Eleanor H. Kuykendall. *Hypatia* 3 (1988) 32–44.

Isherwood, Lisa. *The Power of Erotic Celibacy: Queering Heteropatriarchy*. Queering Theology Series. New York: T. & T. Clark, 2006.

Jantzen, Grace. "New Creations: *Eros*, Beauty, and the Passion for Transformation." In *Toward a Theology of Eros: Transfiguring Passion at the Limits of Discipline*, edited by Virginia Burrus and Catherine Keller, 271–87. Transdisciplinary Theological Colloquia. New York: Fordham University Press, 2006.

Johnson, Elizabeth A. *Quest for the Living God: Mapping Frontiers in the Theology of God*. New York: Continuum, 2007.

Johnson, Luke T. "Friendship with the World/Friendship with God: A Study of Discipleship in James." In *Discipleship in the New Testament*, edited and with an introduction by Fernando Segovia, 166–83. Philadelphia: Fortress, 1985.

Johnson, Mark. *The Meaning of the Body: Aesthetics of Human Understanding*. Chicago: University of Chicago Press, 2007.

Laplanche, Jean. *Life and Death in Psychoanalysis*. Translated and with an introduction by Jeffrey Mehlman. Baltimore: Johns Hopkins University Press, 1976.

Levine, Donald N. *The Flight from Ambiguity: Essays in Social and Cultural Theory*. Chicago: University of Chicago Press, 1985.

Lewis, C. S. *The Four Loves*. New York: Harcourt, Brace, Jovanovich, 1960.

Lorde, Audre. "Uses of the Erotic: The Erotic as Power." In *Sister Outsider: Essays and Speeches*, 53–59. Freedom, CA: Crossing Press, 1984.

Middlesworth, Jean E. "Self-Evaluation for an Ethical Practice." *Massage Therapy Journal* 46 (2007) 119–33.

Miller-McLemore, Bonnie J. "Generativity, Self-Sacrifice, and the Ethics of Family Life." In *The Equal-Regard Family and Its Friendly Critics: Don Browning and the Practical Theological Ethics of the Family*, edited by John Witte, Jr., M. Christian Green, and Amy Wheeler, 17–41. Grand Rapids: Eerdmans, 2007.

Nye, Andrea. "Irigaray and Diotima at Plato's Symposium." In *Feminist Interpretations of Plato*, edited by Nancy Tuana, 197–215. University Park: Pennsylvania State University Press, 1994.

Nygren, Anders. *Agape and Eros*. Translated by Philip S. Watson. New York: Harper & Row, 1969 [1953].

Orr, Deborah. "Diotima, Wittgenstein, and a Language for Liberation." In *Belief, Bodies, and Being: Feminist Reflections on Embodiment*, edited by Deborah Orr et al., 59–80. Lanham, MD: Rowman & Littlefield, 2006.

Person, Ethel Spector. "Sexuality as the Mainstay of Identity: Psychoanalytic Perspectives." *Signs* 5 (1980) 605–30.

Pickstock, Catherine. "*Eros* and Emergence." In *Queer Theology: Rethinking the Western Body*, edited by Gerard Loughlin, 99–114. Malden, MA: Blackwell, 2007.

Pieper, Josef. *About Love*. Translated by Richard and Clara Winston. Chicago: Franciscan Herald Press, 1974.

Plato. *Symposium*. Translated by Alexander Nehamas and Paul Woodruff. Indianapolis: Hackett, 1989.

Purvis, Sally B. "Mothers, Neighbors and Strangers: Another Look at *Agape*." In *Christian Perspectives on Sexuality and Gender*, edited by Elizabeth Stuart and Adrian Thatcher, 232–46. Grand Rapids: Eerdmans, 1996.

PART 3—Power and Sexual Abuse

Sheffield, Frisbee C. C. *Plato's Symposium: The Ethics of Desire*. Oxford: Oxford University Press, 2006.

Tillich, Paul. *Love, Power, and Justice: Ontological Analyses and Ethical Applications*. The Firth and Sprunt Lectures. New York: Oxford, 1954.

Traina, Cristina L.H. "Captivating Illusions: Sexual Abuse and the Ordering of Love." *Journal of the Society of Christian Ethics* 28 (2008) 183–208.

———. *Erotic Attunement: Parenthood and the Ethics of Sensuality between Unequals*. Chicago: University of Chicago Press, 2011.

Vacek, Edward Collins. *Love, Human and Divine: The Heart of Christian Ethics*. Washington: Georgetown, 1994.

van Schalkwyk, Annalet. "Heretic but Faithful: The Reclamation of the Body as Sacred in Christian Feminist Theology." *Religion and Theology* 9 (2002) 135–61.

Weiss, Gail. *Body Images: Embodiment as Intercorporeality*. New York and London: Routledge, 1999.

Yardley-Nohr, Terrie. *Ethics for Massage Therapists*. LWW Massage Therapy and Bodywork Education Series. Philadelphia: Lippincott Williams and Wilkins, 2007.

PART 4

Challenges for Theology and Pastoral Praxis

8

Empowerment in Pastoral Care for Persons with a Psychiatric Disorder
Towards Human Flourishing

Jana Binon

INTRODUCTION

THE DISCOURSE ON EMPOWERMENT is widespread in the contemporary context: from empowerment within companies, to specific empowerment research methods, and empowerment dynamics in care. Although some incentives are given concerning pastoral care, in the pastoral field there are still many opportunities to deepen the concept of empowerment, and to inspire pastoral praxis through its dynamic.

The word "empowerment" is often used and praised in different areas of life, but without a clear understanding of what is meant by an empowering dynamic. Therefore, this contribution starts with exploring the concept of "empowerment." Secondly, attention will be given to the relationship between empowerment and power. In a third movement, a journey will be undertaken to look beyond the first impression of empowerment in terms

PART 4—Challenges for Theology and Pastoral Praxis

of the autonomy of the individual and to explore its broader context. Subsequently, the conditions for enabling empowerment will be elaborated. In all these aspects, the question will be how these ideas can inspire and challenge pastoral care, in particular for persons with a psychiatric disorder. Finally, three main ways of creating an empowering pastoral care will be discussed and some final suggestions will be put forward.

AN EXPLORATION OF EMPOWERMENT

The word empowerment is frequently used to describe one's empowering policy, empowering strategy when dealing with staff, empowering developmental work, or empowering care for vulnerable groups. But do all the actors refer to the same interpretation of empowerment? According to Linkhorst and Eckart, defining the concept is a difficult venture.[1]

The American psychologist Rappaport defines empowerment as "a process, a mechanism by which people . . . gain mastery over their affairs."[2] Empowerment is about control, about taking one's life in one's own hands. Staples refers to empowerment in terms of groups, as well as individuals, who would like to gain control over their lives.[3] Croft and Beresford speak of empowerment as the redistribution of power.[4] Linhorst and Eckart focus especially on the active participation of individuals or groups in the decision making process.[5] They encourage especially vulnerable groups to take part in making decisions in important areas in their lives, for example, psychiatric patients who can have a say in their treatment process. Perhaps they can also be given a voice in shaping the pastoral care that aims at reaching them? To enable this empowering process to take place, Linhorst and Eckart distinguish a set of "enabling" conditions, which will be dealt with in the fourth part of this contribution. Empowerment can vary according to the context and occurs at different levels, both on an individual and a more structural level.

---

1. Linhorst and Eckert, "Conditions for Empowering People with Severe Mental Illness," 279–305.
2. Rappaport, "Terms of Empowerment," 122.
3. Staples, "Powerful Ideas about Empowerment," 30.
4. Croft and Beresford, "The Politics of Participation," 32.
5. Linhorst and Eckert, "Conditions for Empowering People with Severe Mental Illness," 279–305.

The idea of empowerment originates from the working sphere, from the individual employee who should be empowered through perceiving a sense of control, competence, and internalization of the aims set by the employing organization.[6] Empowerment stresses autonomy, delegation, and the so called "elbow space" that enables the individual to be more self-directing. But, according to Glor, it can also be perceived as psychological empowerment, or power sharing.[7] An interesting idea in this regard is Pink's "surprising truth about what motivates us," in which he scientifically demonstrates that the old idea that you work harder and better if you receive a better financial reward seems outdated (at least for work in which cognitive skills are required).[8] What really makes people work more efficiently, contributes to their personal satisfaction, and really motivates them, are autonomy (self-direction, leading to engagement), mastery (challenges, the desire to improve, wanting to make a contribution), and purpose. He mentions a software company where, one day a week, the employees can do whatever they want with whomever they want, and report it back to the group in an informal meeting. Apparently this "elbow space" has provided a boost of creative ideas and innovations that otherwise would not have come up. Enabling this creative autonomous space became part of an empowering movement that connected the person's passion and engagement with efficiency, inspiring work, and work satisfaction. Can this seemingly purely economic strategy also inspire pastoral care? Can it function, not as a way to maximize profit or efficiency, but to maximize inspiration, engagement, and capacities within persons, both pastors and pastoral care receivers? This empowering idea connects with the pastoral idea of a fulfilled Christian, who may act in a more inspiring and prophetic way when motivated and self-directed, than when guided by a heavenly reward.

Empowerment is not only a matter of control, or having power over one's life. It can also include a creative space, engagement, motivation, and purpose. Furthermore, it does not turn people into self-realizing autonomous individuals. Interaction is a crucial part of empowerment. Spierts distinguishes three main characteristics of empowerment, namely its interaction, its process, and limited autonomy, supported by connectedness with others and with the broader society.[9] The focus on interaction and

---

6. Menon, "Psychological Empowerment"; Glor, "About Empowerment," 1–19.
7. Glor, "About Empowerment," 1–19.
8. Pink, *Drive*.
9. Spierts, "De verspreiding van empowerment," 37–39.

PART 4—Challenges for Theology and Pastoral Praxis

connectedness will be dealt with further below and is especially present in the work of the Belgian sociologist Van Regenmortel.[10]

EMPOWERMENT AND POWER

Power over One's life? Three Challenges for Individual Empowerment

Gaining control over one's life, having autonomy and a sense of self-mastery are important aspects of empowerment, but also indicate the factor of power stealing onto the scene. It is precisely the element of power in empowerment that can introduce problems when the notion of empowerment is misunderstood. A first possible problem is the narrowing down of empowerment to the process where an individual, selfish person gains more power for his or her own self-realization, and therefore—perhaps unaware of the misunderstood, narrowed concept—empowerment as a whole is rejected. This attitude is reflected in some historical actions and attitudes of the Catholic church, reacting in a defensive, and often clerical and institutional way against too much "empowerment" of the common people of God. Particular spiritualities within Christianity, such as those that stress the work of divine grace and God at the expense of the individuality and emancipation of the individual faithful, can legitimate such an attitude toward a narrowed down emancipation concept rather than recognizing empowerment in its fullest sense.

A second problem occurs when the power of the community is emphasized at the cost of individual empowerment. In a community (e.g., the L'Arche community where people with a disability live together with people without a disability), an individual's decision can be discouraged in favor of the common good and common goal of the group, according to the American psychologists McDonald and Keys.[11] This concern is often tangible in a church, as well as in every other type of community, for instance a political group or society. The voice of the many overrules the voice of the individual and can therefore repress individual empowerment with a huge potential for power abuse and dictatorial regime.

A third problem is situated on the level of the relationship. Is empowerment creating more equality? According to the South African critical race

10. Van Regenmortel, *Zwanger van empowerment*.
11. McDonald and Keys, "L' Arche."

theorist Hongwane, empowerment can sharpen the power imbalance.[12] For, it is "I," the empowerer, who empowers "you" the empoweree. "I," as empowerer, will hardly empower "you" to such an extent that I need to be empowered myself. Structurally there remains thus a difference in position to ensure the "I" does not become the object of empowerment, for then the process of empowerment would have to start all over again, but with exchanged roles. This structural problem can however, take extreme forms, when the empowerer clings rigidly to his powerful role, and uses empowerment as an excuse, but in fact suppresses the empoweree. Thus the difference between the two partners engaged in empowerment can be maintained and even sharpened.

In giving consideration to empowerment in the relationship between pastor and pastoral caregiver, the French philosopher Foucault and the German theologian Steinkamp point to the danger of pastoral power.[13] In pastoral power, it is the pastor-shepherd who knows what is best for the well-being of the pastoral care receiver, and the care receiver in his turn allows himself to be led by the pastor. In such a shepherd-flock relationship, there seems to be hardly any "empowerment" present. Nevertheless, while claiming to empower the pastoral care "receiver" nowadays, a pastor must be careful not to fall into the same trap of sharpening the power imbalance, between the shepherd who grants empowerment to a certain extent, and the faithful who allow themselves to be empowered in such a way. The notion of *sensus fidelium* is interesting: within Catholic teaching, every Catholic has a kind of common sense about faith and is free to follow his or her conscious . . . yet this *sensus fidelium*, which is potentially empowering, is accepted as long as it is in line with the tradition as expressed through the Magisterium. Empowering . . . and sharpening the power imbalance at the same time.

Dealing with a Power Imbalance

How can one empower the other without sharpening the power imbalance? Hongwane stresses the importance of creating spaces and communities in which the conditions for empowerment are present.[14] Van Regenmortel

12. Hongwane, "Discovering the Academic for Trust's Sake."

13. Foucault, *Was ist Kritik?;* Foucault, "Omnes et singulatim"; Steinkamp, *Die sanfte Macht der Hirten.*

14. Hongwane, "Discovering the Academic for Trust's Sake."

focuses on the very paradox of empowerment: the fact that one cannot empower someone else.[15] People have to empower themselves, but those around them can facilitate the empowerment, open resources, and make an appeal to the hidden resources of the persons involved and the context in which they live. It is the person who is further developed in the empowerment process who bears the responsibility of creating conditions to enable empowerment for the "less empowered." Where Hongwane states that one empowering the other sharpens the power imbalances, Van Regenmortel is of the opinion that one must enable empowerment, rather than empower as such.[16] The empowerer is thus given a special responsibility. Furthermore, the empowering process is also restricted by the rule that empowering someone may not take place at the expense of the empowerment of someone else. Empowerment has its own logic. According to the Dutch psychologist Jacobs, to empower the one, does not mean to disempower the other.[17] Israel is of the opinion that if increasing one's power were to automatically decrease the other's power, empowerment would be met with much resistance.[18] But what is meant with empowerment is a synergetic cooperation that enriches all the parties involved. The notion of an enriching cooperation, however, has not penetrated all fields. For instance, in certain political regimes or church policies, the empowerment of the common people or faithful is perceived rather as a threat toward the establishment than a true mutual equal cooperation.

A good way of dealing with power is first of all to conceive of it not merely in negative or exclusive terms, as a good that, if one person has it, the other one does not. Van Regenmortel underlines the positive approach to power when it is connected to mastery and agency, to community and (inter)connectedness.[19]

In a community, for instance, individual empowerment can be seen as a threat to the common good, but empowerment and gaining more power over one's life in connection with others can also be very positive. In the L'Arche community for instance, the relationship between the assistants and the core members (with a disability), although asymmetrical in nature,

---

15. Van Regenmortel, *Zwanger van empowerment*, 19.

16. Hongwane, "Discovering the Academic for Trust's Sake"; Van Regenmortel, *Zwanger van empowerment*.

17. Jacobs et al., *Op eigen kracht naar gezond leven*.

18. Israel et al., "Health Education and Community Empowerment," 149–70.

19. Van Regenmortel, *Zwanger van empowerment*.

can enable empowerment in an adequate way.[20] Assistants can accord power to the core members and also find meaning in the expressions of the core members in response to that given power. Core members themselves can gain power through their relations with assistants, and through them have a greater access to power channels. So both the assistants (through the meaning they receive in response) and the core members (through their opportunities for and the access to power channels) can be transformed through this empowering process. In what way can this be inspiring for pastoral care with different target groups?

Levels of Empowerment

Van Regenmortel and Jacobs have made distinctions within the concept of empowerment.[21] Empowerment can be found on different levels. On the individual level, empowerment deals with being in touch with one's own capacities and developing skills, and growing in consciousness and confidence. This individual level is described in terms of strength and with a stress on power from within. At collective level, empowerment opens up the resources within one's own surroundings, the social support of friends and family, and the religious and communal support. This empowerment is indicated as "strength" as well and as "power with" in which the process of meaning-making plays a crucial role in the empowerment process and in achieving one's goals. At a political and societal level, empowerment is described in terms of "power" namely the power to make changes possible, beyond the individual level. For instance, to seek to change prejudices, improve accessibility, and influence regulations. This last form, to which the two other levels contribute, is referred to as "power to."

The correspondence with the ideas of the American theologian Stortz is remarkable.[22] She makes a distinction between different forms of power possessed by pastoral leaders. Might these forms of power also connect to forms of "empowerment?" Her first category of "power over" seems to be ruled out, since empowerment is intended precisely to give the control to the other person, and not to take control oneself. Nevertheless, mindful of Hongwane's critique, even when a person deliberately tries to stimulate

20. McDonald and Keys, "L' Arche."

21. Van Regenmortel, *Zwanger van empowerment*; Jacobs et al., *Op eigen kracht naar gezond leven*.

22. Stortz, *PastorPower*.

empowerment, there is a danger of "power over." Power within, Stortz's second category of pastoral power—the charismatic power of a pastoral leader—connects with empowerment at the individual level in two ways. First, "power within" makes the person (for instance the pastoral care receiver) want to empower him or herself through realizing his or her own potential and charisma. The charismatic power of the pastor also indicates the encouraging and empowering dynamic that a pastor can have in enabling empowerment. Finally, the category of "power with" is the most empowering of all. With this term, Stortz refers to the power of co-action, of working together, although such an empowering co-action is not always inclusive to all. As Jacobs and Van Regenmortel focus on the importance of support from the family, from a condition-creating context, and from communal and religious support, "power with" can certainly be linked with collective empowerment.[23] A climate and support that fosters creative power and dynamic can certainly be used to enable empowerment. Furthermore, in a pastoral context, it is important to be aware of the responsibility of the church as a community in the living out of such a collective empowerment, in creating conditions for empowerment (especially for vulnerable groups), and in giving sufficient social support.

A JOURNEY BEYOND FIRST SIGHT

Empowerment is so popular these days that it is possible to use the term without further refinement of what is meant. Some prejudices circulate that can lead to a narrow image of empowerment and an attitude of suspicion or overestimation towards empowerment. Therefore I highlight a few of these prejudices and journey beyond them to discover what empowerment can entail and what the implications of an elaborated concept of empowerment can be for pastoral care.

Mere Autonomy?

Empowerment described in terms of gaining more control over one's life, rightly stresses the notion of autonomy. Pink already mentioned the importance of autonomy, mastery, and purpose for true motivation. Glor similarly

---

23. Van Regenmortel, *Zwanger van empowerment*; Jacobs et al., *Op eigen kracht naar gezond leven*; Stortz, *PastorPower*.

stressed autonomy, self-direction, "elbow room" a desirable future, variety, and so on as important for an empowering process in the workplace.[24] Crucial in empowerment is trust and power sharing, beyond a "delegating" hierarchy. True power sharing in a democratic way, in which people have a voice in the policy, is therefore fundamental. Even though Glor focuses on the individual empowerment of employees, I think this democratic idea of power sharing can be very beneficial for pastoral care on two levels. Firstly, giving the pastors who actually do the concrete work a voice in the decision making process of church policies, pastoral policies, and policies within the institution, would mean a great step forward. It is needless to mention that the empowerment process could transform churches with more involved and empowered faithful as a result. Secondly, pastors can create an environment in the pastoral setting, in which, in practice, in research, in relation to policy concerning their expectations for pastoral care, pastoral care receivers have a voice. This process could foster a truly empowering pastoral policy. Linhorst for instance stresses the importance of autonomy for patients with a psychiatric disorder, who—when certain conditions are met—should have a say in the decision making process, treatment, planning, and policy.[25] Would pastoral care, under certain conditions, also be able to give persons with a psychiatric disorder a say in the pastoral policy, planning, and activities? An empowering patient-centered research on pastoral care in psychiatry, with "hands-on" experts who are involved as pastoral volunteers, patient representatives in pastoral meetings . . . these can be concrete ways of enabling persons with a psychiatric disorder to be more than objects of pastoral care.

Autonomy, emancipation and independence are important features of empowerment, but at the same time they must be considered in the context, in connection with the community, the responsibility of the other, the social context, and interdependence.[26] Autonomy does not exclude dependence or responsibility. On the contrary, dependence on and connectedness with the social contexts are also ways to be empowered, supported, and to achieve more than by managing everything as an autonomous disconnected self. The autonomy spoken of in the concept of empowerment

---

24. Pink, *Drive*; Glor, "About Empowerment," 1–19.

25. Linhorst and Eckert, "Conditions for Empowering People with Severe Mental Illness," 279–305.

26. Van Regenmortel, *Zwanger van empowerment*.

is not a radical, liberal one, but autonomy in connection.[27] The means to strengthen people in this form of empowerment of "autonomy in connection" is according to Van Regenmortel precisely the making of connections between people, groups and organizations, so that persons and (vulnerable) groups are empowered. Religion can play an important role in this work of *religare*, of connecting people and of allowing people to be part of a community that sustains and strengthens them. Pastoral care should provide a platform for autonomy, democracy, and for connecting people in an interdependent network with each other, nature, and God that is uplifting. Beyond the purely liberal approach of autonomy, dialogue, respect, mutuality, and authentic encounters are crucial for empowerment.

The anthropology that grounds empowerment is not the image of the human person as a mere autonomous self, but as a person in connection, enwrapped in a network of relationships. The feminist theologian Beattie stresses the importance of relationality and interdependence, without denying an autonomous subject.[28] Moreover, she connects the human relationality to the divine community of God in the trinity. Relating God's communal nature to that of human persons is not surprising. The question is in what way the consequences of taking care of the others, who are like brothers and sisters, is interpreted. "Caring" for yourself and for others can imply denial of oneself in order to listen to God's will and the humble service and loving charity to the broader community, as pope Benedict XVI mentions.[29] Van Regenmortel pleads for a more empowering way of relating, in which individuals gain more power over their own life, because of being connected to and having important people to support them.[30] How do charity and empowerment, self-denial, and gaining more control, relate to each other?

Merely Individual?

Empowerment is apparently not just a matter of an autonomous individual having control over his or her own life, empowerment goes "beyond" liberal "autonomy" and beyond the individual, as it is precisely in the connections with others that the individual can be empowered. This became clear

27. Ibid.
28. Beattie, *New Catholic Feminism*, 46–47.
29. Benedictus XVI, *Deus caritas est*.
30. Van Regenmortel, *Zwanger van empowerment*.

in Van Regenmortel's notion of "autonomy in connection" as well as in the different levels that were distinguished in empowerment.[31]

The importance of connections, social support, and interdependence for the empowerment process inspires two complementary ways of perceiving empowerment. McDonald and Keys refer to *communal empowerment*.[32] On one hand, they are aware that community can erode empowerment, for instance by discouraging an individual decision if it would challenge the common good or the decision of the group. Tensions may rise between individual agency and cooperation. Yet, on the other hand, according to McDonald and Keys, integrating the sense of community and empowerment is possible. They speak of communal empowerment that encourages such forms of empowerment that do not erode the community, based on a shared relationship of community and union.[33] The relationships grounding such empowerment are based on "being with" each other, rather than "caring for" in an asymmetrical way. In the L'Arche community, for instance, assistants and core members want to travel on a shared journey, beyond the patient-caregiver relationships, and with the acceptance of one's own weaknesses. Egalitarian interpersonal connections, as well as equally shared responsibility are the conditions to create such an empowerment. A person with a disability or with a psychiatric disorder is sooner empowered through the other than that the other prevents the person's empowerment.

Another way to perceive empowerment, referred to by Oduyoye in the context of interreligious dialogue, is *mutual empowerment*.[34] Mutual empowerment highlights what a community or the conversing partners have in common, and how that common heritage empowers them toward a common good. The focus on what is shared and on the common goal can also inspire pastoral care, and care in general, toward vulnerable groups. What does the pastor, what does the caregiver share with for instance the person with a psychiatric disorder? How can the empowerment process take shape toward a common goal, a common concern, and future? Furthermore, in this model of mutual empowerment lies the recognition that the pastor, who has more power, can learn from the other. Experiencing the other as a gift can inspire the empowerment process and also strengthen

---

31. Van Regenmortel, *Zwanger van empowerment*; Jacobs et al., *Op eigen kracht naar gezond leven*.

32. McDonald and Keys, "L'Arche."

33. Ibid., 17.

34. Oduyoye, "'Mutual Empowerment' in Interreligious Dialogue."

the pastor, not merely practically or theoretically, but also theologically, spiritually, personally, and as an inspiration to continue professionally. Thus, without accentuating the difference in position, the empowering process can benefit both pastor and pastoral care receiver without sharpening the difference in position, in honest mutual interaction.

Merely Personal?

How does a person or a group gain more power over his or her or their life? Is empowerment a mere personal matter of one person encouraging the other, creating space, and making an appeal to the person's internal strength?

Obviously, for empowerment to function well, structural efforts should be made, and the right conditions and climate must be created.[35] Empowerment on the structural level entails giving people a voice on a higher policy level,[36] creating the conditions for empowerment to take place[37] and taking on the role of advocacy. As a pastor for instance, it is important to stand up to injustice, to help voiceless people to have a voice, and to advocate what is in the interest of their empowerment. Furniss, who discusses the social context of pastoral care, stresses that in the case of structural evil or powerlessness, pastoral care does not consist of asking the pastoral care receiver to adapt him or herself to the situation and to accept it as it is, but rather to encourage empowerment that will give the person a voice in order to transform inhuman structures.[38] It is the task, not only of the caregiver or pastor, but of every person, to share responsibility, perhaps as a kind of "mutual empowerment" toward a more human society.

Important in this structural empowerment approach is, according to Furniss, the opportunity offered to the pastoral care receiver of having an alternative to being a victim.[39] He stresses the importance of gathering in

---

35. Van Regenmortel, *Zwanger van empowerment*; Jacobs et al., *Op eigen kracht naar gezond leven*; Linhorst and Eckert, "Conditions for Empowering People with Severe Mental Illness," 279–305.

36. Linhorst and Eckert, "Conditions for Empowering People with Severe Mental Illness," 279–305.

37. Ibid., 279–305; Linhorst, *Empowering People with Severe Mental Illness*; Van Regenmortel, *Zwanger van empowerment*.

38. Furniss, *The Social Context of Pastoral Care*, 75–76.

39. Ibid., 77.

groups (such as religious communities, migrant groups, or volunteers) who can function as mediating structures between the individual person and the system, and thus make their voice heard. "Pastoral care," writes Furniss, "assists care seekers in finding a sense of divine vocation and in facilitating their empowerment through participation in mediating structures to have a meaningful impact on their society and its larger structures."[40] Hence, empowerment should not be detached from its structural component.

Mere Strength?

Empowerment can be praised as a happy ending story, in which the person finds strength within himself or herself, is encouraged in that endeavor, and becomes empowered. But is it just a question of "Yes, I can?" There can be a risk of overestimating the person, of unrealism, or worse, of even blaming the person since she is responsible for her own resources, strength, and empowerment process. Van Regenmortel refers to this as the risk of "blaming the victim". If the person is not empowering himself, this will entangle the person in a negative spiral and thus contradict the very logic of empowerment.[41]

Realism is therefore crucial to continue in the empowerment process in an adequate way. It is important to be aware of the human person with his or her strengths, but also with his or her weaknesses and frailty. Denying these would be to deny humanity. Van Regenmortel highlights that empowerment and vulnerability are not two opposite realities, but are in fact interwoven.[42] Empowerment recognizes vulnerability, but especially focuses on the vulnerability within the relations between vulnerable groups and societal institutions.

Pastors often meet pastoral care receivers when they are struggling with existential questions or do not feel in touch with the inner resources they have within themselves for finding strength. I agree with Van Regenmortel that vulnerability and strengths are interwoven. In order to foster an empowering and realistic pastoral care, pastors should make pastoral care receivers aware both of their strengths and of their vulnerability. The vulnerability of a vulnerable group, for instance psychiatric patients who are often seen as powerless and are thus treated accordingly, is a special

---

40. Ibid.
41. Van Regenmortel, *Zwanger van empowerment*, 18.
42. Ibid., 26.

point of attention for pastoral care.[43] How should that vulnerability be dealt with? What sort of vulnerability is individual, when does it have structural roots and how should this complexity be dealt with?

ENABLING EMPOWERMENT

How can empowerment be made possible for people so that they can empower themselves in relation to others and be encouraged in their empowering process? Creating the appropriate climate, working through mediating structures, offering the right conditions, and providing empowering initiatives are ways to foster a realistic and concrete process of empowerment.

Creating a Climate of Empowerment

The seeds of empowerment can only grow in a particular soil. The Afro-American theologian Lartey conceives pastoral care as being such a fertile soil when it begins with what is good within the person, with as its task: "the 'drawing out and building up' of the unnoticed strengths and resources within and around people and communities."[44] Important for an empowering climate is an increasing awareness of those who are oppressed and enable them to question their situation. Pastors play a vital role in this conscientization process, a key process described by Lartey as "a process in which people become more aware of their situation and of the resources they possess to respond to and change things."[45]

Van Regenmortel depicts the empowering landscape as a place where clients or patients are seen as human persons with their resilience, their meanings, and feelings. Where the most vulnerable are given special attention, where there is a lot of space to create, to experience, to care in the right measure, and to care for the caregivers.[46] A climate in which empowerment can spring forth and that uses strength oriented methods, methods oriented toward a positive basic attitude, appropriate participation, and social inclusion. The landscape in psychiatric care, for instance, should fully integrate persons with a psychiatric disorder in the care. According to

---

43. Linhorst, *Empowering People with Severe Mental Illness*.
44. Lartey, *In Living Color*, 58.
45. Ibid., 59.
46. Van Regenmortel, *Zwanger van empowerment*.

the "Taskforce Vermaatschappelijking Geestelijke Gezondheidszorg," the socialization process is a task for the community as a whole, where persons with a psychiatric disorder are seen as active citizens, who can act in society.[47] It is fundamental that they have a feeling of belonging to the society; that care is not only provided within the community, but also throughout the whole community.[48]

A suitable concept for creating the context for empowerment for persons with psychiatric disorders is what Kal elaborates with the Dutch term "kwartiermaken," or as she translates it, "quarter-making."[49] "Quarter-making" refers to creating an open space, a home as a society, in which persons who are perceived as "different" can be fully encountered and welcomed. It indicates an attitude and place of hospitality, where people from diverse worlds meet and influence each other in equality and mutuality in complex multilayered conversations in equality and mutuality. "Quarter-making" aims to create a hospital societal climate, in which opportunities are created for persons with a psychiatric disorder and for all those who are in one way or another excluded from everyday societal life. In this way, pastoral care can offer and contribute to such a hospital empowering climate, offering more opportunities to the pastoral care "receivers" to be more than mere "receivers."

Closely linked to the socialization process and the creation of a climate of hospitality is the movement in psychiatry that focuses on rehabilitation. Interestingly, rehabilitation or recovery does not equal a medical healing, but neither does it imply a mere acceptance of life as it is. According to Anthony, recovery can be perceived as a release from the disastrous consequences of psychiatric conditions and seeking to develop a new meaning and goal in life.[50] Existential questions about the meaning of life, as well as faith and philosophy of life play a vital, but often underestimated role. It seems hard for caregivers to deal with existential questions, and as a consequence, managers, caregivers, and therapists often sideline the existential dimension.[51] This lack of attention for such an important dimension toward recovery and empowerment could offer an opportunity for pastoral care. Pastors are trained to deal with existential questions, and they might

47. Taskforce Vermaatschappelijking Geestelijke Gezondheidszorg, *Erbij horen*.
48. Steyaert et al., *Actief Burgerschap*.
49. Kal, *Kwartiermaken*.
50. Plooy, "Proloog," 10–11.
51. Vergouwen and Kerssemakers, *Vragen naar zin*.

PART 4—Challenges for Theology and Pastoral Praxis

train other staff to be more attentive to this dimension and advocate appropriate structures.

Mediating Structures

How and by whom should an empowering climate be fostered? Furniss and Braithwaite emphasize mediating structures (volunteer groups, religious communities, migrant groups, etc.) as major actors in the empowering process.[52] Furniss describes the need for mediating structures between the family and bigger structures as politics and economy.[53] Braithwaite rightly stresses these mediating structures, as he distinguishes a double dynamic within society today: people who are given less social capital are often provided with big structural institutions, but precisely this group needs flexible, informal networks.[54] Small steps and micro-interventions are ways to bring about a greater structural change.

Conditions for Empowerment

Empowering oneself and raising one's voice is not self-evident for persons with a psychiatric disorder. Linhorst develops therefore seven conditions that must be met for persons with a psychiatric disorder for them to take part in the decision making process within the context of empowerment.[55] The first condition is the necessity that the psychiatric symptoms are under control, so that the clients are free enough to engage in the decision-making process. For this process, a second condition must be met, namely that of teaching the clients some basic decision making skills to be able to function in that process. Then a number of conditions external to the clients must be fulfilled. In what way could pastors contribute in fulfilling these conditions and in involving pastoral care receivers in the pastoral "decision-making process" in developing its strategy and pastoral vision? Access to sources is a third condition, according to Linhorst.[56] Staff must not only enable clients

---

52. Furniss, *The Social Context of Pastoral Care*; Braithwaite, "Emancipation and Hope," 79–98.

53. Furniss, *The Social Context of Pastoral Care*.

54. Braithwaite, "Emancipation and Hope," 79–98.

55. Linhorst and Eckert, "Conditions for Empowering People with Severe Mental Illness," 279–305; Linhorst, *Empowering People with Severe Mental Illness*.

56. Linhorst and Eckert, "Conditions for Empowering People with Severe Mental

to have access to resources, but should also be given the necessary resources to devote attention to the participation and empowerment of clients in the decision-making process. Reciprocal concrete incentives should be taken as a fourth condition, in light of which clients and staff should participate together and where both have an interest in empowering the client.[57] A fifth condition is the decision-making structures and processes that must bring people together in such a way that clients are not mere care receivers, but can also be given an opportunity to contribute.[58] Availability of choices and information is a sixth condition that must be taken into consideration, of which clients should have a range of possibilities to choose from. Finally, there is a need for a supportive organizational culture in the institution that believes in empowerment and in including persons with a psychiatric disorder into the decision making process. Perhaps pastors can also contribute to the awareness and importance of empowerment and promote and support an organizational culture that focuses on participation.

Empowering Initiatives

According to Spierts, the way in which empowerment takes shape is an aim in itself. It is not by theory, but by acting that persons become empowered.[59] But the idea of empowerment as an act of unfolding, positive development can create problems. Some may seek to force such a process through introducing many regulations in connection with it, but by doing so contribute to its failure.[60]

Some initiatives have been taken to put empowerment into practice that are inspiring for pastoral care. Empowerment conferences, for instance, offer "a special space to nurture hope," as Braithwaite puts it.[61] Californian empowering conferences gather youngsters who are in problem situations. They are asked to set the agenda for the conference. Certain goals—and how they want to reach them—are established as the topic of the empowering conference. The youngsters send out the invitations to those who are involved (family, management, social workers, organizations, etc.).

Illness," 279–305; Linhorst, *Empowering People with Severe Mental Illness*.

57. Handler, *Law and the Search for Community*.
58. Ibid.
59. Spierts, "De verspreiding van empowerment," 37–39.
60. Van Regenmortel, *Zwanger van empowerment*.
61. Braithwaite, "Emancipation and Hope," 79–98.

PART 4—Challenges for Theology and Pastoral Praxis

Much attention is devoted to the resources and strengths of the youngsters themselves as a point of departure, and attention is given explicitly to these areas by facilitators. The ultimate goal of these empowering conferences is, according to Braithwaite, "to provide the youth with hope, resources, and a plan. It empowers the youth to determine and set their own goals."[62] Similar initiatives have been taken in the Netherlands with *Eigen kracht conferenties* ("Own Power Conferences"), where people seek for a solution to and a way out of their problematic situation (e.g., teenage mothers, abused youngsters, etc.) within their social network, before reaching out to organized help.[63] Would similar empowering conferences not be an opportunity for other vulnerable groups, such as immigrants or persons with a psychiatric disorder? Pastoral care might play a role in encouraging such initiatives, perhaps in organizing them and in setting up an empowering conference in a pastoral care setting. It would be fascinating to see what would happen if pastoral care receivers could set the agenda, if their strengths and resources could be addressed, and their goals facilitated. Existential questions and goals could be the topic of "pastoral empowerment conferences" in which exploring resources, connecting with others, and receiving support from others play a very crucial role. This would be an empowering way of doing pastoral work and of dealing with existential questions, as well as helping care receivers to gain more control over their life within the context of pastoral care.

Another inspiring example is a church that is opened for all who wish to make use of the building in one way or another. It could be used by support groups, for an empowering conference in small groups amongst vulnerable groups, for benefits, artistic activities, parties organized by the youth, or activities that the persons themselves wanted to set up and reflect upon. In this way, the empowering climate manifests itself in an empowering environment.

Increasingly popular is a way of working that involves active outreach.[64] Care receivers are visited where they are. This has been developed particularly for the care of psychiatric patients in Great Britain, for instance in Birmingham, referred to by Birchwood as "comprehensive community

---

62. Ibid., 88.

63. Van Regenmortel, *Zwanger van empowerment*; Eigen kracht centrale, www.eigenkracht.nl.

64. Van Regenmortel, *Zwanger van empowerment*.

based mental health services."[65] If a caregiver only goes to those people who have explicitly asked for care services, many people are sidelined. This is a problem often encountered within pastoral care: pastoral care "on request" means overlooking so many people who might otherwise benefit. So outreach is very important in order to be actively present, also for those who did not ask for help. But it must be in freedom, as the lurking danger may exist of putting people under pressure, or of claiming superiority or the desire to evangelize, which may cause harm.

"Hands-On" Experts

In psychiatric institutions in the Netherlands, people who have themselves struggled with psychiatric problems have been employed as "hands-on" experts in mental health care.[66] They are the missing link in care, in cooperation with (para) professionals.[67] Apparently the integration of "hands-on" experts within mental health institutions has a very positive effect: the institutions become more flexible, offer more choices to the patients, give more concrete information, and are more concerned with recovery than solely with medical healing.[68] Working with "hands-on" experts might also be a true enrichment for pastoral care: what was important for them, which pastoral initiatives worked and which did not? How can they help in shaping pastoral care and in being involved in pastoral activities and policies?

IMPLICATIONS FOR PASTORAL CARE

Empowerment understood in its rich complexity, in an autonomous and connected way, is beneficial for all kinds of people, especially those who are rendered powerless, such as people with a psychiatric disorder.[69] According to Linhorst, an empowering approach enables such persons to take decisions about their own life and to have the possibility to improve. Moreover, empowerment increases their quality of life and enables them to contribute

---

65. Birchwood, "Comprehensive Community Based Mental Health Services in Birmingham."

66. Knooren and Van Haaster, "Onderwijsprogramma's voor ervaringsdeskundigen," 515–25.

67. Van Regenmortel, *Zwanger van empowerment*.

68. Ibid.

69. Linhorst, *Empowering People with Severe Mental Illness*.

to society (e.g., through voluntary work, engagement in politics, etc.). If empowerment has such a potential for growth and an improved quality of life, it is crucial to implement this idea in pastoral care as well, including the empowering conditions mentioned by Linhorst and the structural challenges.[70] In fact Liégeois already defines pastoral care in itself as "an *empowering* companionship between a client in his or her search for meaning in life and a pastoral counselor inspired by a community and a tradition of faith."[71]

Lartey mentions a form of pastoral care in which empowerment is central, starting from what is already present in the persons concerned and in the community surrounding them.[72] It is not merely a question of supporting the hidden strengths, but also of making people aware of the situation they are in and particularly of oppression and marginalization. It is awareness that can lead to further empowerment. Furniss shares this concern for questioning existing oppressing structures, so that empowerment in pastoral care is not just an individual, but also a structural issue.[73]

How can pastoral care, individually, structurally, theologically, and policy-wise integrate the empowerment idea? Throughout this contribution, different possibilities and implications of the multifaceted reality of empowerment and its conditions have been identified. I have discussed a few ways of integrating pastoral care and empowerment.

Empowering Spirituality

For psychiatric patients, religion and spirituality are often "to be avoided" as their expression of spirituality is considered to be "pathological" according to the practical theologian and Presbyterian minister Swinton.[74] But he notices that patients with a psychiatric disorder often find release, comfort, and a deeper form of spiritual healing in worship, through turning to spirituality. Taking spirituality seriously is, in this context for patients with a psychiatric disorder, crucial.[75] Seen through a particular spirituality, empowerment can be perceived as focusing too much on the human person,

70. Ibid.
71. Liégeois, "Pastoral Counseling in Care Services," 129. My italics.
72. Lartey, *In Living Color*.
73. Furniss, *The Social context of Pastoral Care*.
74. Coyte et al., *Spirituality, Values and Mental Health*.
75. Vergouwen and Kerssemakers, *Vragen naar zin*.

rather than on grace, and thus cause a hesitant or even resistant approach. On the other hand, there is sufficient potential in Christian spirituality to foster an empowerment movement through an empowering spirituality. Firstly, in the context of a Christian spirituality influencing pastoral care, the human person is perceived as being created in the image of God.[76] The focus is on the strengths, the hidden treasures and resources, and the value of the human person, rather than on his or her human weaknesses and defects.[77] Secondly, the idea and dynamic of *theosis* has much potential for empowerment: the human person, created in God's image is called to grow more and more in His likeness, and to be a partaker in the divine.[78] *Theosis* can be interpreted as focusing on God's activity without which we would be lost, but also as a form of "divine empowerment." The person becomes empowered by God to grow and become more God-like. Thirdly, the idea of "connecting" people is closely linked with the idea of empowerment.[79] Pastoral care could play a vital role in the process of connecting people with themselves, with others, with the broader context, and with God, in strengthening and encouraging encounters, and in building up a community. But Swinton notes that there is also a huge challenge for religious and other communities to not become stigmatizing and exclusive, particularly with regard to psychiatric patients.[80] So in the context of the community building dimension of pastoral care, special attention should be given to the way community is built and the kind of connections that emerge.

Empowering Research

Empowerment in pastoral care also implies pastoral research methods that follow this dynamic. Van Regenmortel names a few: patient-centered research, qualitative research, making use of Delphi Research, "hands-on" expert's expertise, etc.[81] Increasingly integrating such a patient-centered approach in pastoral research today, with specific methods for discovering what the pastoral care receivers want and desire, is a vital step in grounding an empowering pastoral praxis. Besides such empowering re-

---

76. Sachs, *The Christian Vision of Humanity*.
77. Lartey, *In Living Color*.
78. Murphy, "Reformed Theosis," 191–212.
79. Van Regenmortel, *Zwanger van empowerment*.
80. Coyte et al., *Spirituality, Values and Mental Health*.
81. Van Regenmortel, *Zwanger van empowerment*.

search methods, theology should also be refined and rethought from an empowering perspective: tackling what oppresses people, taking up those aspects that are uplifting, and going about this by returning to the theological sources and reinterpreting them in today's context, in a realistic and empowering way.

Pastoral Praxis

Empowerment can influence and challenge the everyday praxis of pastoral care, and in this way really make a difference, leaving a history of (paternalistic) shepherding behind. The pastoral praxis must be challenged both on individual, collective, and societal level, questioning pastoral policies, taking up a role of advocacy within institutions, reflecting on the individual pastoral behavior and on how to voice the pastoral care receiver's expectations and experiences (e.g., by means of "empowering conferences," "hands-on experts," outreaching pastoral). Pastoral care should encourage empowerment dynamics and initiatives, as well as being changed by them themselves, and should offer some sort of "empowerment pastoral care."[82]

CONCLUSION: TOWARDS HUMAN FLOURISHING

The rich complexity of empowerment, with its implications for pastoral care, especially for persons with a psychiatric disorder, has been discussed. Its colorful palette of autonomy, control, connectedness, and social support, on different levels, has shown a reality that is worthy to be taken into account in current pastoral care. However, attention should be given to developing a realistic approach, one that neither under nor overestimates the persons involved, is alert for power abuse, and that creates conditions that enable empowerment.

For vulnerable groups such as psychiatric patients, empowerment is especially important in different life spheres, so why not also in pastoral care? Implementing empowerment in pastoral care can be seen as building on something that is already present and at the same time rethinking pastoral research methods, spirituality, theology, and the concrete daily praxis. It is a far-reaching task, extending beyond the more "supportive" attitude of

82. Lartey, *In Living Color*.

an individual pastor. Nevertheless, I believe empowerment can truly enrich pastoral care and make it more finely tuned to the needs of the pastoral care "receivers." The special value and contribution of empowerment to the quality of life should encourage pastors to take an empowering pastoral care so that people can flourish.

BIBLIOGRAPHY

Beattie, Tina. *New Catholic Feminism, Theology and Theory*. London: Routledge, 2006.
Benedict XVI. *Deus Caritas Est*. December 25, 2005. http://www.vatican.va/holy_father/benedict_xvi/encyclicals/documents/hf_ben-xvi_enc_20051225_deus-caritas-est_en.html.
Birchwood, Max. "Comprehensive Community Based Mental Health Services in Birmingham: Evidence, Experience and the Importance of Engaging Young People." Unpublished lecture during the conference "Geestelijke Gezondheid, Kiezen of Delen." Gent, Belgium (14/09/2010).
Braithwaite, John. "Emancipation and Hope." *Annals of the American Academy of Political and Social Science* 592 (2004) 79–98.
Coyte, Mary Ellen, *et al. Spirituality, Values and Mental Health: Jewels for the Journey*. Gateshead: Athenaeum, 2007.
Croft, Suzy, and Peter Beresford. "The Politics of Participation." *Critical Social Policy* 35 (1992) 20–44.
Eigen Kracht Centrale. www.eigen-kracht.nl.
Foucault, Michel. *Was ist Kritik?*. Berlin: Merve, 1992.
Foucault, Michel. "Omnes et singulatim. Zu einer Kritik der politischen Vernunft." In *Gemeinschaften. Positionen zu einer Philosophie des Politischen*, edited by Joseph Vogl, 65–93. Frankfurt: Suhrkamp, 1994.
Furniss, George M. *The Social Context of Pastoral Care: Defining the Life Situation*. Louisville: Westminster John Knox, 1994.
Glor, Eleanor. "About Empowerment." *The Innovation Journal: The Public Sector Innovation Journal* 10 (2005) 1–19.
Handler, Joel F. *Law and the Search for Community*. Philadelphia: University of Pennsylvania Press, 1990.
Hongwane, Vussy. "Discovering the Academic for Trust's Sake: In Search of Sustainable Empowering Partnerships between Academy and Community." Unpublished lecture during the DPR conference. Greenwich, UK (30/3/2010).
Israel, Barbara A., *et al.* "Health Education and Community Empowerment: Conceptualizing and Measuring Perceptions of Individual, Organizational, and Community Control." *Health Education Quarterly* 21 (1994) 149–70.
Jacobs, Gaby, *et al. Op eigen kracht naar gezond leven: Empowerment in de gezondheidsbevordering: concepten, werkwijzen en onderzoeksmethoden*. Utrecht: Universiteit voor de Humanistiek, 2005.
Kal, Doortje. *Kwartiermaken: Werken aan ruimte voor mensen met en psychiatrische achtergrond*. Amsterdam: Boom, 2001.
Knooren, Jean, and Harrie Van Haaster. "Onderwijsprogramma's voor ervaringsdeskundigen." *Maandblad Geestelijke Volksgezondheid* 62 (2008) 515–25.

PART 4—Challenges for Theology and Pastoral Praxis

Lartey, Emmanuel Y. *In Living Color: An Intercultural Approach to Pastoral Care and Counseling*. London: Jessica Kingsley, 2003.
Liégeois, Axel. "Pastoral Counseling in Care Services: Between Confidential Space and Integrated Care." *Counseling and Spirituality* 25 (2006) 127–40.
Linhorst, Donald. M., and Anne Eckert. "Conditions for Empowering People with Severe Mental Illness." *The Social Service Review* 77 (2003) 279–305.
Linhorst, Donald M. *Empowering People with Severe Mental Illness: A Practical Guide*. New York: Oxford University Press, 2005.
McDonald, Katherine E., and Christopher B. Keys. "L'Arche: The Successes of Community, the Challenges of Empowerment in a Faith-Centered Setting." *Journal of Religion, Disability and Health* 9 (2005) 5–28.
Menon, Sanjay. T. "Psychological Empowerment: Definition, Measurement, and Validation." *Canadian Journal of Behavioural Science* (1999) 161–64.
Murphy, Gannon. "Reformed Theosis." *Theology Today* 65 (2008) 191–212.
Oduyoye, Mercy A. "'Mutual empowerment' in interreligious dialogue." Unpublished Lecture during Ethical Conference: From Trent to the Future. Trente, Italy (24/7/2010).
Pink, Dan. *Drive: The Surprising Truth About What Motivates Us*. New York: Riverhead books, 2009.
Plooy, Annette. "Proloog." In *Passagecahier. Herstel, empowerment en ervaringsdeskundigheid van mensen met psychische aandoeningen*, edited by Wilma Boevink et al. 9–13. Amsterdam: SWP, 2006.
Rappaport, Julian. "Terms of Empowerment/Exemplars of Prevention: Towards a Theory for Community Psychology." *American Journal of Community Psychology* 15 (1987) 121–44.
Sachs, John R. *The Christian Vision of Humanity: Basic Christian Antropology*. Minnesota: The Liturgical Press, 1991.
Spierts, Marcel. "De verspreiding van empowerment." *Tijdschrift voor de Sociale Sector* 53 (1999) 37–39.
Staples, Lee H. "Powerful Ideas about Empowerment." *Administration in Social Work* 14 (1990) 29–42.
Steinkamp, Hermann. *Die sanfte Macht der Hirten. Die Bedeutung Michel Foucaults für die praktische Theologie*. Mainz: Matthias Grünewald, 1999.
Steyaert, Jan, et al. *Actief Burgerschap: Het betere trek- en duwwerk rondom publieke dienstverlening*. Eindhoven: Fontys Hogescholen, 2005.
Stortz, Martha E. *Pastor Power*. Nashville: Abingdon, 1993.
Taskforce Vermaatschappelijking Geestelijke Gezondheidszorg. *Erbij horen: Advies Taskforce Vermaatschappelijking Geestelijke Gezondheidszorg*. Utrecht: Trimbos-instituut, 2002.
Van Regenmortel, Tine. *Zwanger van empowerment: Een uitdagend kader voor sociale inclusie en moderne zorg*. Eindhoven: Fontys Hogescholen, 2008.
Vergouwen, Lia, and Jacques Kerssemakers. *Vragen naar zin: Het perspectief van de GGZ-cliënt*. Tilburg: KSGV, 2004.

9

The Meaning of Informed Consent in Pastoral Counseling

Axel Liégeois

THIS PAPER INVESTIGATES THE meaning of informed consent in pastoral counseling. Its perspective is determined by three elements. The object of our investigation is the encounter and conversation between a pastor and a patient. The context is the field of health care in which pastoral counseling happens. And the approach of our study is by way of an ethical analysis and evaluation.

We begin our investigation with a description of the asymmetry and power imbalance in the pastoral relationship and with an ethical analysis of this power imbalance. Then we explore the concept of informed consent through the literature of medical ethics, patients' rights, and pastoral ethics and make some feasible applications. Thereafter, we affirm that not only the consent of the patient, but also the intention of the pastor is essential to deal with power in an ethical manner. By way of conclusion we formulate ten statements.

PART 4—Challenges for Theology and Pastoral Praxis

ASYMMETRY AND POWER IMBALANCE

Pastoral counseling is the encounter and conversation between a pastor and a patient. The counseling is grounded in the relationship between these two persons. One of the most important characteristics of this relationship is its asymmetry and power imbalance.[1]

Asymmetry

The pastoral relationship may well be a mutual one, in the sense that both partners are involved and communicate with each other. The relationship can also be considered as one of equals, in the sense that both partners enjoy the same dignity as human persons. However, they are unequal in terms of their relative position within the pastoral relationship: the one is the pastor and the other is the patient. Asymmetry characterizes the relationship in that the partners have an unequal position.

We can clarify this unequal position by referring to three characteristics of the pastor's identity, more precisely the ecclesiastical, the professional, and the personal character of his or her identity.[2] To begin with, the pastor holds an official position, a ministry in the church. This gives the pastor the authority to act and to speak on behalf of the community. In some cases, this authority may originate from an even more exalted source, since the patient may regard the pastor as being the direct representative of God, which can lead to the ascribing of all kinds of "superhuman" qualities to the pastor. Moreover, the pastor not only holds a ministerial position, but also has a professional status. The pastor is a theological and spiritual expert as well as a professional counselor in matters of meaning and faith. This implies much knowledge and skill in these matters. The pastor also belongs to the group of care providers who collaborate in teams and networks and who share information, even potentially confidential information. Finally, the pastor is a human person, a man or a woman who has grown toward a personal religious conviction and spirituality, in dialogue with the faith tradition and the contemporary culture. Therefore, he or she can be

---

1. Cf. Doehring, *Taking Care*, 74–103; Gula, *Just Ministry*, 117–55; Lebacqz, *Professional Ethics*, 109–23; Lebacqz and Diskrill, *Ethics and Spiritual Care*, 72–77; Neuger, "Power and Difference," 65–85; Schenderling, *Beroepsethiek voor pastores*, 195–201; Trull and Carter, *Ministerial Ethics*, 90–97.

2. Heitink, *Practical Theology*, 310–24.

an example or a witness for many people who attach great importance to spirituality and faith.

The patient who seeks pastoral counseling is placing great reliance on the ecclesiastical, professional, and personal position of the pastor. At the same time, the patient is in a vulnerable and dependent position.[3] The patient is vulnerable because he or she has a question, a need, or a problem that is difficult to solve on his or her own. Or the patient would like to share an intimate life experience, of which he or she is perhaps ashamed. The patient is vulnerable because he or she will need to reveal a personal matter and disclose sensitive information. This makes the patient dependent on the support of the pastor and on confidence in the pastor.

Power Imbalance

This unequal position creates an inequality or imbalance in the relationship. This imbalance is inevitably a power imbalance. Power means the ability to influence or control other people. Power can be very evident, as in the physical or psychological abuse of a patient. It can also be very subtle in the use of words, in the non-verbal attitude, or by the desire to be available or to help the patient, without really involving him or her. Obviously, the pastor has more power. In particular situations, the patient can also exercise limited power over the pastor and the pastor can feel very powerless and helpless. Despite this possibility, the power imbalance is usually to the advantage of the pastor because of the structure of their relationship.

Indeed, the unequal position and the power imbalance are structural facts. They are inescapable facts in the pastoral relationship as well as in any other caring and helping relationship. Unequal position and power imbalance belong to the inherent structure of any professional relationship. They anticipate the manner in which pastor and patient relate to each other. They are structural facts and not immediately an ethical matter.

Premoral Evil and Moral Evil

From an ethical point of view, it is helpful to make a distinction between the "premoral" dimension on the one hand and the "moral" dimension on

---

3. van Heyst, "Professional Loving Care," 199–217.

the other hand.[4] This distinction refers to the ambiguity of the human action. All human actions contain some features that have the potentiality of improving the well-being and quality of life of human beings and some features that potentially threaten it. According to Gula, these features are premoral goods "to the extent that these features enhance the potential for human goodness and growth," and they are premoral evils "to the extent that these features frustrate the full potential for promoting the well-being for persons and their social relations."[5]

We consider the unequal position and the power imbalance as premoral evils. On the one hand, they are evaluated as "evil" because they do not improve the potential for the well-being of human persons. The reason is that on a philosophical and anthropological level all human beings are considered as fundamentally equal. The *Universal Declaration of Human Rights* affirms that "all human beings are born free and equal in dignity and rights."[6] And from a theological perspective, all human beings are created in the "image of God."[7] Unequal position and power imbalance hence have the potentiality for threatening the fundamental equality of human persons. On the other hand, unequal position and power imbalance are qualified as "premoral" because they are inevitable features in human actions. These facts are not immoral or unethical, but premoral or pre-ethical. Their potentiality becomes reality, and thus moral or ethical, through human actions.

This insight has important consequences for the pastor's moral behavior. The moral or ethical character of the pastor's action depends on how he or she deals with the premoral evil of unequal position and power imbalance.[8] The pastor's intention or purpose should not be to engage in the pastoral relationship for his or her own benefit, but for the benefit of the patient. This implies firstly that the pastor should deal with the power imbalance in a way that does not harm the patient. Here the principle of non-maleficence is at stake. This secondly implies that the pastor should

---

4. Gula, *Reason Informed by Faith*, 269–70; Janssens, "Ontic Evil and Moral Evil," 133–56; Janssens, "Ontic Good and Evil," 70–82.

5. Gula, *Reason Informed by Faith*, 269.

6. General Assembly of the United Nations, "Universal Declaration of Human Rights," art. 1.

7. Genesis 1:26–27. Cf. Gula, *Reason Informed by Faith*, 64–66.

8. See below on the "sources of morality."

handle power in a way that is to the advantage of, or helps, the patient. Here we refer to the concept of empowerment.

Empowerment

Empowerment is an important concept in the social sciences and in psychosocial care.[9] We understand empowerment in an ethical way as enhancing responsibility, giving another person more power and strength so that he or she is better able to assume responsibility in his or her life. Hence, the pastor's intention or purpose should be to empower the patient, to make him or her more powerful. The patient is then better able to assume his or her own responsibilities. At the same time, the pastor can redress the imbalance of power within the pastoral relationship. Empowerment is an important characteristic of the pastoral relationship.

Consequently, we define pastoral counseling as an empowering companionship between a pastor and a patient.[10] In the relationship, the patient searches for meaning and/or faith in life, while the pastor, inspired by the Christian tradition and community, accompanies him or her. Empowerment expresses the purpose of pastoral counseling: the pastor empowers the patient in his or her own quest for meaning and/or faith in life. In other words, the purpose of pastoral counseling is to encourage and strengthen the patient so that he or she is able to understand meaning and/or faith in life more clearly and to experience them more deeply.

An important consequence of these reflections on power is that the person who has the greater power in the relationship also bears the greater responsibility toward that relationship.[11] Because of the fact of the unequal position, the pastor has the greatest power and the greatest responsibility. This imposes a twofold responsibility on the pastor: the responsibility not to abuse the power, or not to harm the patient, and the responsibility to empower the patient in his or her quest for meaning and/or faith in life. In order to give substance to the idea of empowerment and to redress the imbalance of power in the pastoral relationship, we can refer to the concept of informed consent. Asking for informed consent can be considered as the pre-eminent means of respecting the patient's autonomy.

---

9. Cf. Van Regenmortel, *Empowerment en participatie*, 9–19.
10. Liégeois, "Pastoral Counselling in Care Services," 129.
11. Gula, *Just Ministry*, 133.

PART 4—Challenges for Theology and Pastoral Praxis

INFORMED CONSENT

The main goal of this paper is to explore the possibilities and limits of informed consent as a means of adjusting the imbalance of power. Therefore, we investigate this concept through several sources in literature and examine the meaning of informed consent in pastoral counseling.

The Principle of Informed Consent

In their book *Principles of Biomedical Ethics*, Beauchamp and Childress have developed an authoritative view of informed consent.[12] In their opinion, the meaning and justification of informed consent is to be found in the principle of respect for autonomy. They remark that initially, from the 1950s on, informed consent was considered as a way to protect the patient from potential harm. But since the 1970s, the primary purpose of informed consent has been to improve the patient's autonomous choice. In this latter period, they observe in the 1990s a shift of emphasis from the care provider's obligation to disclose information, to the patient's quality of understanding and consenting.[13]

Beauchamp and Childress are very principled. They distinguish seven elements in informed consent. First, they propose two "threshold elements" or preconditions, namely (1) the patient's "competence" to understand and to make a decision and (2) the "voluntariness" in deciding. They subsequently make a distinction between three elements of information, specifically (3) the care provider's "disclosure" of material information, (4) the "recommendation" of a certain intervention, and (5) the patient's "understanding" of the former elements of disclosure and recommendation. Finally, they consider two elements of consent, namely (6) the patient's "decision" in favor of a certain intervention and (7) the "authorization" of that chosen intervention.[14] Based on these elements, informed consent can be conceptualized as the voluntary decision and authorization of a competent patient in favor of a certain intervention, on the basis of the understanding of the information about and the recommendation concerning that intervention.

---

12. Beauchamp and Childress, *Principles of Biomedical Ethics*, 117–40.
13. Ibid., 117–18. Cf. Faden et al., *A History and Theory of Informed Consent*, 114–50.
14. Beauchamp and Childress, *Principles of Biomedical Ethics*, 117–35.

Although Beauchamp and Childress highlight and prefer informed consent, they also give some attention to other forms of consent. They propose surrogate decision-making in order to protect patients who are not able to give consent, based on advance directives, or made by the family, the care providers, an ethics committee or the judicial system.[15] They also briefly mention other forms of consent, without elaborating them: expressed, tacit, implicit or implied, and presumed consent.[16]

Planned and Unplanned Pastoral Counseling

It is not easy to apply the well-defined concept of informed consent to pastoral counseling. In some situations, pastoral counseling is a planned activity with a series of sessions. The pastor and the patient can then talk about the nature and the purpose of pastoral counseling, and they can make appointments to meet. Information and consent are part of the process of planning the counseling sessions.

But in most situations, pastoral counseling is not planned this way. It has an accidental or occasional character. Pastor and patient meet by chance and in an unintentional way. They engage in a conversation, and no specific attention is given to providing information and giving consent. It is very artificial, and the request of an express informed consent for the encounter may be counter-productive. Nevertheless, the spontaneous conversation can be the starting point for further planned conversations or appointments.

Although informed consent could be very important in pastoral counseling, it is not easy in practice: perhaps it is achievable for planned pastoral counseling, but it will seldom be practicable for unplanned counseling. Therefore, we continue our exploration of literature on patients' rights in order to find concepts of informed consent that are more applicable to pastoral counseling.

---

15. Ibid., 185–90.
16. Ibid., 107–8.

PART 4—Challenges for Theology and Pastoral Praxis

Patients' Right to Informed Consent

An authoritative document concerning patients' rights is *The Convention on Human Rights and Biomedicine* of the Council of Europe.[17] This is a legal and political document with a global relevance in health care throughout the European Union.

The Convention affirms the already well-established rule of informed consent in medical law and medical ethics. It states that "an intervention in the health field may only be carried out after the person concerned has given free and informed consent to it."[18] The Explanatory Report clarifies that the word intervention is to be understood in the "widest sense" so that "it covers all medical acts."[19] According to the Convention, consent has two important characteristics, namely being informed and being freely given. Informed consent means that consent is given on the basis of objective information. The care providers give "appropriate information as to the purpose and nature of the intervention as well as on its consequences and risks."[20] The information should be given beforehand, and thus precede the intervention. The information should also be appropriate, this means "sufficiently clear and suitably worded" for the patient.[21] Free consent means that no pressure is applied from any person. Freedom implies that the patient "may freely withdraw consent at any time."[22]

Various Forms of Consent

The Explanatory Report develops the idea that consent may take various forms: express or implied.[23] This explanation is very important for the

17. Council of Europe, "Convention on Human Rights and Biomedicine." The European Committee of Ministers adopted the Convention on 19 November 1996 and its Explanatory Report on 17 December 1996. The Convention was opened for signature on 4 April 1997. Australia, Canada, the Holy See, Japan and the United States of America also took part in the Convention's preparation and are obligated to take a stand on it. The Convention had a determining influence on many national acts on patients' rights, such as the Belgian act of 22 August 2002. Cf. Liégeois et al. "An Ethics of Deliberation," 73–75.

18. Council of Europe, "Convention," art. 5.

19. Council of Europe, "Explanatory Report," nr. 34.

20. Council of Europe, "Convention," art. 5.

21. Council of Europe, "Explanatory Report," nr. 36.

22. Council of Europe, "Convention," art. 5.

23. Council of Europe, "Explanatory Report," nr. 37.

purpose of pastoral counseling. The Report states that "express consent may be either verbal or written," and that the form "will largely depend on the nature of the intervention."[24] The Report affirms that "it is agreed that express consent would be inappropriate as regards many routine medical acts," and that "the consent is therefore often implicit, as long as the person concerned is sufficiently informed."[25] For the inverse situations, the Report explains that "in some cases, however, for example invasive diagnostic acts or treatments, express consent may be required," and that "the patient's express, specific consent must be obtained for participation in research or removal of body parts for transplantation purposes."[26]

Implicit Consent for Pastoral Counseling

The Explanatory Report makes clear that express informed consent is probably not necessary, and that implicit consent is likely to be sufficient for pastoral counseling. There are several arguments. First, the Report asserts that informed consent is necessary for "medical acts."[27] Is pastoral counseling a medical act? Certainly, pastoral counseling is an act in the context of health care and may have beneficial effects on the patient's health. But in our opinion, pastoral counseling is not a medical act, because otherwise we confuse the specific contribution of the disciplines in health care. The disciplines should be distinguished and recognized in their identity and specificity, in the knowledge that they are interconnected and complementary. Consequently, care providers should work in an interdisciplinary way, but may not mix the disciplines.

Secondly, the Explanatory Report asserts that express consent may be required for "invasive diagnostic acts or treatments" and should be obtained for "participation in research."[28] It is clear that pastoral counseling does not belong to these types of interventions. On the other hand, the Report supports the possibility of implied consent, especially for routine medical acts. This possibility may sometimes be applicable to pastoral counseling.

24. Ibid.
25. Ibid.
26. Ibid.
27. Cf. above on the explanation of the word intervention, and note 19.
28. Cf. above on express consent, and note 24.

PART 4—Challenges for Theology and Pastoral Praxis

Nevertheless, for non-invasive interventions the consent might be implicit "as long as the person concerned is sufficiently informed."[29]

This is an important statement in respect to pastoral counseling. When express consent is not achievable, in either written or verbal form, an implicit consent is practicable for pastoral counseling. But there is an important condition: the patient should be sufficiently informed.

Protection of Patients Not Able to Consent

The Convention continues with some articles on the protection of patients who are not able to give consent for a certain intervention. An adult may be considered unable to consent "because of mental disability, a disease or similar reasons."[30] These reasons refer to situations in which the patient is "unable to formulate his or her wishes or to communicate them."[31] The Convention then establishes a first condition concerning the protection of the patient: the intervention must be "for his or her direct benefit."[32] The second condition concerns the surrogate consent, for a minor as well as for an adult, and implies "the authorization of his or her representative or an authority or a person or body provided by law."[33]

Nevertheless, the patient is not ruled out. For a minor, his or her opinion "shall be taken into consideration as an increasingly determining factor in proportion to his or her age and degree of maturity."[34] For an adult, he or she "shall as far as possible take part in the authorization procedure."[35] This means that, for patients, it will be necessary "to explain to them the significance and circumstances of the intervention and then obtain their opinion."[36]

Moreover, the Convention pays attention to the patient's advance directives. It asserts that "previously expressed wishes related to a medical intervention by a patient who is not, at the time of the intervention, in a

---

29. Cf. above on implicit consent, and note 25.
30. Council of Europe, "Convention," art. 6.3.
31. Council of Europe, "Explanatory Report," nr. 43.
32. Council of Europe, "Convention," art. 6.1.
33. Ibid., art. 6.2 (minor) and 6.3 (adult).
34. Ibid., art. 6.2.
35. Ibid., art. 6.3.
36. Council of Europe, "Explanatory Report," nr. 46.

state to express his or her wishes shall be taken into account."[37] This is the case with progressive diseases. According to the Explanatory Report taking the wishes into account "does not mean that they should necessarily be followed."[38] The reason may be that "the wishes were expressed a long time before the intervention and science has since progressed."[39]

Pastoral Counseling with Patients Not Able to Consent

The question arises whether surrogate consent is necessary for pastoral counseling with patients who are not able to consent. At first sight, it seems to be necessary. Pastoral counseling should be for the direct benefit of the patient and a representative should consent. However, is it reasonable to ask the representative's express consent when the patient's implicit consent would be sufficient, but is actually impossible? Or is it sufficient to take into consideration the wishes and opinion of the patient in proportion to age, degree of maturity, and degree of capacity to consent?

The answer is not easy. We give three considerations. First, it is unquestionable that the patient should be involved in giving consent as far as he or she is able to do so. This remains the best way to respect the wishes and the autonomy of the patient. A second consideration is that the representative should be asked for consent for a planned series of pastoral counseling. Unfortunately, this is rarely practicable for an unplanned or incidental pastoral encounter or conversation. A third consideration is that the patient's advance directives should be taken into account. Of course it is not necessarily the case that the patient has expressed advance directives concerning pastoral counseling. But, whatever the case should be, the pastor can assess whether pastoral counseling is in line with the fundamental choices the patient has made during his or her life. If there is a contra-indication, the pastor should withdraw from providing pastoral counseling.

Probably, the best answer to the problem of pastoral counseling with patients who are unable to consent is a combination of the three considerations: in so far as it is possible, the patient's current consent, the representative's consent as far as this is feasible, and the patient's advance directives in so far as these have been previously expressed. Nevertheless, we continue our exploration of the literature on pastoral ethics

---

37. Council of Europe, "Convention," art. 9.
38. Council of Europe, "Explanatory Report," nr. 62.
39. Ibid.

in order to find practical concepts of consent that are easily applicable to pastoral counseling.

Pastoral Ethics

The results of our exploration of literature on pastoral ethics and professional ethics for pastors have been disappointing: in professional ethics and professional codes for pastors, informed consent is not a topic of discussion.[40] Of course, respect is a key concept. But this does not imply the duty to ask for an informed consent. As far as we know, only two manuals bestow attention on the question.

In the manual *Christian Counseling Ethics*, Horace Lukens deals with the question of informed consent.[41] He spells out a number of specific items that the therapist should provide for the client as a part of informed consent: "information about the services provided," "goals of therapy and procedures to be used," "financial issues," "confidentiality," "qualifications," and "other pertinent information."[42] Furthermore, Thomas Rodgerson proposes similar items: "the nature and risks of therapy, the alternatives to treatment, the qualifications and values of the counselor, the nature or the fees and the policies regarding cancellations, the limits to confidentiality, ant the right to terminate."[43] The content as well as the terminology indicates clearly that both authors focus on (Christian) therapists and a planned series of sessions and not specifically on pastors.

More interesting is the chapter on "Permission for Mission" in the book *Gentle Shepherding: Pastoral Ethics and Leadership*, by Joseph Bush.[44] He begins with a clear statement regarding pastors and informed consent. He asserts that "fortunately, unlike other types of health care professionals, pastors do not normally have to get written permission from each person in

---

40. For literature on professional ethics for pastors, cf. note 1. Among the most important codes for pastors, cf. American Association of Christian Counselors, "Code of Ethics"; American Association of Pastoral Counselors, "Code of Ethics"; Canadian Association for Spiritual Care, "Code of Ethics for Spiritual Care Professionals"; Netherlands Association of Spiritual Counsellors in Care Institutions, "Professional Standard Spiritual Counsellors."

41. Lukens, "Essential Elements for Ethical Counsel," 43–56.

42. Ibid., 50–51 passim.

43. Rodgerson, "Pastoral Counseling and the Informed Relationship," 398.

44. Bush, *Gentle Shepherding*, 44–69. Cf. Bush, "Informed Consent and Parish Clergy," 427–36.

his or her congregation to exercise pastoral ministry to these individuals."⁴⁵ We should remark that Bush refers here to "clergy" working in a parish or congregation and not to pastors or chaplains in a hospital or care service. Nevertheless, his perspective is very interesting. In his opinion, informed consent can be established verbally rather than in writing. Moreover, he considers informed consent as an ongoing conversation of establishing informed consent.⁴⁶

Establishing Informed Consent

According to Bush, informed consent in pastoral counseling occurs largely through the conversation between pastor and patient. It involves both parties and both should listen and speak with care. Careful listening by the pastor means that the pastor listens sensitively to the patient so as to hear his or her expectations and to clarify the nature of these expectations with the patient.⁴⁷ Careful speaking means that the pastor communicates honestly about the kind of pastoral counseling he or she can offer as an appropriate response to the expectations.⁴⁸ This implies that the pastor is fully aware of the limits of pastoral counseling. Therefore, the pastor makes clear that other kinds of care are available and is ready to refer the patient to another care provider.

Through this conversation, informed consent is established. A written consent is not necessary; a verbal consent is sufficient. Bush does not clearly affirm, but it seems that, in his opinion, the verbal consent is rather an implicit than an express consent. Establishing informed consent happens through the whole conversation. The pastor should be attentive that he or she receives and retains informed consent.

Informed Consent as a Dialogical Process

In our view, we consider establishing informed consent as a "dialogical process."⁴⁹ Pastoral counseling is a process of dialogue between the pastor

45. Ibid., 48.
46. Ibid., 187, n. 8. Bush refers to Welfel, *Ethics in Counseling and Psychotherapy*, 111–15.
47. Ibid., 63–64.
48. Ibid., 64–68.
49. Cf. Liégeois, *Waarden in dialoog*, 59–61.

and the patient, through which informed consent is established. An important element of this dialogical process is providing and receiving information. The pastor informs the patient by introducing himself or herself as being pastor and, when appropriate, by explaining the purpose, possibilities, and limits of pastoral counseling. The patient, on his or her part and when suitable, informs the pastor about his or her own expectations. If necessary, the pastor might help to clarify the patient's expectations. In this way, the expectations and the possibilities can be fine-tuned through the dialogue. Together, pastor and patient inform each other through the process of pastoral counseling.

Based on this mutual information, another important element of the dialogical process is giving and receiving consent. The consent can be positive as well as negative, by means of an informed consent, or an "informed refusal." Through the dialogical process, the pastor should "create an opportunity" for the patient to consent to or to refuse pastoral counseling. The creation of that opportunity by the pastor is crucial. Moreover, the consent or refusal can take various forms, express or implicit, verbal or non-verbal. The pastor should be very attentive in order to detect both the verbal as well as the non-verbal signs of consent or refusal. Non-verbal signs of consent or refusal can be communicated through emotional expressions or body language.

Informed consent, in our view, may not be considered as a decision and authorization that is provided at a given moment. On the contrary, informed consent is an ongoing process through the dialogue and the counseling. During the whole process of counseling, pastor and patient inform each other concerning the possibilities and expectations. On the basis of this shared information, they continuously give shape to and participate in the process of pastoral counseling. Yet, it is the pastor's responsibility to be attentive to the patient's verbal and non-verbal signs of consent or refusal, and to respect them.

FURTHER THAN INFORMED CONSENT

Although informed consent is very important for pastoral counseling, in our opinion it is insufficient for guaranteeing an ethical way of dealing with asymmetry and power imbalance. Good reason is to be found for this at the core of Christian ethics. It brings to light that we should not only focus on the patient, but also on the pastor.

The Sources of Morality

In the tradition of Christian ethics, we find the theory of the so-called "three sources of morality."[50] As the name suggests, this theory postulates that there are just three sources of morality: the intention of the person acting, the object or the act-in-itself, and the circumstances surrounding the action. These three elements determine the "ethical" quality of the human action. The intention is the "internal part" of the human action; it is the "end" or the "purpose" of the action and gives "personal meaning" to the action. The act-in-itself is the "external part" of the human action; it is the "means-to-an-end" of the action and can be easily observed. Finally, there are the circumstances in which the action is realized and that include the consequences of the action.[51] The human action as a whole consists of the three elements: act, intention, and circumstances.

According to the theory of the three sources of morality, the ethical evaluation of the human action is also based on these three elements. The act cannot be evaluated without considering the intention of the person acting. Two similar acts may have a different moral quality depending on the intention of the person acting. Different intentions may confer different evaluations of human actions. Consequently, proportionality is necessary between the intention and the act. An act cannot represent any intention and, vice versa, an intention cannot be realized in whatever act. The end does not justify all means. Only an act congruent with or in proportion to the intention can adequately fulfill or express that intention.

The proportion is therefore the criterion for evaluating the ethical quality of the human action as a whole, considering the three sources: the act should be proportionate to the intention, taking the circumstances into account. Gula affirms in a clear way that "only by considering the action in reference to the intention within the total context of its qualifying circumstances, we can determine the true moral meaning of the action."[52]

---

50. For an explanation of the sources of morality, cf. *Catechism of the Catholic Church*, nr. 1749–1754; Gula, *Reason Informed by Faith*, 265–67; Janssens, "Ontic Evil and Moral Evil," 116–33. The three sources of morality are: the *finis operantis* (intention), the *finis operis* (object), and the *circumstantiae* (circumstances). The basis of these three sources of morality can be found in the description of the human act by Thomas Aquinas, *Summa Theologica*, IaIIae, q. 18, a. 2–4.

51. Gula, *Reason Informed by Faith*, 265.

52. Ibid., 267.

part 4—Challenges for Theology and Pastoral Praxis

This ethical vision can be applied to the question of dealing with power in pastoral counseling.

The Proportionality of Pastoral Counseling

The three elements can be easily distinguished in pastoral counseling. The act is the process of pastoral counseling between pastor and patient. The circumstances are determined by the asymmetric relationship and the power imbalance between pastor and patient. The intention is twofold. Both the patient and the pastor have a certain intention in pastoral counseling.

Until now, we have focused on the patient's perspective. The intention of the patient is usually personal and determined by his or her expectations. From the patient's perspective, the act of pastoral counseling should be proportionate to his or her intention, taking into account the circumstances of the pastoral relationship. For the pastor, it is impossible to know how the patient evaluates the proportionality between his or her own intention and the counseling process in the given relationship. The only way to come to know the patient's evaluation is by asking his or her informed consent, presuming that the patient will only consent if there is proportionality.

Now it is time to move on to the pastor's intention and the proportionality between the pastor's intention and the process of pastoral counseling in the context of the asymmetric relationship. What is the intention of the pastor? Is the act of counseling, in the given context of the relationship, a proportionate expression or fulfillment of the purpose of pastoral counseling?

The Complexity of the Intention

An intention is an end, a purpose that a person is seeking to achieve. We have already touched on the purpose of the pastoral counseling in our earlier description and definition: it is the empowerment by the pastor of the patient in his or her own quest for meaning and/or faith in life.[53] In other words, the purpose of pastoral counseling is to encourage and strengthen the patient so that he or she is able to understand meaning and/or faith in life more clearly and to experience them more deeply. The intention of the pastor is justified to the extent to which it aims at this purpose.

---

53. Cf. above on empowerment, and note 10.

A particular problem in this respect is the fact that human intentions are seldom unambiguous. Our actions are hardly ever motivated by one single intention. On the contrary, psychology has demonstrated that the motivation of human behavior is multi-causal and can be influenced by many different factors. In particular, transference and counter-transference in the relationship between pastor and patient can play a crucial role.[54] Through the process of transference, the patient projects onto the pastor a number of unfulfilled wishes or unresolved problems stemming from relationships with other important people in his or her life. Through the process of counter-transference, the pastor projects a number of his or her own unfulfilled wishes and unresolved problems back onto the patient.

As a result, a pastor might sometimes attempt to enter into a relationship with a patient in order to help that person. But in fact, through that relationship, the pastor is seeking to satisfy his or her own desires for contact or to find solutions to his or her emotional problems. This distorts the professional relationship that has as its purpose the empowerment of the patient and may lead to unjustifiable or inappropriate behavior. Alternatively, a pastor may genuinely believe that asking the patient for certain information is justified in terms of achieving the purpose of the pastoral counseling. But in fact, the pastor is interested in that information because it refers to similar facts or events in his or her own life, or because the pastor has become curious about the life story of the patient, or because the pastor recognizes a person he or she is acquainted with in the patient's environment. The pastor then becomes intrusive in the patient's private life and betrays the trust the patient has given. Therefore, the pastor needs to learn how to deal with his or her own desires and problems in the pastoral relationship.

Moral Integrity

As a consequence, we can reasonably expect a pastor to behave with integrity.[55] This ethical virtue comprises two elements. First, integrity is the ability and the quality of acting in such a way that there is a correspondence between the intention and the act. This entails a correlation between what the pastor feels and thinks on the one hand, and what he or she says and does on the other hand. The pastor must only do things and say things that

---

54. Hartung, "Transference," 1285–86.
55. Musschenga, *Integriteit*, 167–93.

agree with his or her own feelings and opinions. Secondly, integrity is the ability and the quality of acting in accordance with values and norms. It implies that there is no discrepancy between what the pastor postulates in ethical terms and what he or she actually does. If the pastor possesses integrity, he or she will be regarded as being trustworthy, honest, and reliable.

Integrity is important for all human beings, but for the pastor the question of integrity goes much deeper. By virtue of the pastor's ecclesiastical, professional, and personal character, the pastor refers to and witnesses to the higher reality of the sacred or to a personal God. This implies that a pastoral relationship creates a kind of spiritual sanctuary, an open space in people's hearts and minds that encourages trust and surrender to God. This sacred or divine space must be protected at all costs and must not be desecrated by inappropriate pastoral counseling on the part of the pastor.

Emotional Integrity

Moral integrity presupposes that the pastor has already attained a high level of emotional integrity. First, the pastor should possess a high degree of self-knowledge. This is necessary in order to be aware of his or her desires and needs and the role that these can play in the processes of transference and counter-transference. Moreover, good self-knowledge also makes it easier to recognize when certain dominant emotions run the risk of leading to inappropriate behavior.

This brings us to the pastor's self-care. One of the pastor's tasks is to ensure his or her own physical, emotional, social, and spiritual well-being. Being comfortable and content with the experience of one's own private and professional life is an important precondition for keeping one's feelings and needs detached from one's professional relationships. If the pastor is not able to do this, he or she may need external support and guidance.

This support can be provided in a general way through formation and training in dealing with power imbalances and informed consent. But often, a more personal guidance is needed. The pastor can seek this help from a colleague or a friend, or by making use of the existing supervision and intervision procedures, or, when necessary, by undergoing psychotherapy. The advice of an external person might help the pastor to clarify his or her own desires and needs, permitting the person to function more effectively at both a personal and a professional level.

CONCLUSION

In this paper we have discussed the meaning of informed consent in pastoral counseling. We conclude with ten statements.

1. The asymmetry or unequal position of pastor and patient in the pastoral relationship creates an imbalance of power. This unequal position is due to the ecclesiastical, professional, and personal character of the pastor's identity and the vulnerable and dependent position of the patient.

2. The unequal position and power imbalance are structural facts. From an ethical point of view, they can be considered as "premoral" evils. They become "moral" goods or evils depending on the way the pastor deals with them. This implies that the pastor may not harm the patient, but should empower the patient.

3. We define pastoral counseling as an empowering companionship between a pastor and a patient. Empowerment expresses the purpose of pastoral counseling: the pastor strengthens the patient in his or her own quest for meaning and/or faith in life. In order to empower the patient, the pastor should request the informed consent of the patient.

4. Medical ethics describes informed consent as the voluntary decision and authorization given by the competent patient in favor of a certain intervention, based on the understanding of the information on and recommendation of that intervention. This concept can only be applied in the case of planned sessions of pastoral counseling.

5. Patient's rights make clear that various forms of informed consent can be used in pastoral counseling. Express consent, either written or verbal, is not always achievable. Implicit consent can be appropriate, as long as the patient is sufficiently informed. This implicit consent can be applied to unplanned or incidental pastoral counseling.

6. Some patients are not able to consent. Nevertheless, the pastor can involve the patient in giving consent as far as he or she is able to do so. For planned sessions of pastoral counseling, the pastor can ask a surrogate informed consent from a representative. The pastor can also search for advance directives concerning pastoral counseling or assess whether pastoral counseling is in line with the patient's fundamental options.

PART 4—Challenges for Theology and Pastoral Praxis

7. Pastoral ethics demonstrate that establishing informed consent is a "dialogical process" of mutual listening and speaking. The pastor gives information regarding the possibilities and the limits of pastoral counseling, and the patient regarding his or her expectations. The pastor creates opportunities in which the patient can consent or refuse in an express or implicit, verbal or non-verbal way. Informed consent is an ongoing process.

8. The sources of morality make clear that for the evaluation of a human action, the act should be proportionate to the intention, taking the circumstances into account. The proportionality of pastoral counseling depends on the patient's informed consent and on the pastor's intention.

9. The intention of the pastor should be the empowerment of the patient. But human intentions are multi-causal and influenced by transference and counter-transference. Therefore, the pastor should learn how to deal with his or her own desires and problems in the pastoral relationship.

10. Moral integrity is an important virtue for the pastor. It is the ability and quality of acting in correspondence with his or her intention and with values and norms. Moral integrity presupposes emotional integrity. Therefore, the pastor needs self-knowledge, self-care, and when necessary, external support.

BIBLIOGRAPHY

American Association of Christian Counselors. "Code of Ethics," 2004. www.aacc.net.
American Association of Pastoral Counselors. "Code of Ethics," 2010. www.aapc.org.
Beauchamp, Tom, and James Childress. *Principles of Biomedical Ethics*. 6th ed. New York: Oxford University Press, 2009.
Bush, Joseph E. *Gentle Shepherding: Pastoral Ethics and Leadership*. St. Louis: Chalice, 2006.
———. "Informed Consent and Parish Clergy." *The Journal of Pastoral Care and Counseling* 57 (2003) 427–36.
Canadian Association for Spiritual Care. "Code of Ethics for Spiritual Care Professionals," 2011. www.cappe.org.
Catechism of the Catholic Church. Rev. ed. London: Chapman, 1999.
Council of Europe. "Convention for the Protection of Human Rights and Dignity of the Human Being with regard to the Application of Biology and Medicine: Convention on Human Rights and Biomedicine." Brussels: European Treaty Series—No. 164, 1996. http://conventions.coe.int/treaty/en/treaties/html/164.htm.
———. "Explanatory Report." Brussels: European Treaty Series—No. 164, 1996. http://conventions.coe.int/Treaty/EN/Reports/Html/164.htm.
Doehring, Carrie. *Taking Care: Monitoring Power Dynamics and Relational Boundaries in Pastoral Care and Counseling*. Nashville: Abingdon, 1995.
Faden, Ruth, Tom Beauchamp, and Nancy King. *A History and Theory of Informed Consent*. New York: Oxford University Press, 1986.
General Assembly of the United Nations, "Universal Declaration of Human Rights," 1948. http://www.un.org/en/documents/udhr/index.shtml.
Gula, Richard. *Just Ministry: Professional Ethics for Pastoral Ministers*. New York: Paulist, 2009.
———. *Reason Informed by Faith: Foundations of Catholic Morality*. New York: Paulist, 1989.
Hartung, Bruce M. "Transference." In *Dictionary of Pastoral Care and Counseling*, edited by Rodney J. Hunter, 1285–86. Nashville: Abingdon, 1990.
Heitink, Gerben. *Practical Theology: History, Theory, Action Domains: Manual for Practical Theology*. Grand Rapids: Eerdmans, 1999.
Janssens, Louis. "Ontic Evil and Moral Evil." *Louvain Studies* 4 (1972–73) 115–56.
———. "Ontic Good and Evil: Premoral Values and Disvalues." *Louvain Studies* 12 (1987) 62–82.
Lebacqz, Karen. *Professional Ethics: Power and Paradox*. Nashville: Abingdon Press, 1985.
Lebacqz, Karen, and Joseph D. Diskrill. *Ethics and Spiritual Care: A Guide for Pastors, Chaplains, and Spiritual Directors*. Nashville: Abingdon, 2000.
Liégeois, Axel. "Pastoral Counselling in Care Services: Between Confidential Space and Integrated Care." *Counselling and Spirituality* 25 (2006) 127–40.
———. *Waarden in dialoog: Ethiek in de zorg*. Leuven: LannooCampus, 2009.
Liégeois, Axel, and Marc Eneman. "An Ethics of Deliberation, Consent and Coercion in Psychiatry." *Journal of Medical Ethics* 34 (2008) 73–76.
Lukens, Harace C. "Essential Elements for Ethical Counsel." In *Christian Counseling Ethics: A Handbook for Therapists, Pastors and Counselors*, edited by Randolph K. Sanders, 43–56. Downers Grove: InterVarsity Press, 1997.

PART 4—Challenges for Theology and Pastoral Praxis

Musschenga, Albert W. *Integriteit: Over de eenheid en heelheid van de persoon.* Utrecht: Lemma, 2004.

Netherlands Association of Spiritual Counsellors in Care Institutions. "Professional Standard Spiritual Counsellors," 2005. www.vgvz.nl.

Neuger, Christie C. "Power and Difference in Pastoral Theology." In *Pastoral Care and Counseling: Redefining the Paradigms*, edited by Nancy J. Ramsey, 65–85. Nashville: Abingdon Press, 2004.

Rodgerson, Thomas E. "Pastoral Counseling and the Informed Relationship." *The Journal of Pastoral Care* 45 (1991) 389–98.

Schenderling, Jacques. *Beroepsethiek voor pastores.* Budel: Damon, 2008.

Trull, Joe E., and James E. Carter. *Ministerial Ethics: Moral Formation for Church Leaders.* Grand Rapids: Baker Academic, 2004.

van Heyst, Annelies. "Professional Loving Care and the Bearable Heaviness of Being." In *Naturalized Bioethics: Toward Responsible Knowing and Practice*, edited by Hilde Lindemann, Marian Verkerk, and Margaret Urban Walker, 199–217. Cambridge: Cambridge University Press, 2009.

Van Regenmortel, Tine. *Empowerment en participatie van kwetsbare burgers: Ervaringskennis als kracht.* Amsterdam: SWP, 2010.

Welfel, Elizabeth R. *Ethics in Counseling and Psychotherapy: Standards, Research and Emerging Issues.* 2nd ed. Pacific Grove, CA: Brooks/Cole, 2002.

Contributors

Jana Binon is writing a dissertation on pastoral care within a psychiatric context at the Faculty of Theology and Religious Studies, KU Leuven, Belgium.

Roger Burggraeve is emeritus professor in Christian ethics, with a focus on ethics of marriage and sexuality. He taught at the Faculty of Theology and Religious Studies, KU Leuven, Belgium.

Annemie Dillen is associate professor of practical and empirical theology at the Faculty of Theology and Religious Studies, KU Leuven, Belgium. She coordinates a research project on power and pastoral care.

Carrie Doehring is Associate Professor of Pastoral Care and Counseling at Iliff School of Theology, Denver, Colorado.

Stefan Gärtner is assistant professor in practical theology at the Faculty of Catholic Theology at the University of Tilburg, the Netherlands.

Emmanuel Lartey is professor of pastoral theology, care, and counseling at Candler School of Theology, Emory University, Atlanta, Georgia.

Axel Liégeois is professor of pastoral theology at the Faculty of Theology and Religious Studies, KU Leuven, Belgium. He holds the Chair Canon

Contributors

Triest on Pastoral Care of People with Mental Illness or Disability (Brothers of Charity). He is ethical advisor for the Brothers of Charity, Gent (Belgium).

Didier Pollefeyt is vice rector of education at the KU Leuven, Belgium. As professor at the Faculty of Theology and Religious Studies, his research is in catechetics, religious education, Jewish-Christian relations, and post-Holocaust studies.

Machteld Reynaert obtained her PhD at the Faculty of Theology and Religious Studies, KU Leuven, Belgium. Her research was about power, children and pastoral theology. She works at the same university on a project about Catholic identity.

Cristina Traina is Professor of Religion, Department of Religious Studies, Northwestern University, Evanston, Illinois.

Anne Vandenhoeck is assistant professor in pastoral theology and pastoral care at the Faculty of Theology and Religious Studies, KU Leuven, Belgium.

Index

A

Abissath, Mawutodzi K. · 79, 97
abuse · xiv–xvi, 44, 46, 57, 59, 60, 63, 65, 67, 72, 82, 93, 103, 105, 125, 164
    justification of · 109
    of power · ix, xii, 3, 9, 15, 19, 102, 119, 122, 124, 126, 135, 138, 141, 150, 168, 173, 175
    sexual · x, xv, xviii,83, 87, 104, 109, 123, 124
Adriaenssens, Peter · xiv, xx
African
    culture · 91
    religion · 93
agape · 133
Agyemang, Fred · 91, 97
Akan · 79
Alexander, Veerman L. · 16, 143
Altemeyer, Bob · 67, 76
ambiguity of the human action · 174
American Association of Christian Counselors · 182, 191
American Association of Pastoral Counselors · 182, 191
Amodio, David M. · 63, 64, 76, 77
anger · 105
Arendt, Hannah · 45, 46, 51
Aristotle · 139, 140, 142
Asad, Talal · 71, 77
Asante · 94, 95
Ashanti · 94, 95, 97

asymmetry · 5, 6, 13, 18, 21, 25, 27, 34, 40, 41, 43, 70, 72, 78, 81, 88, 102, 124, 133, 152, 157, 172, 173, 184, 186, 187, 190
Augustine · xiii, xx, 24
authenticity · 119
autonomy · 8, 25, 89, 148, 149, 150, 154–56, 169, 176, 177, 182,

B

Baart, Andries · 47, 51
Barr, James · 134, 142
Bauer, Christian · 33, 51, 53
Bauman, Zygmunt · 47, 51
Beattie, Tina · 156, 169
Beauchamp, Tom · 176, 177, 191
Benedict XVI · 140, 142, 156, 169
Benhabib, Seyla · 72
Benjamin, Ben E. · 138, 142
Beresford, Peter · 148, 169
bipolar structure · 32
Birchwood, Max · 164, 165, 169
Black, Peter · 64, 92, 134, 142
blaming the victims · 111
Blodgett, Barbara · 134, 142
Boileau, David · 73, 77
Bolten, Mart P. · 118, 120
Bolz, Nobert · 48, 51
Braithwaite, John · 162, 163, 164, 169
Brewer, Marilynn B. · 62, 77

Index

Brock, Rita Nakashima · 134, 142
Bröckling, Ulrich · 47, 51
Brouwer, Rein · 39, 44, 46, 51
Browning, Don S ·15, 143
Bruinsma, De Beer, Joke · 6, 15
Bucher, Rainer · 30, 40, 48, 50, 51
Burggraeve, Roger · 16, 57, 59, 68, 69, 71, 77, 115, 116, 117, 120, 121, 193
Bush, Joseph E. · 182, 183, 191
Büttgen, Philippe · 18, 27

C

Cabezón, Jose Ignacio · 62, 77
Campbell, Alistair · ix, xx
Canadian Association for Spiritual Care · 182, 191
care
    deficit model of · 42
    intercultural · 67
careful speaking · 183
Carter, James E · 142, 172, 192
Catechism of the Catholic Church · 185, 191
Chanter, Tina · 137, 139, 140, 142
chaplain · 15, 28, 29, 30, 34, 38, 39, 40, 41, 42, 43, 44, 45, 47, 50, 58, 71
Chevallier, Philippe · 18, 26, 27
Childs, Brian H. · 49, 50, 51
Christian spirituality · 167
clericalism · 14
community and empowerment · 157
consent
    expressed · 179
    free · 178
    patient's advance directive · 181
    implicit · 179
    informed · 176, 178, 182, 183
    patient's current · 181
    representative's · 181
    surrogate · 180
Cooper-White, Pamela · 5, 124, 125, 141, 142
Cornu, Ilse · 117, 120
Costa, Mario · 136, 142
CouncilofEurope · 178, 180, 181, 191

counseling · 23, 29, 30, 34, 38, 39, 40–46, 48–51, 93, 127, 128, 183
Cowley, Catherine · 140, 142
Coyte, Mary Ellen · 166, 167, 169
Clinical Pastoral Education · 58, 65, 71, 75
Croft, Suzy · 148, 169

D

Davie, Grace · 30, 51
DeRidder, Hugo · 101, 120
de-ecclesiologizing · 25
Demasure, Karlijn · xx, 14
demonizing · 107
Demoulin, Stephanie · 63, 77
deontology · 111
dependency · 45
deterministic view · 111
Devine, Patricia G. · 64, 77
Devisch, Ignaas · 9, 15
dialogical process · 183
Diedrich, W. Wolf · 73, 77
Dillen, Annemie · xx, 15, 16, 19, 53, 193
Diskrill, Joseph D. · 172, 191
Doehring, Carrie · 15, 33, 44, 52, 172, 191, 193
domination · 93
    three types of · 85
Drechsel, Wolfgang · 42, 52
Duckitt, John · 63, 77
Dueck, Alvin · 68, 77

E

Eckert, Anne · 148, 155, 158, 162, 170
Eigen KrachtCentrale · 169
Eigenkrachtconferenties · 164
Ellison, Marvin M. · 134, 142
empathy · 72
empowerment · 148, 175
    collective · 154
    conditions of · 162
    conducive climate of · 160
    initiatives of · 163

Index

mediating structures of · 162
minimalistic understanding of · 156
redesigning research of · 167
Ephraim Amu · 91
eros · 133
evil
    moral and premoral · 174
exploitation · 93

F

Faden, Ruth · 176, 191
Farley, Wendy · 135, 138, 142
Ferder, Fran · 135, 142
Foucault, Michel · xvii, xx, 4,6, 7, 9, 11,
    13, 15, 17-27, 31–33, 35, 36, 52,
    53, 79, 80, 81, 84, 85, 95, 97, 123,
    142, 151, 169, 170
fragmentation
    male characteristic · 116
    technique of · 115
Franck, Georg · 48, 49, 52
French, John R.P. · 4, 72, 77
Freud, Sigmund · 130–32, 142
Furniss, George M. · 158, 159, 162, 166, 169

G

Gabbard, Glen O. · 115, 120
Ganzevoort, Ruard · 5, 12, 14, 16
Gärtner, Stefan · xi, xx, 10–13,16, 30, 39, 52, 123, 126
Geluk, Hans L. C. · 112, 120
General Assembly of the United Nations · 191
genocide · 82
Gilson, Anne Bathurst · 134, 142
Glor, Eleanor · 149, 154, 155, 169
Graham, Elaine · 76, 77
Greenberg, Jeff · 63, 77
Greenwald, Carole A. · 39, 52
Guggenbühl-Craig, Adolf · 82, 83, 97
Gula, Richard · 172, 174, 175, 185, 191

H

Habermas'theory · 72
Halbe, Jorn · 47, 52
Handler, Joel F. · 163, 169
hands-on-experts · 165
Hansen, Robinson, Linda · 43, 52
Hartung, Bruce M. · 187, 191
Haslinger, Herbert · 38, 43, 52
Heitink, Gerben · 172, 191
Heyward, Carter · 5, 134, 142
Hochschild, Michael · 34, 52
Hoge, Dean R. · 40, 52
Hogue, David · 68, 77
Holler, Linda · 138, 142
holocaust · 82
Hongwane, Vusi · 151, 152, 153, 169
Howe, Mary Blye · 134, 142
Hübenthal, Christoph · 45, 52, 53
Hunsberger, Bruce · 67, 76

I

images of self · 129
impotency · 11
integrity
    emotional · 188
    moral · 187
    personal and vocational life · 126
intention · 186
intimacy · 117
Irigaray, Luce · 136, 137, 142, 143
Isherwood, Lisa · 134, 143
Israel, Barbara A. · 19, 21, 138, 152, 169

J

Jacobs, Gaby · 152, 153, 154, 157, 158, 169
Jähnichen, Trugott · 38, 52
Janowski, Gudrun · 43, 52
Janssens, Louis · 174, 185, 191
Jantzen, Grace · 137, 143
Johnson, Elizabeth A. · 58, 65, 130, 138, 143

Index

Johnson, Luke T. · 143
Johnson, Mark · 127, 129, 131, 139, 143
Jones Eddie Harmon · 77
Jung · 82, 84, 96
Jurgrau, Thelma · 101, 120

K

Kal, Doortje · 161, 169
Kämpfer, Horst · 46, 52
Karle, Isolde · 34, 39, 41, 45, 52
Karrer, Leo · 38, 39, 53
Keller, Catherine · 69, 77, 142, 143
Kerssemakers, Jacques · 161, 166, 170
Keys, Christopher B. · 150, 153, 157, 170
King, Nancy · 18, 191
Klessmann, Michael · 37, 53
Knooren, Jean · 165, 169
Kofi Busia · 94
Korem, Albin K. · 79, 97
Körver, Sjaak · 38, 53

L

L' Arche community · 150, 152
Laplanche, Jean · 131, 143
Lartey, Emmanuel · 13, 68, 78, 160, 166–68, 170, 193
Lebacqz, Karen · 73, 172, 191
Levinas, Emmanuel · 22, 57, 68–70, 72, 73, 76-78, 119, 121
Levine, Donald N. · 127, 143
Lewis, C.S. · 139, 140, 143
Lieberman, Matthew D. · 63, 76
Liégeois, Axel ·13, 16, 166, 170, 176, 179, 185, 192,
Lincoln, Bruce · 71, 78, 142
Linhorst, Donald M. · 148, 155, 158, 160, 162, 163, 165, 166, 170
Loomer, Bernard M. · 60, 61, 66, 78
Lorde, Audre · 134, 143
Lukens, Harace C. · 182, 191
Lumen Gentium · 13
Luther, Henning · 42, 53

M

Magyar, Gina M. · 61, 78
Marlet, Johannnes J. C. · 116, 120
McCleary, Daniel F. · 67, 78
McDonald, Katherine E. · 150, 153, 157, 170
media as polarizing agent · 106
Menon, Sanjay T. · 149, 170
metaphor · 14, 17, 20, 31
Middlesworth, Jean E. · 138, 143
Miller-McLemore, Bonnie · 6, 16, 134, 143
moralizing attitude · 108
Morgan, Virginia R. · 73, 78
Moskowitz, Gorden B. · 64, 78
Moyaert, Paul · 112, 120
Murphy, Gannon · 167, 170
Musschenga, Albert W. · 187, 192
mutuality · 5, 6, 8, 30, 34, 59, 61, 69, 70, 76, 115, 133, 134, 139, 140, 152, 156 -158, 161, 172, 184, 190
Mveng, Englebert · 90, 97

N

Netherlands Association of Spiritual Counsellors in Care Institutions · 192
Neuger, Christie C. · 4, 13, 16, 33, 53, 172, 192
Nolte, Kristina · 48, 53
Nye, Andrea · 137, 143
Nygren, Anders · 133, 134, 136, 143

O

Oduyoye, Mercy · 157, 170
Orr, Deborah · 137, 143

P

paradox
  anthropological · 115

of agential and receptive power · 73
of professional helpers · 82
Pargament, Kenneth I. · 62, 78
Parsons, Thomas D. · 68, 77
pastoral
   culture of experts · 44
   ethics · 182
   guidance · 32
   relationship · 15, 16, 7, 10, 14, 37, 49, 50, 61, 102, 103, 117, 172, 188
   role · 37, 40, 59, 128, 138
   work · 18, 19, 22
pastoral care · 10, 12, 15, 17–19, 22, 24, 27, 29, 30, 33, 34, 37-47, 49–51, 57, 65, 71, 76, 84, 102, 116, 119, 133, 148, 149, 154, 157, 158, 161–63, 165, 166, 193, 194
   market model · 47
   theological foundation · 119
pastoral caregiver · 10, 12, 14, 15, 81, 102, 116
   position of · 80, 103
pastoral care receiver
   suffocationg pastoral care giver · 110
pastoral counseling
   defined · 175
   opportunity to refuse · 184
   planned and unplanned · 177
patient
   protection of · 180
   patient-centered approach · 167
   rights of · 178
Pattison, Stephen · 37, 53
Paul, Saint · 83
pedagogicaldereliction · 109
Person, Ethel Spector · 124, 143
Petter, Karin · 43, 53
philia · 133
physical touching · 104, 112
Pickstock, Catherine · 136, 143
Pieper, Josef · 139, 140, 143
Pink, Dan · 149, 154, 155, 170
Plato · 136, 137, 143, 144
Plooy, Annettte · 161, 170
Poling, James N. · 5, 16, 69, 70, 78

Pollefeyt, Didier · xix, xx, 33, 41, 53, 112, 113, 119, 121, 123, 124–26, 138, 141, 194
Pope Francis · x
Pope, Sonne · 107, 121
Pott, Martin 50, 51, 53
power · 4, 11, 12
   agential · 59
   amorality of · 109
   as taboo · 10–12, 13, 15
   expressions of · 8
   hierarchical · 11
   imbalance 173
   pastoral · 18, 36, 151
   positive · 13
   relational · 61
   traditional · 30
powerlessness · 113
prejudgments · 62
Presbyterian Church · 58, 91
priesthood · 13
   process-relational theology · 69
professionalism · 38, 42
proportionality · 186
propping · 130
Prothero, Stephen · 71, 78
Purvis, Sally B. · 134, 143

R

Ragsdale, Katherine · 5, 14, 16
Rappaport, Julian · 148, 170
Raven, Bertram H. · 72, 77
Redekop, Calvin · 4, 11, 12, 13, 16
Remmelzwaal, Albert J. · 44, 45, 53
Rendle, Gilbert · 39, 53
Reuter, Ingo · 42, 50, 53
Rieger, Joerg · 71, 78
Rodgerson, Thomas E. · 182, 192
Rodolfa, Emil · 107, 121
Rogers, Carl · 71
Rutter, Peter · 109, 121

Index

S

Sachs, John R. · 167, 170
Sander, Hans Joachim · 34, 53
Schenderling, Jacques · 172, 192
Schilderman, Hans · 39, 53
Schlamelcher, Jens · 47, 53
Schmälzle, Udo F. · 48, 50, 53
self-affirming prejudice · 63
self-awareness · 31, 33, 39, 40, 62, 81, 124, 125, 130
self-justification · 112
Sennett, Richard · 35, 54
sensus fidelium · 151
shadow · 83, 96
Sheffield, Frisbee C. C. · 136, 144
shepherd see pastor also priest · ix, x, xv, 17, 18, 19–23, 32, 33, 36, 46,
    motivations of · 66
Smith, James K. A. · 9, 13, 16
Sohnen-Moe, Cherie · 138, 142
Spierts, Marcel · 149, 163, 170
Staples, Lee H. · 148, 170
Steck, Wolfgang · 43, 54
SteinhoffSmith, Roy H. · 5, 6, 14, 16
Steinkamp, Herman · 7, 9, 10, 16, 32, 34, 54, 151, 170
Stenger, Hermann · 38, 54
Stephan, Walter · 63, 78
Steyaert, Jan · 161, 170
stigmatization · 108
Stortz, Martha Ellen · xii, xx, 4, 7, 12, 16, 37, 45, 54, 153, 154, 171
subjugation · 8, 23, 85, 86, 88, 92, 93, 96
supervision · 19, 14, 65, 75, 76, 118, 188
Surzykiewicz, Janusz · 47, 54
Swinton, John · 166
symmetry · 72

T

Tajfel, Nemri · 62, 78
theosis · 167
Tillich, Paul · 139, 144
Traina, Cristina L.H. · 6, 122, 135, 144
Tran, Jonathan · 7, 16

transference · 187
Trull, Joe E. · 172, 192
Turner, John C. · 62, 78

V

Vacek, Edward Collins · 134, 135, 136, 139, 141, 144
Van Damme, Caroline · xii, xx
Van Haaster, Harrie · 165, 169
van Heyst, Annelies · 173, 192
Van Regenmortel, Tine · 150, 151, 152, 153, 154, 155, 156, 157, 158, 159, 160, 163, 164, 165, 167, 170, 175, 192
van Schalkwyk, Annalet · 134, 144
Verelst, Lieve · 109, 121
Vergouwen, Lia · 161, 166, 170
Vermaatschappelijking Geestelijke Gezondheidszorg, Task force · 161, 170
Vosman, Frans · 40, 54
vulnerability · 96, 101, 103, 105, 119, 125, 159, 160

W

Weber, Max · xx, xxi, 3, 4, 6, 7, 12, 16
Weiss, Gail · 129, 130, 131, 144
Welfel, Elizabeth R. · 183, 192
wellbeing · 81
Wenger, Jasqueline E. · 40, 52
Williamson, Marianne · 86, 97
Wittrahm, Andreas · 42, 54

Y

Yardley-Nohr, Terrie · 144
Young, Iris Marion · 72, 78, 169

Z

Zulehner, Paul M · 31, 54

www.ingramcontent.com/pod-product-compliance
Lightning Source LLC
Chambersburg PA
CBHW070256230426
43664CB00014B/2552